The Parent's Success Guide™ to Baby Names

Edited by P. Mourouzis

WILEY

Wiley Publishing, Inc.

The Parent's Success Guide™ to Baby Names

Published by
Wiley Publishing, Inc.
111 River St.
Hoboken, NJ 07030-5774
www.wiley.com

For general information on our other products and services or to obtain technical support, please contact our Customer Care Department within the U.S. at 800-762-2974, outside the U.S. at 317-572-3993, or fax 317-572-4002.

Wiley also publishes its books in a variety of electronic formats. Some content that appears in print may not be available in electronic books.

Library of Congress Control Number: 2003115750

ISBN: 0-7645-5924-9

Manufactured in the United States of America

10 9 8 7 6 5 4 3 2

Contributors

Pam Mourouzis has been editing *For Dummies* books for more than ten years. She's done yoga with model Stephanie Seymour, author of *Beauty Secrets For Dummies;* lunched with motivational speaker Zig Ziglar, author of *Success For Dummies;* and traded notes on basketball with former coach and commentator Digger Phelps, author of *Basketball For Dummies.* Her husband, Matt McClure, is a freelance writer. Together, they maintain their creativity in naming by thinking up alternate monikers for their "baby," a 6-year-old Beagle mix officially named Emerson.

George R. Stewart was a teacher and Berkeley Fellow at the University of California. During his lifetime, he wrote many scholarly works and several bestsellers, including *Storm, Fire, Earth Abides,* and *Names on the Land.*

Publisher's Acknowledgements

Some of the people who helped bring this book to market include the following:

Editor: Kelly Ewing

Acquisitions Editors: Holly Gastineau-Grimes, Joyce Pepple

Cover Photo: © Getty Images

Interior Design: Kathie S. Schnorr

Table of Contents

Chapter **1**

Fussin' about the Perfect Name for Your Baby

In This Chapter

☺ Understanding the importance of a name

☺ Discovering tips for naming your children

☺ Avoiding baby-naming pitfalls

William Shakespeare once wrote, "What's in a name? That which we call a rose/By any other name would smell as sweet." And though he certainly had a point, you have to admit that If a rose were actually called a foot, you'd probably have a different opinion of how it smells!

That's something to keep in mind when thinking of names for your children. You may have the sweetest little boy in the world, but if you name him Adolf, it simply won't matter how sweet he is. The negative historical significance of that name will follow your child for the rest of his life. At the very least, you may get quizzical looks from other parents when you introduce him; at worst, he'll be teased until he can't stand it anymore, especially in history class.

Naming children comes down to two things: common sense and a little forethought. In this chapter, you discover some common-sense advice for naming your children, as well as what to keep in mind when making your decision.

First Things First: Using This Book

As a parent-to-be, you may think that the typical 40-week pregnancy seems like a *long* time — but as many parents will tell you, that time goes fast! Soon-to-be parents have many things to take care of before Baby arrives, one of the most important being to select a name. With hundreds and hundreds of names to choose from, this task may seem overwhelming. That's where this book comes in!

This book is part of a series called The Parent's Success Guide™. Its main purpose is to help you, a busy, multitasking mom (or dad!), make some positive changes in your life as a parent — in a minimum amount of time.

Brought to you by the makers of the world-famous *For Dummies* series, this book provides straightforward advice, hands-on information, and helpful, practical tips about baby names. The goal is to give you the information you need to make your decision *without* requiring a considerable amount of your valuable time.

Keep the following points in mind as you use this book:

✿ For each name, we list the origin and then the meaning, unless the history of the name is so vague and convoluted that it's just impossible to tell. In these cases, we venture a hypothesis if a reasonable one exists; otherwise, we simply say "Origin and meaning unknown."

✿ For some names, we list derivatives, variations, and similar-sounding names that might also appeal to you in bold type.

✿ When another name relates to the name at hand, we put it in all capital letters so you'll know that you can look up its entry for more information.

✿ Our primary source of information about names' popularity is the Social Security Administration, which publishes lists of the 1,000 most common names for baby girls and boys from 1991 to the present, according to applications for Social Security cards. To search the lists for yourself, make your way to www.ssa.gov/OACT/babynames/.

While reading this book, you'll see these icons sprinkled here and there:

 This icon points out advice that saves time, requires less effort, achieves a quick result, or helps make a task easier.

 This icon signifies information that's important to keep in mind.

 This icon alerts you to areas of caution or danger — negative information you need to be aware of.

Knowing a Name's Importance

There are no rules for naming a baby; in fact, you can name your children pretty much anything you want. But if there were any rules, the most important one would probably be this: "Remember that your children have to live with their names for the rest of their lives." And that's a long time.

So try not to be cavalier in choosing your children's names. For example, don't give your child a particular name simply because you like it or because it's the latest fad. Your taste in names may change or the name may go out of fashion — and then you (and your kid) are stuck with a name you no longer like or that's no longer popular. And by all means, steer clear of names that you think are funny, because your child probably won't find the humor in it.

 Your child's name will become part of his or her identity, part of who he or she will become. So do yourself and your child a favor — choose a name that has some significance to you and your family and will have significance to your child.

Mulling over the origin and meaning

Most names have an origin and a meaning that often date back centuries. The *origin* is simply the language or dialect in which the name was probably heard first. For example, older names that you may think of as Italian or French in origin may actually come from Latin — the root of many western European languages. Most names have origins deep in some ancient language while wearing a much more recent form. A good example is Shane — an English form of an Irish borrowing of an English borrowing of a French borrowing of a Latin borrowing of a Hebrew name.

On the other hand, some names that are popular today haven't always been used as names. People find names in places, such as America or Madison, and even in words that have pleasant meanings, like Summer and Precious.

The *meaning* of a name often signifies from what or where the name came. For example, the meaning of the name Ashton is "from the ash tree." Almost anything or any place can serve as the basis for a name.

Sometimes, especially in the case of names from biblical or mythological sources, the meaning may actually be a description of the first-known person or character to carry the name. Here are a couple of examples:

❀ **Marcus:** Derived from Mars, the Roman god of war, so the meaning of Marcus is "warlike."

❀ **Raphael:** Means "God has healed," which relates to the biblical story of how the archangel Raphael had the power to heal.

When choosing a name for your child, paying attention to the name's origin and meaning isn't a bad idea. If you want your child's name to be an indication of your family's ethnic roots, you may want to restrict your selections to names with a particular origin, such as Irish/Gaelic or Russian. When considering the meaning, you may want to choose a name with a meaning that has some significance to you. Granted, it's impossible to tell what kind of person your child will grow up to be, but that doesn't mean that you can't engage in some old-fashioned wishful thinking.

Sounding out the name

This may sound like a no-brainer, but you may want to keep in mind that you, your child, your child's teachers, and everyone else should be able to say your child's name without difficulty. If, for example, you name your child Aloysius — fine name that it is — most people will probably have trouble spelling or saying the name. Aloysius is not spelled like it's pronounced (al-lo-WISH-us). Some people may try to pronounce it as it's spelled, as in "al-LOY-see-us." This mispronunciation may lead to some embarrassing moments for your child!

 If you have a fairly simple last name, like Brown or Smith, you're better able to "get away with" using a more complicated name. If your last name is long and tricky to pronounce, do your child a favor and choose a simple first name to offset it.

Another important step is to practice saying the name with your last name. There should be a rhythm to it; it should roll off the tongue effortlessly. After all, you'll be using your child's full name when he or she gets into trouble, right? As in "John Wesley Smith, clean up that mess. Now!" You don't want to be stumbling over "Aloysius Maynard Hazelton," do you?

 Be careful when putting together a first name that ends with the letter with which the last name begins, as in Pam Matthews. The repeated consonant can sound muddy when run together.

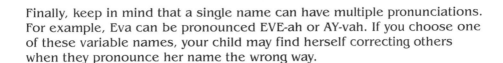
Finally, keep in mind that a single name can have multiple pronunciations. For example, Eva can be pronounced EVE-ah or AY-vah. If you choose one of these variable names, your child may find herself correcting others when they pronounce her name the wrong way.

Deciding on a common or unique name

Choosing a common name versus a unique name often means a choice between a traditional name with historical significance and a modern name that hasn't quite caught on. Both options have advantages and disadvantages:

- **Common names:** These names can often be found in the Bible, in mythology, or in classic works of literature. For example, the common — and immediately recognizable — names James, Matthew, and Mark draw added significance from their use in the Bible. Common names are also less likely to become super-popular and then go out of style. The disadvantage of using common names is that they can be seen as unoriginal or just plain "been there, done that."

- **Unique names:** Often, these names are derived from objects or locations, such as Paris or Robin. The advantage is that it sets your child apart from others, and the name gains added significance by having a well-known association. The disadvantage is that the name probably won't have much historical significance and may become trendy, which makes them anything *but* unique. For example, Madison, which hasn't been around very long, has climbed to the No. 2 spot in popularity. You may not want your daughter to have the same name as three other girls in her class!

 A way to have the best of both worlds is to choose a common last name with a great deal of significance and use it as your child's first name. Last names of historical figures — such as Lincoln and Truman — carry with them the prestige of those historical figures but have the virtue of not being used very often as first names.

Contemplating the spelling of the name

Some names come with a variety of spellings — often due to how the name appears in different languages or because a parent long ago wanted to distinguish her child's name from the common form. For example, Megan is also spelled Meagan or Meghan. Marcy may also be spelled Marci, Marcee, or Marcie.

Choosing among different spellings of a single name is really a matter of aesthetics, unless the different spellings denote differences in the name's origin. For example, Alain is the French spelling of Alan; if your family doesn't have French roots, you may not want to choose Alain. Or you may find Alain to be unique and beautiful because of those roots.

A word of caution: These names can easily be misspelled, especially if you go with a less common form. Megan is the most common spelling of the name. If you choose Meghan instead, rest assured that others will drop the *h* a good portion of the time. However, the extra letter does make the name distinctive; just keep in mind that Meghan will often have to correct the spelling of her name.

Combining a First and Middle Name (or Two)

The truth is, you do *not* have to give your child a middle name. No law says that you have to, and no one is going to haul you off to jail if you don't. But giving your child a middle name (or two — there's no limit) can add significance to your child's name. And your child may end up with a name he or she would be proud to put on the cover of the next Great American Novel!

For example, consider Edgar Allan Poe — he wouldn't be the same if he had been just Edgar Poe. Or Ed Poe, for that matter. Or how about Louisa May Alcott? Louisa Alcott seems a little plain, doesn't it?

A middle name has another advantage: If your child ends up hating the first name, he or she has a second option. Using an initial for the first name along with the middle name looks pretty cool, too! It worked for J. Edgar Hoover, didn't it?

Here are a few hints for giving your child a middle name — and making it work with the rest of his or her name:

❀ **Make the middle name more unique.** Because middle names don't get used every day, they can be a great way to get creative without giving your child a lifelong burden to bear.

❀ **Honor the mother's family by using her maiden name.** Not only does this add to the uniqueness of your child's name, but it will also endear you to the mother's family!

❀ **Consider either parent's first or middle name.** This is a great way to pass along a little bit of yourself, without the apparent egotism that some perceive in naming your child directly after yourself.

☺ ☺ ☹ ☺ ☺ ☹ ☺ ☺ ☹ ☺ ☺ ☹ ☺ ☺ ☹ ☺ ☺ ☺ ☺ ☹ ☺

❀ **Think about initials.** Patrick Ian Garnett may sound just dandy to you, but you don't want your son to have to suffer through grade school with the initials P.I.G.

Of course, the same advice for matching up a first name and a last name applies here: Sound out the full name to make sure that it flows nicely.

Naming Your Baby after You or Someone Else

Although you risk being called a copycat, naming your child after someone else has distinct advantages — and disadvantages.

A junior dilemma

There's absolutely nothing wrong with giving your baby your name or your spouse's name and sticking a "Jr." at the end of it. The passing down of names to sons indicates a strong family tradition. (Generally, only boys are given their fathers' names and become Juniors.) However, be prepared for some criticism, whether it's overt or not. Keep these points in mind when you're considering the "Jr." option:

❀ **Others may view you as unoriginal.** They may think that you couldn't come up with an original name. But don't let this deter you from making your child a Junior; just be prepared for this kind of attitude.

❀ **Your child will be called "Junior" at some point in his life.** Some kids don't mind; others hate it. Remember how Indiana Jones got his first name: The young Henry Jones, Jr., hated being called Junior by his father so much that he started calling himself Indiana — after the family dog.

❀ **Your child may be ridiculed.** If his schoolmates ever find out that he's a Junior, watch out! Relentless teasing will ensue!

❀ **It can create confusion.** Some Jrs., IIs, and IIIs report that their records get mixed up with their fathers' and grandfathers'. In this electronic age, documents like credit histories are often based on names, and same names can cause trouble.

 One way to avoid the Junior issue is to nickname the child something else, perhaps a shortened form of his middle name. For example, if a father and son are both named James Theodore and the father goes by Jim, the son's nickname can be Ted. Then no one will ever know your child's deep, dark secret!

Negative associations

Naming your child after yourself or a family member is a pretty safe choice, unless that family member happens to be one of those skeletons in the family closet. Naming your child after a famous celebrity or historical figure, however, is another matter entirely and can have a negative impact on how others view your child.

Of course, for nearly every given name out there, you can find a famous person with that name; avoiding associations with the famous people who carry your child's name will be nearly impossible. Often, these associations are positive — movie stars, athletes, political figures, famous authors, and so on. You really can't go wrong with a name like Harrison (after actor Harrison Ford or President Benjamin Harrison) or Margaret (after former British Prime Minister Margaret Thatcher or author Margaret Mitchell).

A few names have gained such negative significance that you really want to shy away from them. Adolf is one such name. Another example may be to avoid a combination of first and middle names that result in the initials O.J. However, these are really rare cases; you shouldn't avoid good, strong names like Jack or Jeffrey simply because they were the first names of the two of the most notorious serial murderers in history. The best advice: Just be aware of the associations and use your best judgment.

If your last name is the same as a famous person's, you may want to avoid giving your child the first name of that famous person, too. You may think it's cute, but your child may not feel same way. If your last name is Kennedy and you name your son John, he will go through life as John Kennedy. That may be fine for you, but your son may not care for that association, especially if he grows up to be a Republican!

Creating a Family of Names

If you know that you're going to have a slew of kids or you want to find a visible way to create family unity, you may want to make all your children's names alike in some way. Doing so has the advantage of creating an even tighter bond between your children. Here are a few examples of how you can create a "family of names":

❀ **All names start with the same initial or sound.** For example, you can have two boys named Michael and Matthew and two girls named Meredith and Marie. This can be especially fun if you and your spouse have names that begin with that letter or sound as well.

❀ **All names come from a single source.** The Bible has always been a popular source for creating this kind of name family. For example, you can name your children for famous biblical personalities:

Abraham, Isaac, David, and so on. Or you can name your children after your favorite authors, such as James (for James Joyce), John (for John Steinbeck), Elizabeth (for Elizabeth Barrett Browning), and Virginia (for Virginia Woolf).

✾ **All names come from your own family.** For example, if you plan to have four children, you could give them the names of all four grandparents. But be aware of the political ramifications: Don't choose names from only one side of your family; mix and match from both sides of the family.

Beware the twin trap! Your twins may get badly teased if you name them with cutesy couplets, such as Brad and Chad or Cindy and Mindy. Let them have their own identities — give them unique names. However, you do want them to sound like they're related. Don't give one daughter a traditional name like Sarah and the other a modern name like Trinity.

Knowing the Sex Beforehand — or Not

Of course, it's your family's personal decision whether you want to know the sex of your baby before it's born. Some parents want to know so that they can plan ahead — such as painting the baby's room pink or blue, buying boy or girl baby clothes, and, yes, even choosing one baby name rather than having to come up with two. Plus, it gives the baby an identity even before he or she is born — instead of just being "it," the baby is Katie or Carter, for example. Other parents want to leave it up to nature and preserve the surprise for the delivery room. This section offers some baby-naming tips for whichever situation you're in.

Knowing ahead of time

Knowing the sex of your baby before it's born gives you plenty of time to come up with names. You can do research; you can get advice from others; and you can make love-hate lists of names. The advantage is that you're prepared. The disadvantage is that you may be *too* prepared.

Ideally, you can narrow down your choices to two or three beforehand, and when your baby is born, you realize that the choices you made are perfect for the little one you're holding in your arms. However, keep in mind that it doesn't always happen that way. For example:

✾ You may look at the little tyke and decide that none of the names seems to fit. Say that you're set on the name Emily. But when you see your little girl for the first time, you say, "She doesn't *look* like an Emily. She looks like a Rachel. But I hate the name Rachel!"

Stranger things have happened. Remember, right after your child is born, you and your family will be filled with all sorts of emotions, and the logical, cool decisions you made beforehand may end up going out the window.

❀ The doctor may have been wrong in determining the sex of your baby. It's rare, but it does happen. So you spent all that time coming up with the perfect girl's name only to find a little boy in your arms — and it's back to the ol' drawing board!

If you know the sex ahead of time, the best advice is not to get too attached to the name you select and have a few backups just in case. You may even want to plan for the unlikely event that your doctor made a mistake and decide on both a boy's name and a girl's name. You can always use the other one the next time around!

Waiting for the surprise

A lot of parents want to be surprised. They want to feel that rush of excitement when the doctor exclaims, "It's a (fill in the blank)!"

Waiting for the surprise means that you have double the prep work to do. Instead of one list of names, you make two. You decide on likely candidates for each sex and narrow it down to a few possibilities. But remember, don't get too attached to the names you pick, and have some backup choices just in case.

Keeping Nicknames in Mind

Like it or not, your child will probably develop a nickname (or several), unless you decide on a very short name. A nickname will likely be a shortened version of the full name, such as Bill or Will for William or Beth or Liz for Elizabeth. This kind of nickname is different from a pet name. (You know how dreadful those can be, especially if your pet name was Princess or Squeaky.)

 Your child's friends, aunts, uncles, cousins, grandparents, and teachers — pretty much everybody — will want to call your child by a nickname. Most of the time, a nickname is a sign of endearment, or it indicates the other person's wish to interact on a more familiar level.

So take nicknames into consideration. You may always call your son Jacob, but plenty of others will want to call him Jake. Exotic Francesca may well turn into the rather ordinary Fran. Also, beware the dreaded adding of a "y" or "i" to the end of a name or nickname. Benjamin, for example, can easily become Benny or (gasp!) Benji.

Coming Up with a List of Names You Like

Having hundreds of names in this book to choose from may seem overwhelming. To start narrowing down the field a bit, use Table 1-1 to record some of the names that you like. Remember that if you're not planning to find the sex of your baby ahead of time, you should fill out two worksheets — one for a boy and one for a girl. After you complete Table 1-1, try ranking the names in order of preference.

 It may be helpful if both you and your spouse or partner fill out Table 1-1 separately and then compare notes. With any luck, you may end up with a couple of common choices between you.

Table 1-1 Favorite Names

Name	Nicknames	Origin	Meaning	Pros	Cons

The Top 100 Names Being Used Today

If you're curious to know which are the most popular names in the United States, the Social Security Administration's Web site, www.ssa.gov/OACT/babynames/, is probably the best resource. At the site, you can pull up lists of the top 1,000 (or 500, 100, 50, or 10) names from every year since 1990. You can also track the popularity of a single name over the years since 1990; review the top five names by state; and find the top names (based on much smaller samples) by year and decade dating back to 1880. The data is based on applications for Social Security cards.

Table 1-2 lists the top 100 names from 2002, the most recent year available.

Table 1-2 Top 100 Names from 2002

Rank	Boys	Girls
1	Jacob	Emily
2	Michael	Madison
3	Joshua	Hannah
4	Matthew	Emma
5	Ethan	Alexis
6	Joseph	Ashley
7	Andrew	Abigail
8	Christopher	Sarah
9	Daniel	Samantha
10	Nicholas	Olivia
11	William	Elizabeth
12	Anthony	Alyssa
13	David	Lauren
14	Tyler	Isabella
15	Alexander	Grace
16	Ryan	Jessica
17	John	Brianna
18	James	Taylor
19	Zachary	Kayla
20	Brandon	Anna
21	Jonathan	Victoria
22	Justin	Megan
23	Christian	Sydney
24	Dylan	Chloe
25	Samuel	Rachel
26	Austin	Jasmine
27	Jose	Sophia
28	Benjamin	Jennifer

Rank	Boys	Girls
29	Nathan	Morgan
30	Logan	Natalie
31	Kevin	Julia
32	Gabriel	Kaitlyn
33	Robert	Hailey
34	Noah	Destiny
35	Caleb	Haley
36	Thomas	Katherine
37	Jordan	Nicole
38	Hunter	Alexandra
39	Cameron	Maria
40	Kyle	Savannah
41	Elijah	Stephanie
42	Jason	Mia
43	Jack	Mackenzie
44	Aaron	Allison
45	Isaiah	Amanda
46	Angel	Jordan
47	Luke	Jenna
48	Connor	Faith
49	Luis	Paige
50	Isaac	Makayla
51	Brian	Andrea
52	Juan	Mary
53	Jackson	Brooke
54	Eric	Katelyn
55	Mason	Rebecca
56	Adam	Madeline
57	Evan	Michelle
58	Carlos	Kaylee
59	Charles	Sara

continued

☺ ☻ ☹ ☺ ☻ ☹ ☺ ☻ ☹ ☺ ☻ ☹ ☺ ☻ ☹ ☺ ☺ ☻ ☹ ☺

Table 1-1 Top 100 Names from 2002 *(continued)*

Rank	Boys	Girls
60	Sean	Kimberly
61	Gavin	Zoe
62	Alex	Kylie
63	Aidan	Aaliyah
64	Bryan	Sierra
65	Nathaniel	Amber
66	Jesus	Caroline
67	Ian	Gabrielle
68	Steven	Vanessa
69	Cole	Alexa
70	Timothy	Trinity
71	Cody	Danielle
72	Adrian	Erin
73	Seth	Autumn
74	Sebastian	Angelina
75	Devin	Shelby
76	Lucas	Gabriella
77	Richard	Riley
78	Blake	Jada
79	Julian	Lily
80	Patrick	Melissa
81	Trevor	Jacqueline
82	Jared	Angela
83	Miguel	Ava
84	Chase	Isabel
85	Dominic	Bailey
86	Antonio	Ariana
87	Xavier	Jade
88	Jeremiah	Melanie
89	Jaden	Courtney

☺ ☺ ☹ ☺ ☺ ☹ ☺ ☺ ☹ ☺ ☺ ☹ ☺ ☺ ☹ ☺ ☺ ☺ ☹ ☺

Rank	Boys	Girls
90	Alejandro	Leah
91	Jeremy	Maya
92	Jesse	Ella
93	Garrett	Jocelyn
94	Diego	Leslie
95	Mark	Claire
96	Owen	Christina
97	Hayden	Lillian
98	Victor	Evelyn
99	Bryce	Gabriela
100	Riley	Catherine

Chapter 2

Bailey, Brian, or Brent? Names for Boys

In This Chapter

☺ Choosing today's most popular boys' names

☺ Looking for something a little more unique

☺ Deciphering the origins and meanings of the names you like

Your son's name will be part of his identity forever, so you want to choose a name that he'll be proud to bear for a lifetime. In this chapter, you find hundreds of options, from traditional names like Aaron and Adam to newer, trendier options like Brayan and Brock.

A

Aaron: Origin and meaning uncertain. Some sources say that Aaron comes from Hebrew and means "enlightened" or "to sing." In the United States, Aaron appeared throughout the period of the popularity of Old Testament names. After the mid-19th century, its popularity declined, but it remains a viable name today. Among well-known Aarons, Aaron Burr mortally wounded Alexander Hamilton in an 1804 duel. Aaron Spelling has produced many hit TV shows, including *Beverly Hills 90210, Fantasy Island, The Love Boat*, and *Charlie's Angels*. Baseball legend Hank Aaron also comes to mind. Alternate spellings are **Aron, Arron,** and **Erron.**

Abraham: Hebrew; "father of a multitude." During the popularity of Old Testament names, Abraham was current but never common; **Abram** also appeared occasionally. A slight increase in popularity occurred near the beginning of the 19th century, including "Old Abe" himself, Abraham Lincoln (born in 1809). By the Civil War, however, Abraham was becoming old-fashioned, and it has remained rare in spite of hero worship of the

☺ ☺ ☹ ☺ ☺ ☹ ☺ ☺ ☹ ☺ ☺ ☹ ☺ ☺ ☹ ☺ ☺ ☹ ☺

Great Emancipator. Today, the name is far from extinct, but it's by no means widespread. Abraham is the more common form in modern times, sitting at No. 204 in the Social Security Administration's most recent list.

Adam: Hebrew; meaning uncertain. In its opening passage, the Book of Genesis uses the Hebrew word *adam* in at least three senses: first, as the name of a particular man; second, for man in the general sense; and third, for the color red. Some scholars even take the meaning to be "earth" or "likeness." The name's popularity has been on something of a roller coaster throughout the centuries. It was quite popular throughout the British Isles, but this usage failed to survive the Reformation. Although it didn't become obsolete, Adam became rare. In America, it held a precarious but tenacious position. At Harvard, for example, there was rarely a year without at least one student named Adam, and probably never a year when there were more than two in one class. One reason for its lack of popularity was Adam's association with the idea of Original Sin, a doctrine that the Puritans respected highly. In the late 18th century, Adam became popular again, but then, perhaps because of its old-fashioned associations, it waned once more early in the 20th century. Today, the name is quite common. Modern-day Adams of note include comedic actor Adam Sandler and rocker Adam Duritz of the band the Counting Crows.

Addison: English; "son of Adam." Although Addison is suitable for a boy or a girl, today it's more popular for girls. A famous male Addison is James Addison Baker III, who served as President Ronald Reagan's chief of staff during his first term and then as Secretary of the Treasury in Reagan's second term. He successfully managed the campaign of President George H. W. Bush and served as his Secretary of State, where he aided in the effort to bring peace to the Middle East.

Adrian: Latin; "of the Adriatic." You may be surprised to hear that this name has been among the top 100 baby names for more than a decade. Several popes have carried the name Adrian. One notable example was Pope Adrian IV, who was the first (and only) pope from Britain. Another was Pope Adrian VI, who was the only Dutch pope. From the music world, Sir Adrian Boult was a British conductor who served as music director of the BBC and conductor of the London Philharmonic Orchestra during the mid-20th century. If you're a fan of musicals from the 1920s and 1930s, you may recognize the work of fashion designer Adrian Gilbert, who was discovered by Irving Berlin when studying in Paris and became one of Broadway's and Hollywood's leading costume designers of the era. In fact, you can thank him for popularizing shoulder pads and dolman sleeves! An alternate spelling is **Adrien,** the form used by Adrien Brody, the youngest man to win a Best Actor Oscar for his role in Roman Polanski's film *The Pianist.*

Aidan: Gaelic, Old Irish; "to help." St. Aidan epitomized the definition of his name as someone who desired to help others. An Irish monk from a

☺ ☺ ☹ ☺ ☺ ☹ ☺ ☺ ☹ ☺ ☺ ☹ ☺ ☺ ☹ ☺ ☺ ☺ ☹ ☺

Gaelic monastery, he was called upon by Northumbria's King Oswald to create a church and monastery on the island of Lindisfarne in 635 AD. He became the first bishop of the church he established and later became known as the apostle of Northumbria. A modern-day Aidan of note is Aidan Quinn, an actor known for his powerful yet sensitive performances in such films as *Legends of the Fall* and *Benny & Joon.* He received an Emmy nomination for his performance in *An Early Frost,* which was the first television movie to deal with AIDS. Nicknames and derivatives of Aidan include **Adan, Aden, Aiden, Ayden,** and **Eden.**

Alan: Breton; meaning uncertain, possibly "handsome." Alan was the name of a fifth-century bishop of Quimper in Brittany, which was an area of Gaelic speech. The name later became current, especially in Scotland. In America, it has been primarily a family name, but in the late 20th century, it became somewhat popular as a given name. Today, both Alan and **Allen** are among the top 250 names in use. **Allan** appears as well. Notable bearers of this name include actor Alan Alda and Federal Reserve Chairman Allan Greenspan.

Albert: German; "noble and bright." Albert was used in England during the Middle Ages but fell out of use in the early modern period, to be revived after the marriage of Queen Victoria to the German Prince Albert in 1840. As Prince Consort, he became highly popular among the English, and curiously, his name became much more popular than hers ever did. The popularity of Albert has waned in recent years, but it remains a viable name. The Spanish version, **Alberto,** is even more popular. In its evolution, Albert developed two different familiar forms — **Bert** in Britain and **Al** in the United States. Famous Alberts include physicist Albert Einstein and humanitarian and theologian Albert Schweitzer.

Alden: Old English; from the name Ealdwine, meaning "old friend." Everyone knows who Neil Armstrong is, but very few people know that his middle initial *A,* which makes an appearance on the plaque on the Apollo 11 lunar lander, stands for Alden. A former test pilot, Armstrong was the commander of the Apollo 11 flight and became the first human to set foot on the moon in 1969, when he uttered his famous words, "One small step for man, one giant leap for mankind." Another noteworthy Alden is J. Alden Weir, an American Impressionist painter of the late 19th century and early 20th century. Alden Nowlan was a 20th-century poet, novelist, and playwright who had a busy career, having written three plays and 24 books in 27 years. This name isn't popular today, but its nice meaning and positive associations make it worthy of consideration.

Alexander: Greek; from *alex-,* "defend," and *ander,* "man." It's an additional name or title borne by Paris in *The Iliad.* Alexander was common in later classical Greece, partly because of Alexander the Great, who, in the Middle Ages, became the hero of a cycle of romances. Some 20 saints also bear the name. Nevertheless, Alexander never really flourished in England.

In Scotland, however, it was borne by three successive kings (1214–1285) and became generally used. In the American colonies, Alexander may even have been employed as a test for Scottish influence. Historically, **Sandy** is a nickname for Alexander, not (as common belief now runs) a nickname for someone with so-called "sandy" hair. Today, the name is often shortened to **Alex.** Notable Alexanders include Revolutionary War figure Alexander Hamilton, telephone inventor Alexander Graham Bell, and gameshow host Alex Trebek.

Alexis: Greek; "helper, defender." Alexis is a borrowing from the French, which in turn took it from Russian or some other language of eastern Europe. In the United States, this name, which originally was a male name, is generally thought of as female — it was No. 5 on the most recent list of the top baby names — but it has become increasing popular for boys as well. If the trend continues, it's poised to break into the top 150 names in coming years. Historian and political scientist Alexis de Tocqueville, a Frenchman, is known for his work *Democracy in America.*

Alfred: Old English; "elf counsel." In spite of the Christianization of the Anglo-Saxons, pagan customs lingered, such as the belief in elves as friendly supernatural creatures, and "elf" was a recognized name component. In addition, the royal family regularly used names beginning with *A.* After the Norman Conquest, the name Alfred went out of use. It reappeared in the late 18th century, when interest revived in the Anglo-Saxon heritage. In the United States, the name dates from about 1780. It rose in popularity early in the next century, but after 1870, its popularity fell off rapidly over the course of a few decades, and by 1950, it was seldom used. One difficulty has been the lack of a comfortable short form. Albert tends to monopolize Al, and Frederick dominates Fred. The British solution of using **Alf** remains a Briticism to most Americans in spite of Alf Landon, candidate for president in 1936. Americans also know this name well because of Alfred Hitchcock, who directed dozens of suspense films, a few of the most acclaimed being *Notorious, Rear Window, Psycho,* and *The Birds.* Today, the Spanish form **Alfredo** is more common than its English counterpart.

Alistair: Scottish; "defender of men." Alistair is the Gaelic version of ALEXANDER. Alistair Cooke, the venerable figurehead of *Masterpiece Theatre,* embodies the British host. Alistair MacLean wrote many important and popular war novels, including *Force Ten from Navarone* and *Where Eagles Dare.* **Alistaire** and **Alister** are two common variations.

Allan, Allen: See ALAN.

Alvin: Old English; a merging of Aelfwine, which means "elf + friend," and Ethelwine, which means "noble + friend." The name apparently wasn't in use for long. Its "revival" in the late 19th century may not have been an actual revival but a coinage. It seems to be essentially an American form and has achieved some popularity since the late 19th century; today, it

Chapter 2: Bailey, Brian, or Brent? Names for Boys

☺ ☺ ☹ ☺ ☺ ☹ ☺ ☺ ☹ ☺ ☺ ☹ ☺ ☺ ☹ ☺ ☺ ☺ ☹ ☺

barely cracks the top 500. Alvin is sometimes shortened to **Al.** The most famous Alvin may be the mischievous character in the animated TV show *Alvin and the Chipmunks.* Also noteworthy is Alvin Ailey, who was a pioneering choreographer in the field of modern dance.

Amos: Hebrew; "carried." Amos was one of the minor prophets and a book of the Bible. It was a fairly popular name in early New England throughout the period when biblical names were popular. The most famous Amos may be Famous Amos, the cookie maker. *Amos n' Andy* was a wildly popular radio show from 1928 to 1943.

Andre: French; "manly." Andre is the French form of ANDREW. Famous Andres include Andre Agassi, the Las Vegas native who, early in his professional tennis career, became as famous for his hometown-inspired wardrobe as for his fearless play on the court. But this tennis champion proved that he had substance by winning (to date) seven Grand Slam tournaments. Actor Andre Braugher is known for his daring portrayal of detective Frank Pembleton on the television drama *Homicide.* Composer and conductor Andre Previn achieved much success with his first opera, *A Streetcar Named Desire,* which won him a Grammy Award. Another bravely creative Andre was French author Andre Gide, whose prolific writing career won him the Nobel Prize for Literature in 1947. This Andre is best known for his novels *The Immoralist* and *The Counterfeiters.* **Andres,** a Spanish form, is slightly more popular than Andre today.

Andrew: Greek; "manly." Andrew entered the Christian tradition as the name of the apostle and saint who became the patron of both Scotland and Russia. Although the association with Scotland began at an early date, it was possibly more formal than popular. Scottish immigrants brought this name with them to America, but it wasn't much used until the mid-19th century, when it became fairly common, doubtless because of the popularity of Andrew Jackson. The name Andrew has failed to develop a one-syllable form, but the nickname **Andy** is almost universal — in fact, today it's considered an independent name as well. Famous Andrews and Andys include U.S. President Andrew Johnson, industrialist and philanthropist Andrew Carnegie, TV star Andy Griffith, and *60 Minutes* commentator Andy Rooney.

Angel: Greek; "messenger." Angel was originally more common for males than for females, but Puritans preferred to add the *o.* **Angelo** took root in Italy and has remained popular there. In English-speaking countries, Angelo had, for the most part, replaced Angel as a man's name. However, with the growth of the Latino population in the United States, Angel (generally pronounced "an-HEL") is gaining strength once again. Angelo Dundee was Muhammad Ali's boxing mentor.

Angus: Gaelic; possibly "unique strength." Angus has failed to attain popularity in the United States, where it's classified as a rare name, but if you're an Anglophile, it's a unique option to consider. In Scotland, it's sometimes shifted to **Aeneas,** as if from the name of the Trojan hero. Angus Young plays guitar for long-time hard rockers AC/DC.

Ansel: A variant of **Anselm,** which is Germanic ("god helmet"), chiefly used among the Lombards and brought to England by Anselm (himself a Lombard) when he became Archbishop of Canterbury in the late 11th century. This name is rare in the United States. Ansel Adams was a highly regarded 20th-century photographer, known for his photographs showcasing the natural beauty of Yosemite National Park and other such places.

Anthony: Latin; meaning unknown. Derived from a Roman *gens* (family) "Antonius." The modern usage of this name is chiefly due to St. Antony of Padua, a Franciscan monk who is known as the patron of the lower animals. Shakespeare based his tragedy *Antony and Cleopatra* on Marc Antony, a relative of Julius Caesar. In the United States, the inclusion of the letter *h* has influenced the pronunciation, and the *th* pronunciation is now the more common one. The name has been consistently popular throughout the 20th century and into the 21st — in 2002, it reached No. 12. Notable bearers include actor Anthony Hopkins, writer Anthony Burgess, and Supreme Court Justice Anthony Kennedy. **Tony** is a common nickname.

Antonio: Latin; meaning unknown. Antonio is a popular variation of ANTHONY, who, according to myth, lived alone in the wild for more than 80 years during the third century. The actor Antonio Banderas, who starred in such films as *Desperado* and *Spy Kids* and is married to actress Melanie Griffith, is a well-known Antonio.

Archibald: German; a typical two-element name, made up of *ercan,* "true," and *bald,* "bold." It was an established name among the Normans, but it failed to survive in England, except in the North, and especially among the wide-ranging Normans of southern Scotland, where it became common. In America, Archibald appears in some colonial listings, where it's considered evidence of Scottish influence. It has scarcely survived on its own, coming to be associated with Algernon and other such names of aristocratic (and decadent) suggestions. **Archie,** however, was well Americanized, although it, too, remains uncommon. The most famous holder of this name is arguably one of two fictional characters: either TV's Archie Bunker or comic book teen Archie Andrews.

Arnold: German; from *arin,* "eagle," and *vald,* "power." It's found occasionally from the later 18th century onward, sometimes from the family name. The name Arnold is only marginally popular today, although it has served actor and now politician Arnold Schwarzenegger well. **Arnie** is a common nickname — but don't try calling Schwarzenegger that!

Arthur: Origin and meaning uncertain. The origin of the name has been the subject of much controversy — and so has everything else about King Arthur. The name may be from that of a Roman family, recorded as

☺ ☺ ☹ ☺ ☺ ☹ ☺ ☺ ☹ ☺ ☺ ☹ ☺ ☺ ☹ ☺ ☺ ☺ ☹ ☹ ☺

Artorius, but various Celtic origins have been plausibly proposed. Its origin from the legendary King Arthur is, however, certain. The name was nearly extinct in the 17th century, but increased interest in the Middle Ages, and the general Romantic approach to life, gradually brought the name back into use in Britain, and its association with the Duke of Wellington assured its popularity. In the United States, it began to appear about 1780 and grew steadily, peaking in popularity during the early 1900s. As the 20th century advanced, the name, as is to be expected, came to seem old-fashioned, and its popularity declined steadily; by the middle of the century, Arthur was considered uncommon. Variants include **Arturo** and the nicknames **Art** and **Artie.** Among well-known Arthurs, science-fiction author Arthur C. Clarke penned *2001: A Space Odyssey,* jazz pianist Art Tatum earned accolades for his prodigious musical talent, and cartoon aardvark Arthur captures the hearts of many American children today.

Ashton: English; "ash (tree) village." Although Ashton has become a common boys' name in recent years, ranking 203rd in the 2002 list of the most popular names in the United States, it's also used for girls. A famous male Ashton is Ashton Kutcher, the young comedic star of TV's *That '70's Show* and — who could forget? — the movie *Dude, Where's My Car?* An alternate spelling is **Ashten. Asher** also appears now and then.

Augustus: Latin; "venerable, consecrated." In the United States, it regularly appears as **Gus.** It's commonly taken from the German form **August** and has never been wholly embraced into general usage in the United States. The association with the mighty Augustus Caesar, though, makes it worthy of consideration if you're looking for a lofty name. Pulitzer Prize winning playwright August Wilson wrote *Fences* and *Piano Lessons.*

Austin: Latin; "venerable, consecrated." A derivative of AUGUSTUS, perhaps the most famous Austin today is actually a fictional character — Austin Powers, the "international man of mystery" characterized by comedic actor Mike Myers in (to date) three popular films. A couple of other significant Austins include Austin Flint, a physician who founded Buffalo Medical College and helped found Belleview Medical College in New York City, and Austin Clarke, an Irish playwright and poet of the early 20th century. This name also conjures up images of Texas's capital city, which got its name from land developer Stephen F. Austin. A variant of Austin (with literary associations to boot) is **Austen.**

Avery: French; "elf + friend." A borrowing of ALFRED, this name can be male or female, but, as with many androgynous names, today it's used more often for girls than for boys. For example, Tom Cruise's ambitious and, it turns out, unsupportive girlfriend at the beginning of the movie *Jerry Maguire* (played by John Travolta's real-life wife Kelly Preston) is named Avery.

Ayden: See AIDAN.

Ten long and flowery names

A long name can sound dignified and formal. If you're looking for these qualities in a name, consider the following options. But think twice if your last name is long as well; you don't want to give your child a lifetime of hand cramps from writing out all those letters!

* Alexander
* Benjamin
* Demetrius
* Emmanuel
* Giovanni
* Jeremiah
* Maximilian
* Nathaniel
* Sebastian
* Zachariah

B

Bailey: English; "bailiff." A common last name, Bailey has become an increasingly popular first name. In the television show *Party of Five*, the character Bailey Salinger, played by actor Scott Wolf, served as the force that kept the family together. A few more Baileys of note include geologist Bailey Willis, whose research into earthquakes in the early 20th century earned him the nickname "Earthquake Willie." In his studies, he concluded that there are no scientific ways to predict earthquakes, which led to improvements in building codes in earthquake-prone regions. Alternate spellings include **Baylee** and **Bailee,** although these forms may be more appropriate for girls than for boys.

Bartholomew: Hebrew; "son of Tolmai." As one of the apostles, St. Bartholomew was venerated in England during the later Middle Ages, and his name was popular. Like other New Testament names (partly because of its length, perhaps), it failed to maintain that popularity in America, although the recurring short forms **Bart** and **Bat** indicate its use in the 19th century. It's scarcely considered current today, although wise-cracking cartoon character Bart Simpson has kept it alive in popular culture.

Benjamin: Probably Hebrew; "son of the right hand." The original name may have been applied to a tribe. The use as a baptismal name arose

Chapter 2: Bailey, Brian, or Brent? Names for Boys

☺ ☹ ☹ ☺ ☹ ☹ ☺ ☹ ☹ ☺ ☹ ☹ ☺ ☹ ☹ ☺ ☺ ☹ ☹ ☺

among English Puritans of the early 17th century. Brought to America by immigrants to the Puritan colonies, the name Benjamin flourished — in New England in the 17th century, for example, Benjamin was regularly in the top ten. The reasons for this popularity are difficult to figure out. The biblical story is an appealing one — the child orphaned of his mother in childbirth, the solace of an elderly father. Benjamin was probably a name given after the death of the mother in childbirth, an all too frequent reality in those years. After 1700, its popularity fell off, and it made the top ten for the last time in the 1720s. The decline sharpened after the mid-19th century, when the influence of Benjamin Franklin began to wane. As a folk hero, Franklin's only rival was George Washington, and in some respects, Franklin even exceeded Washington. After 1890, the name was rare throughout the country. Its use revived in the mid-20th century, however, and today, it's at a very respectable No. 28. The most common (and, many would say, appealing) nickname is **Ben; Benny** and **Benji** are also used. Famous Bens and Benjamins include actor Ben Affleck, whose films include *Good Will Hunting* and *Pearl Harbor*; actor Benjamin Bratt, Julia Roberts' former flame; and Benny Goodman, the legendary clarinetist and bandleader.

Bernhard: German; "bear-bold." The Normans largely propagated this typical Germanic name. In the United States, it's probably to be considered a family name that is occasionally used as a given name. The variant **Bernard** is more common in the United States. Bernard Shaw gained fame for his coverage of the Gulf War for CNN.

Bertram: German; "bright raven." Brought into English usage by the Normans. It has been less current in America than in Britain. The American use of the name may be from Romantic tastes of the 19th century rather than from a continuing tradition from the Anglo-Saxon. Variants include **Bert** and **Bertrand,** as in the philosopher Bertrand Russell.

Bill, Billie, Billy: See WILLIAM.

Blaine: Welsh; from the name Bleddyn ("wolf"). Also English; a nickname for "a swelling" or a place name for a hill. Magician David Blaine's hip, contemporary, and in-your-face skills are making magic popular again, and in places besides the Las Vegas strip. Ohio's Blaine Wilson harnessed ambition and strength that enabled him to become one of the greatest male gymnasts ever to compete for the U.S. in the Olympic Games in 1996 and 2000. The name has never been especially popular, although it remains in the top 500 in use today. Alternate spellings include **Blane, Blayne,** and **Blain.**

Blake: English; "black." It means the reverse in Old English, "fair, pale." Whatever the meaning, the name is fairly popular today — it's been in the top 100 for more than a decade. Visionary British poet and artist William Blake's works, such as *Songs of Innocence* and *The Marriage of Heaven and Hell,* solidified his reputation as a profound, original genius. Film

☺ ☻ ☹ ☺ ☻ ☹ ☺ ☻ ☹ ☺ ☻ ☹ ☺ ☻ ☹ ☺ ☺ ☻ ☹ ☺

director Blake Edwards kept audiences laughing and swooning for 40 years with such classics as *Breakfast at Tiffany's, The Great Race, Victor/Victoria,* and the unforgettable slapstick of Inspector Clouseau in the *Pink Panther* movies.

Bo: English, French; "beautiful," "handsome." The meaning of this name is a direct translation of the French word *beau.* It has served as both a boys' name and a girls' name, although it's never been particularly popular. Beautiful Bo Derek is famous for her role in the movie *10,* opposite Dudley Moore — the scene of her running down the beach in cornrows is likely to remain one of the best known in film for some time to come. Among male Bos, Bo Jackson was the first athlete to play two professional sports at the same time: baseball with the Kansas City Royals and football for the Los Angeles Raiders.

Bob, Bobby: See ROBERT.

Braden: English; as derived from the name BRAD, Braden means "from the broad valley" or "broad." Braden also translates from the Irish surname O'Bradain, which comes from a Gaelic word for "salmon." This name has seen a tremendous rise in popularity in the last ten years, jumping nearly 250 spots to 169th in 2002. Its numerous variations include **Bradan, Braddon, Bradene, Bradon, Bradyn, Braeden, Braedon, Brayden,** and **Braydon.**

Bradley, Brad: English; "broad clearing, meadow." The name Bradley has been used mostly in the United States. The shortened form **Brad** appears on its own almost as regularly. The name gained great popularity with General Omar Nelson Bradley, who commanded an Army group in Europe during World War II. Current Brads include mega-star Brad Pitt and young actor Brad Renfro, who starred in the film version of John Grisham's *The Client.* And what's a Brad list without Brad Bradley (he starred in *The Martian Chronicles*)? Other, less common spellings include **Bradd, Bradlee,** and **Bradleigh.**

Brady: English; "broad island." Brady began as a surname and eventually became a first name in the United States. Could *The Brady Bunch* have had something to do with its current popularity among parents who came of age during the show? Perhaps. Noted Civil War photographer Matthew Brady is a famed Brady. Occasionally used for girls as well, the name is sometimes spelled **Bradey.**

Brandon: English; "broom-covered hill." **Branden** is a somewhat more modern version of Brandon, which remains a very popular name in the United States, perhaps coming into national circulation in the 1980s because of TV executive Brandon Tartikoff. The late actor Brandon Lee (son of martial arts master Bruce Lee) kept the name alive in pop culture in the early 1990s; like his father, he died young, from gunshot wounds

☺ ☺ ☹ ☺ ☺ ☹ ☺ ☺ ☹ ☺ ☺ ☹ ☺ ☺ ☹ ☺ ☺ ☺ ☺ ☹ ☺

that he received during the filming of the movie *The Crow*. **Brand** may be considered a nickname, although it's more likely an English borrowing of an independent name meaning "sword, fire-brand."

Braxton: English; "brock's settlement" (*brock* was another word for badger). Originally a surname, it made the switch to first name. R&B singing star Toni Braxton is a notable Braxton in the United States. Apropos of this book, it should be noted that 19th-century English doctor John Braxton Hicks "discovered" contractions.

Brayan: See BRIAN.

Brendan: Gaelic; from an Irish borrowing of the Welsh word *brenhin*, meaning "king." In the United States, this name has appeared chiefly in Irish context. Actor Brendan Fraser has starred in numerous films, including *With Honors* and *Gods and Monsters*. Alternate spellings include **Brenden** and **Brendon.**

Brent: English; "from high on the hill." Sports broadcaster Brent Musburger's talented and dynamic play-by-plays make him a prominent voice in college football and basketball telecasts. Its popularity has fallen of late, but the name remains in the top 400 in use for baby boys. Similar names include **Brendt**, **Brenten**, **Brentley**, **Brently**, and **Brenton.**

Brett: English, French; a native of Britain or the Brittany region of France. Other origins are possible as well. Sometimes spelled **Bret,** this name, like BRENT, isn't as common as it once was. It was in the top 100 as recently as 1990, but today, it holds the 200th slot. Ernest Hemingway boosted the popularity of this name by introducing Lady Brett Ashley as his beautiful and independent heroine in *The Sun Also Rises*, although it's seldom used as a girls' name in modern times. Green Bay Packers quarterback Brett Favre, having taken his team to two consecutive Super Bowls, remains the NFL's only three-time Most Valuable Player.

Brian: Breton; "high, noble." It's also a family name. Brian flourished in England during the Middle Ages, but it soon fell into disuse. Revived in the 20th century, it's fairly popular today, consistently appearing among the top 50 names in the U.S. Alternate spellings include **Bryan; Brayan** is a hip variation. Famous Brians include filmmaker Brian De Palma, actor Brian Dennehy, and Beach Boys singer Brian Wilson. Singers Bryan Adams and Bryan Ferry (formerly of Roxy Music) use the *y* spelling.

Brock: English; a variant of **Brook,** which means "one who lives by the river or stream" or "badger." Given its meaning, Brock would be an especially good name for a University of Wisconsin graduate (the school's nickname: Badgers). This name has achieved moderate popularity in the United States, reaching into the mid-200s. Curiously, it isn't connected to any well-known celebrity, which many parents may consider a big plus.

Brody: Scottish Gaelic; "ditch," "from the muddy place." Brody was once a surname, but it's gaining popularity because of its brevity and uniqueness. Actor Adam Brody, starring in many popular teenage angst vehicles, is a popular Brody, as is Adrien Brody. Like the name itself, actor Brody Hutzler is an up-and-comer. Some variations include **Brodie, Brodee,** and **Brodey.**

Bruce: Origin and meaning unknown. Various possible origins exist for the surname Bruce, from Brix in La Manche to Le Brus in Calvados, but linguists can't pin down the exact origin due to a lack of evidence. In most Americans' minds, Bruce is considered primarily a given name. Its popularity has slipped in recent years, but it remains among the top 500 names in use. Noteworthy Bruces include rock and roller Bruce Springsteen, kung fu master Bruce Lee, and decathlete Bruce Jenner.

Bryan: See BRIAN.

Bryce: Origin and meaning unknown. Bryce can be traced to the fifth-century saint Britius or Bricius, whose name is most likely Gaulish. In recent years, the name has cracked the list of the 100 most popular boys' names in the United States. Lovers of the West may associate it with southern Utah's Bryce Canyon Natural Park, which features dramatic red rock formations called "hoodoos." An alternate spelling is **Brice.**

Ten short-and-sweet names

Do you want to make sure that no one takes your child's beautiful given name and shortens it to something you can't stand? Or do you have a long and complex last name that you'd like to balance with something simpler? Try giving your baby one of these five-letters-or-fewer names that are virtually impossible to shorten:

- Alec
- Brock
- Clay
- Dane
- Gage
- Kai
- Jake
- Max
- Reese/Reece
- Ty

Bryson: This name is a surname from BRYCE ("son of Bryce"). Humorist and travel writer Bill Bryson and R&B vocalist Peabo Bryson are notable bearers of the surname. Today, it's growing in popularity as a first name, perhaps because Brian/Bryan just seems too plain.

Byron: A variant of **Byrom,** a surname meaning "dweller of the cowshed." This not-so-pleasant meaning may or may not be why this name is not especially popular these days; it barely cracks the top 500. One of the most versatile and respected poets of the Romantic period, Lord Byron created the timeless lover *Don Juan.* The poet's daughter, Ada Byron, became a mathematician and scientist who wrote a theory of how an engine might calculate numbers. Albeit long before the technical revolution, Ada Byron's theory is widely accepted as the first computer program. US Senator Byron Dorgan is a Democrat from North Dakota.

C

Caleb: Hebrew; "faithful," "bold." Caleb is found in the Old Testament; he was a leader of the Israelites. It has weathered the test of time as a popular boy's name, and in the late 1990s was among the top 50 most used names. In George Eliot's novel *Middlemarch,* Caleb Garth is the honest, hard-working foil to pretentious townspeople. An alternate spelling is **Kaleb,** and **Cal/Kal** and **Cale/Kale** are nicknames.

Calvin: Latin; "bald." As a Protestant reformer, John Calvin was a respected and even heroic figure among both Congregationalists and Presbyterians, but more so among the latter. He believed in predestination — the idea that one's life is already mapped out. Vice President Calvin Coolidge became the 30th President of the United States upon the death of President Warren Harding in 1923. In more recent years, this name become synonymous with American fashion designer Calvin Klein, whose jeans — and the sexy line "Nothing comes between me and my Calvins" — brought stardom to actress Brooke Shields in the 1970s. The comic strip *Calvin and Hobbes* features impish boy Calvin and his stuffed tiger, Hobbes, who is certainly real to him. This name isn't wildly popular today, but it regularly appears at about 200th on the Social Security Administration's list of top baby names. Calvins are often called **Cal** for short.

Cameron: Scottish Gaelic; "crooked nose." Despite a less than appealing meaning, both male and female namesakes are accomplished individuals. Among males, Cameron Crowe is the Oscar-winning screenwriter for the semi-autobiographical movie *Almost Famous,* about his experiences writing for *Rolling Stone* magazine as a teenager, and the renowned writer, director, and producer of other movies, including *Fast Times at Ridgemont High* (also semi-autobiographical) and *Vanilla Sky.* **Camron** is an alternate spelling, and nicknames include **Cam, Kam,** and **Kammer.**

Parent's Success Guide to Baby Names

☺ ☹ ☺ ☺ ☹ ☺ ☺ ☹ ☺ ☺ ☹ ☺ ☺ ☹ ☺ ☺ ☹ ☺ ☺ ☹ ☹ ☺

Carl: German; "a man." Its etymology is the same as that of CHARLES, but its later history is quite distinct. The earlier (German) spelling **Karl** is often used, especially among immigrant groups, to whom the name was generally confined until about 1850. Its popularity rose sharply about 1880, doubtless due to the rise in German prestige following the victorious war of 1871–1872 and the general expansion of German influence on the west. Especially in its C spelling, it was well entrenched by World War I, escaping most of the reaction against things German that appeared under wartime conditions because people no longer thought of the name as solely German. Like CHAD, Carl is unusual in that it has no common short form or diminutive — a situation many people find appealing. (No silly nicknames!) Noteworthy Carls include astronomer Carl Sagan, psychiatrist Carl Jung, and writer Carl Sandburg, whose popular poems include "Chicago" and "Fog."

Carlos: German; "a man." Carlos is a variant of the Latin Carolus (CHARLES). It rarely occurs as a Romantic or literary form, but the name has been consistently popular in the United States in recent years, ranking between 54th and 62nd for 12 years running. Carlos Santana won nine Grammy awards for his album *Supernatural.*

Carson: English; the exact meaning is unknown, but it's likely from an unidentified nickname with "son" added. What began as a surname is gaining in popularity as a first name for either a girl or boy — it cracked the top 100 for boys for the first time in 2001. Frontiersman Kit Carson is one of the first notable Carsons in the United States, after whom Carson City, Nevada, is named. Popular talk show host Johnny Carson may be the best-known Carson ever. However, the younger you are, the more likely you are to have grown up with MTV personality Carson Daly instead.

Carter: English; from the family name, which springs from "a man who drives a cart." The name developed some glamour in the 1970s because of the social status of certain branches of the former First Family. In the past decade, the name has skyrocketed in popularity, jumping 400 places on the Social Security Administration's list of the most common names and nearing the top 100 in 2002. Dr. John Carter of TV's *ER* is a well-known holder of this name, although Carter serves as his surname rather than his given name.

Casey: Irish; "war vigilant." In American usage, this name probably derives from a condensed form of the Irish surname O'Casey. It may also come from a nickname based on the initials *K.C.* (similarly to the conversion of Olympic athlete J. C. Owens' name to "Jesse"). The best-known poem about baseball is *Casey at the Bat;* the most famous locomotive engineer hero is Casey Jones, who died in the line of duty. Music fans worldwide know the voice of Casey Casem, and Casey Affleck, Ben's younger brother, is known for his roles in such films as *Ocean's Eleven* and *200 Cigarettes.* (Casey is actually his middle name; he won't say what his first name is.)

Chapter 2: Bailey, Brian, or Brent? Names for Boys

☺ ☺ ☹ ☺ ☺ ☹ ☺ ☺ ☹ ☺ ☺ ☹ ☺ ☺ ☹ ☺ ☺ ☹ ☺

Variations include **Kaycee, Kayce, Caycee, Kaysee, Kayse,** and **Kacey;** nicknames include **Kase** and **Case.**

Chad: Brittonic; possibly meaning "warrior." From Ceadda, the name of a bishop in the seventh century who later attained sainthood. This name is probably a 19th-century revival in England. Today, it's less popular than it used to be, having fallen from near 100th in 1991 to 312th in 2002. "Hanging chads" were at the center of the 2000 presidential election controversy, and undoubtedly those named Chad faced some teasing because of the connection. Actor Chad Lowe, brother of Rob and husband of Academy Award winner Hilary Swank, has appeared in many films, including *Oxford Blues* and *Unfaithful.* Chad is also the name of a country in Africa.

Chandler: English; "candlemaker." You can probably think of someone you know with the surname Chandler — if not, just think of author Raymond Chandler, who is best known for his Phillip Marlowe detective mysteries, such as *Farewell, My Lovely* and *The Big Sleep.* This name is less common as a first name, although the popularity of the fictional Chandler Bing on the hit TV sitcom *Friends* may change that. This Chandler, portrayed with comedic excellence by actor Matthew Perry, is always ready with a quick-witted remark and is an integral part of the success of the show.

Charles: German; "a man." This name was borne by the famous Frankish leader Charles Mattel (who died in 741) and by Charlemagne — that is, Charles the Great (who died in 814). The Frankish form was put into Latin as Carolus. From this form, with the retention of the final *s* and some phonetic shifting, the Old French developed Charles, which continued to be a common name among the French. But the French and the Normans were at war again and again, and from the Norman point of view, Charles became a hostile name. Its road to England began in France and detoured through Scotland. The young Scottish princess named Mary was betrothed in 1548 to the heir apparent of France and went to live in that country. The princess — later known as Mary Queen of Scots — married her Frenchman but provided no heir to the French throne. After a few years, her husband was killed, and she returned to Scotland, where she continued to speak French and otherwise to follow Gallic customs. With her second husband, a Scottish nobleman, she had a son, whom she christened Charles James. On maturity, the baby became known to history as James the First of England and Sixth of Scotland. King James gave his second son, born in 1600, the name Charles; no one knows why. Then, when Prince Henry died in 1612, everything changed. Charles was now destined to be king of both England and Scotland. In any society, the name of the monarch gains tremendous publicity, and so did Charles from 1612 onward, especially after that king's accession in 1625. The name, however, became involved in a civil war, and the large body of Puritans rejected it. In America, Charles remained a rare name until about 1780, in which decade Charles (barely) made the top ten in a tie with DANIEL for tenth place. But, from then on, it was ever upward. In the 1840s, Charles was the most used name on the Harvard

☺ ☺ ☹ ☺ ☺ ☹ ☺ ☺ ☹ ☺ ☺ ☹ ☺ ☺ ☹ ☺ ☺ ☺ ☹ ☺

roster (a barometer of its general popularity). In that whole period, however, we find no great American hero named Charles. The popularity of the
name seemed to build up by a self-generated momentum. The nickname
Charlie developed regularly enough, and in 1745, the Jacobites were
singing a song, "Charlie Is My Darling." But there was no short form until
the Americans began to use **Chuck,** which scarcely became popular until
the end of the 19th century. All in all, Charles has the most remarkable
history of any English names. Famous Charleses include writer Charles
Dickens, musician Charles Mingus, entrepreneur Charles Schwab, actor
Charlie Chaplin, and Prince Charles, The Prince of Wales.

Chase: English; "chase, hunt." From a French nickname for a hunter, this
name is a common surname that has begun to be used as a first name as
well. Since 1996, Chase has ranked among the 100 most popular names
for boys. Among men with the surname Chase, actor Chevy is probably the
most well known. Having achieved stardom on TV's Saturday Night Live, he
moved on to films, playing key roles in such comedies as *Vacation* and
Fletch.

Christian: English; "of the Christian faith." While this name's religious connotation is obvious, it has become increasingly popular as a boy's name,
without necessarily being tied to its religious significance. From the world
of acting, one well-known holder of this name is Christian Slater, whose
roles in such films as *Heathers, Pump Up the Volume,* and *Interview with
the Vampire* have made him a sought-after actor in Hollywood. Another
actor, Christian Bale, enjoyed modest success in Hollywood until his dis-
turbing portrayal of serial killer Patrick Bateman in *American Psycho* cata-
pulted him to stardom. His subsequent roles in *Captain Corelli's Mandolin*
and *Reign of Fire* have established him as one of Hollywood's up-and-
coming talents. One of the world's most beloved storytellers is Hans
Christian Andersen, the children's author from Denmark best known for
his fairy tales "The Ugly Duckling," "The Tinderbox," and "The Tin Soldier."
And French fashion designer Christian Dior became "the most recognized
name in fashion," especially after he created the "New Look" for women in
1947. **Cristian** and **Kristian** are alternate spellings.

Christopher: Greek; "Christ bearer." Originally meaning merely a
Christian, its literal sense inspired the story of the stalwart saint who carried the Christ-child across a stream. In the United States, the name has
been remarkable for its stability, being present in nearly every list from
Raleigh's colony onward. It fails to match the great popularity of the name
in England since 1950 but nevertheless has continued to be used. It
stands high and reached the top ten in many 20th-century lists. Notable
Christophers include explorer Christopher Columbus, believed to be the
first European to sail across the Atlantic and land on American soil;
musician Chris Isaak, whose sultry ballads make many a female fan
swoon; actor Christopher Reeve, who played Superman in several films;
and English dramatist Christopher Marlowe, a contemporary of
Shakespeare. Nicknames include **Chris** and **Cris.**

Chapter 2: Bailey, Brian, or Brent? Names for Boys

☺ ☺ ☹ ☺ ☺ ☹ ☺ ☺ ☹ ☺ ☺ ☹ ☺ ☺ ☹ ☺ ☺ ☺ ☹ ☺

Clarence: Latin; "clear," "luminous." The name Clarence became popular in the United States during the 1860s, probably because of some special event that occurred around that time, most likely in England. Like other feudal names (such as PERCY and SIDNEY), it suffered in the long run from its suggestions of a no-longer-powerful aristocracy. Mark Twain, always careful with his names, used Clarence for a character in *A Connecticut Yankee in King Arthur's Court* (1889) — it apparently had weak and unheroic suggestions for Twain. (Incidentally, that book was written during the time of the greatest popularity of the name Clarence.) Its use fell off in the 20th century, until it became rare. During that century, Clarence Darrow rose to prominence as a lawyer, while Clarence Thomas became the second African American appointed to the U.S. Supreme Court.

Clark: English; "clerk." Being common as a family name and being simple to pronounce, Clark has been a fairly common given name, although it's not particularly popular today. An alternate spelling is **Clarke.** Perhaps the most famous Clark is a fictional character: Clark Kent, a.k.a. Superman. Clark Gable was an early superstar, earning an astounding salary of $211,000 a year from MGM after he won an Oscar for Frank Capra's *It Happened One Night.* One of his most famous roles was that of Rhett Butler in *Gone with the Wind* — he was the first actor to utter the word *damn* in a motion picture.

Clay: English; from the family name, to denote a person who lived near a clay pit. The longtime popularity of Henry Clay helped to establish Clay as a given name in the 19th century. **Clayton** is the common long form of this name, and heroic Clayton Moore is probably better known as his TV alter-ego, *The Lone Ranger.* Clay Aiken remains America's favorite runner-up; even if he didn't win *American Idol 2,* his debut album and his commitment to charity work solidify his winning personality. Country music also boasts a few Clays: Clay Davidson, Clay Jeffrys, and Clay Walker, who is battling multiple sclerosis and has become a spokesman for research on the disease.

Clifford: English; "(from the) ford of a cliff." The Cliffords were a notable English aristocratic family, and the name became known through its use in Shakespeare's historical plays and in other poetry, especially through Rosamund Clifford, the "fair Rosamund" of song and story. The name made its American appearance in the later 19th century, but remained rare. Often shortened to **Cliff.** John Ratzenberger played the know-it-all postal carrier Cliff Clavin on TV's *Cheers.*

Clinton: English; "a hill." **Clint** is the common nickname, as well as a given name in its own right (although Clinton is the more popular of the two; it peaked at No. 156 in the 1980s). Living legend Clint Eastwood's film career spans more than six decades, but he still found time to serve as mayor of Carmel-by-the-Sea, California. In the 1990s, superstar Clint Black took Nashville by storm, helping to launch the widespread popularity of country music.

☺ ☹ ☺ ☺ ☹ ☺ ☺ ☹ ☺ ☺ ☹ ☺ ☺ ☹ ☺ ☹ ☺ ☺ ☹ ☺

Clyde: Gaelic; from the family name. As a given name, it appeared in the later 19th century and, for some reason, exclusively in the United States. Being limited to American usage, it's sometimes taken as a typically American name. It remains viable, although it certainly isn't popular with today's parents. Basketball great Clyde "The Glide" Drexler was known for his considerable vertical leap during an NBA career that spanned the 1980s and '90s.

Coby: See KOBE.

Cody: Origin uncertain; "helpful." U.S. Army Scout "Buffalo Bill" Cody had an international reputation and helped create a lasting image of the American West, thus giving the "Wild West" its name. Today, world-champion bullrider Cody Custer uses his fame to reach people on a deeper, more spiritual level. Who knows whether it's the Wild West connection that draws parents to choose this name; whatever the reason, Cody has been quite popular in recent years. In 1991, it cracked the top ten, and today it sits at a respectable No. 71.

Colby: English; meaning unknown. Colby is suitable for a boy or girl, though it is much more popular for the former. In 2002, Colby ranked as the 125th most popular name for boys. Enthusiastic Colby Donaldson of TV's *Survivor: Australia* exhibited a winning personality and gentlemanly poise (not to mention good looks), even after coming in second.

Cole: Old English; from the name Cola, which derives from a root word meaning "coal." Its meaning may not be all that glamorous, but Cole's popularity is rising in the United States; in 2002, it was No. 69 on the Social Security Administration's list of baby names. Cole Porter, commonly referred to as the best American songwriter ever, is credited with composing such treasures as "My Heart Belongs to Daddy," "Don't Fence Me In," "Night and Day," and many more. The daughter of Nat King Cole, Natalie Cole emulated her father's smooth, jazzy sound and won seven Grammy awards by composing a duet with her late father, re-releasing his hit "Unforgettable." Although **Coleman** and **Colman** aren't etymological variants of Cole, they may appeal to you as alternatives to the shorter Cole. **Colson** is a possibility as well.

Colin: English; a diminutive of NICHOLAS. The name remained rare in the United States until recently; today, it's poised to break the top 100, and it's been among the top 150 names for more than a decade. Harlem-born Colin Powell (who pronounces it "KO-lin" rather than the usual "KOLL-in") may be the primary reason for this rise; he has served as President Ronald Reagan's national security adviser and as Secretary of State under George W. Bush. Handsome actor Colin Firth has starred in such films as *Shakespeare in Love* and *Bridget Jones's Diary*. The name is sometimes spelled with two *l*'s — and Collin is nearly as popular as Colin.

Colton: English; "town belonging to a man named Cola, Koli, or Cula." The several towns with this name weren't named for the presence of coal, but

Chapter 2: Bailey, Brian, or Brent? Names for Boys

for the presence of a man named Cola. In the last ten years, Colton has never dropped below 129th in popularity, according to statistics compiled by the Social Security Administration.

Connor: Irish, "wolf/hound lover." Connor was also the name of an early king of Ulster. Irish folklore tells of King Connor's tragic love for Deirdre. Today, *Star Trek* fans know Connor Trinneer as the chief engineer on *Enterprise*. Both Connor and Conner are among the top 200 boys' names in use, with Connor being the more popular of the two, at 48th place in 2002. Another possible spelling is **Conor.**

Cooper: English; "barrel maker." In the surname category, famous Coopers include actors Gary and Jackie, as well as "Welcome to My Nightmare" rocker Alice. The small and sporty Mini Cooper is one of the cars of the moment. Although the current roster of celebrities doesn't include any first-name Coopers, the name is gaining popularity in the United States, currently holding 196th place.

Corey: Irish; meaning unknown. Corey is likely derived from a blending of Irish surnames with various meanings. Detroit Lions fullback Cory Schlesinger was named as an alternate to the Pro Bowl in 2002, and Toronto Blue Jays fans know Cory Lidle, the team's starting pitcher. Adolescents during the 1980s will remember actors Corey Haim and Corey Feldman, who have failed to achieve the success as adult actors that they did as teens. Variations include **Cory, Cori, Corie, Corri, Corrie,** and **Corry.**

Craig: Scots; from the place name ("crag," in English). It is derived from the family name and has become fairly common in America as a given name in the 20th century, though its popularity has waned over the last decade.

Cristian: See CHRISTIAN.

Curtis: French; "courteous." Much more common as a surname than as a first name (think of actor Tony Curtis, actress Jamie Lee Curtis, and a host of other famous Curtises), a few well-known, first-named Curtises can be found. Pro Bowl running back Curtis Martin has proved more than courteous with his talent; his New York Jets teammates can count on him to rush for at least 1,000 yards every season. Another Curtis of note is musician Curtis Mayfield, one of the most beloved Motown artists of the 20th century. His best known songs include "Gypsy Woman," "Superfly," and "If There's a Hell Below, We're All Gonna Go." This name has been declining in popularity over the last decade; today, it's near 300th place.

Cyril: Greek; "lordly." This name is borne by several saints, chiefly associated with the Eastern Church. It has been rare in the United States. In fact, it was not among the 1,000 most popular boys' names in 2002.

Cyrus: Persian; "throne," probably with the idea of "royal, kingly." In the Bible, this name refers to the great founder of the Persian Empire, whose policies favored the Israelites. Although a number of references to him in the Bible are friendly, his name is not recorded as having been adopted by the Israelites. It was, however, used in America. Cyrus is not to be considered merely another biblical name, since information about him was abundant in the writings of Herodotus and Xenophon. In fact, Cyrus is almost counterbiblical, since it's outside the main current of the Bible and since it was much better known from lay works. Cyrus didn't appear until around 1750, when the full sweep of the biblical names was over — another indication of its being counterbiblical. After 1750, it remained viable for a century and can still be found today. Cyrus Vance, for example, was the Secretary of State in the Carter administration.

D

Dakota: Native American; "friend, ally." An alternate spelling is **Dakotah.** Although there aren't any famous Dakotas or Dakotahs, it's likely that a few will appear in coming years, as this name has ranked as high as 59th in the last decade.

Dale: English; "dale" (valley). Favored for its short and euphonic form, this name attained popularity as a given name in the mid-20th century. NASCAR fans will always remember the late Dale Earnhardt, while his racing legacy lives on in the form of his son, Dale Jr.

Dalton: English; "from the farm in dale," "from the valley town." This is yet another example of a last name that's gaining popularity as a first name. As yet, there aren't any prominent men with the given name Dalton to speak of. But as a last name, Dalton has a couple of well-known associations. English physicist John Dalton changed scientific wisdom when he theorized about the existence of atoms. And suave Timothy Dalton played the debonair 007, James Bond, and has been favorably compared to Sir Lawrence Olivier.

Damian: Greek; "tame." This name has made its way up the charts in the past ten years, climbing 100 spots in a decade. Baseball fans will delight to know that Chicago Cubs catcher Damian Miller may one day get the chance to play against Baltimore Orioles pitcher Damian Moss. **Damion** is an alternate spelling.

Damon: Greek; "tame." Curiously, Damon is less popular than the similar DAMIAN; it consistently hovers at around 300th place. Comedian and actor Damon Wayans got his start on TV's *In Living Color,* and since then has appeared in many films, including *Last Action Hero* and *Major Payne.* See also DAMIAN.

Daniel: Hebrew; "God is my judge." The question may be raised as to whether there are two names here. Dan may be merely the short form of Daniel, or it may be from the name of the Israelite tribe. In any case,

☺ ☺ ☹ ☺ ☺ ☹ ☺ ☺ ☹ ☺ ☺ ☹ ☺ ☺ ☹ ☺ ☺ ☺ ☹ ☺

names derived from the tribe would have been few, and Dan is usually to be considered as being from Daniel. This name is Hebrew, "God (is) judge." It is the name of a book of the Bible, which takes its name from one of the prophets. This prophet is the leading character in the spectacular and widely spread story commonly known as "Daniel in the lions' den." From such a background, Daniel naturally passed over to being a name used by early Christians. Though falling off with the general decline of Old Testament names in the 19th century, Daniel did not (as many names did) vanish altogether, apparently now being established as a regular American name, having lost its biblical connection. The nicknames **Dan** and **Danny** have also survived. Dan Quayle served as U.S. vice-president under George Bush, Sr. Other notable Daniels include litigator and politician Daniel Webster, American pioneer Daniel Boone, and actor Daniel Day-Lewis.

Dante: Italian; "lasting, enduring." A short form of **Durante;** derivatives include **Dantae, Daunte,** and **Dantel.** The most notable bearer of this name was Dante Alighieri, the medieval Italian poet who wrote *The Divine Comedy,* famous for its graphic description of Hell known as "Dante's Inferno." Football fans admire Daunte Culpepper, quarterback of the Minnesota Vikings.

Darius: Persian; "to (up)hold, sustain." The name appears in the Bible, but its associations are with the great Darius of Persia, known more from the tales of Herodotus than from the Bible (see CYRUS). Darius used to be an extremely rare name, but it did appear occasionally in the 19th century. Today, however, the name has become more common; although it has slipped a bit in the last five or so years, it peaked at 159th place. Darius Rucker has scored multiple musical hits as the lead singer for the band Hootie and the Blowfish.

Darren: Gaelic; from one or more patronymic surnames, possibly O'Dearain, meaning "great, large." This name isn't as common as it has been in the past, but it's still in use in the United States. Character actor Darren McGavin achieved fame as one of television's most dependable performers. The role he will always be known for will be the reporter Carl Kolchak in the 1970s TV series *The Night Stalker.* A fictional Darren was the often-befuddled Darren Stevens on the 1960s sitcom *Bewitched,* portrayed first by Dick York and then by Dick Sargent. This Darren usually got himself into some predicament that Samantha would have to help him get out of — quite a change of pace from the typical television of the decade.

David: Hebrew; "darling, beloved," and thus be a kind of honorific nickname. As an outstanding biblical lay-hero, David would have been likely, under any circumstances, to be a much used name. It had the particular fortune to be the name of the archbishop (sixth century) who became the patron saint of Wales. It was also borne by two kings of Scotland in the Middle Ages. The name thus came to have solid patriotic support in Wales and Scotland, in addition to its biblical aid. A mild popularity of the name spread also to England, and it was in regular use at the time of the

☺ ☹ ☺ ☺ ☺ ☺ ☺ ☺ ☺ ☺ ☺ ☺ ☺ ☺ ☺ ☺ ☺ ☺ ☺ ☺ ☺

Reformation, circa 1540. It suffered in popularity among the Puritans, with whom David's notorious sins would have had a strong negative influence. Once settled in their new home, the Puritans seemed to view David's sins more lightly. Among 675 Boston births from 1630 to 1675, David failed to rank in the top ten by slipping into 11th place — just below Richard and just above Jacob. The highest popularity of David yet established for the 18th century (1781) is in the officers of eight regiments of the Connecticut Line where the name stands in a second-place tie with Samuel and William. Along with the other Old Testament names, David faded out in the later 19th century, and in the early 20th century it was rare. It revived sharply after 1930. The reasons for this popularity are obscure. Famous Davids include talk-show host David Letterman, rocker David Bowie, and illusionist David Copperfield. A common nickname is **Dave.**

Dean: English; from the family name, which originates from someone associated with a dean — that is, a church official. In the United States, the word is more widely known in its academic usage, but we may question whether this connection has influenced naming. The brevity of the name has been a factor in its popularity, together with its resemblance to the popular names Don and Dan. Actor Dean Martin was a member of the Rat Pack, along with Frank Sinatra and Sammy Davis, Jr., among others. Dean Cain starred as Superman on TV's *Lois & Clark.*

Dennis: Greek; "wild, frenzied." It's ultimately derives from the name of the Greek god Dionysius. By the beginning of the Christian era, personal names from that of the god were already in use, and a man of that name was among the early converts. This Dionysius the Areopagite, according to tradition, attained sainthood and was martyred in Paris. As a result, he was much venerated in France, and when his cult spread to England, his name appeared in English most commonly as Dennis. As the name of a nonbiblical saint, Dennis ceased to be a popular name in the Reformation period. Pretty much throughout American history, the name lay dormant, but it enjoyed something of a renaissance in the later 20th century — possibly from the popularity of the cartoon Dennis the Menace. Actor Dennis Hopper's career has spanned 50 years, with appearances in films such as *Rebel Without a Cause, Easy Rider, Blue Velvet,* and *Hoosiers.*

Derek: Dutch; the equivalent of the German name Diederich, which is from Theodoric and means "ruler of the people/tribe." The name probably survived from the early Dutch settlers, but it's generally been rare. Since peaking at close to 50th place in the 1980s, it has fallen out of the top 100. An alternate spelling is **Derrick,** which, along with its more common cousin, is among the top 250 names in the United States today. Derek Jeter is an All-Star infielder for the New York Yankees. In the 1960s, guitar legend Eric Clapton fronted a band called Derek & The Dominos.

Desmond: Irish; after a region in Ireland, meaning "South Munster." This name has never been especially popular, but one particular association might make it particularly appealing to African-American parents: South African priest Desmond Tutu won the Nobel Peace Prize in 1984 for his

Chapter 2: Bailey, Brian, or Brent? Names for Boys

☺ ☺ ☹ ☺ ☺ ☹ ☺ ☺ ☹ ☺ ☺ ☹ ☺ ☺ ☹ ☺ ☺ ☺ ☹ ☺

striving to end apartheid using compassion and faith rather than hatred and violence. Tutu's actions are largely credited with the desegregation that has taken place in South Africa.

Devin: Several origins and meanings possible. English nickname meaning "devine." Also, one of two Irish given names meaning respectively "stag, ox" or "black." It's a variation of DEVON, which is named after the county in England. Pro basketball's Devin Brown earned Rookie of the Year honors in 2003 while playing for the San Antonio Spurs. Variations include **Devon** and **Deven.** Both the *i* and the *o* spellings are among the top 200 names in use today, with Devin ranking 75th.

Diego: Possibly Greek; "teacher." This name broke into the top 100 for the first time in 2002. Considered the greatest Mexican painter of the 20th century, artist Diego Rivera is credited with reintroducing fresco painting into modern art and architecture. The name may also make you think of San Diego, which is known for having some of the sunniest weather in the United States.

Dillon: Old German; meaning unknown. The name also closely resembles the more common DYLAN, whose origin is Welsh. Probably the most famous Dillon of this spelling is in the last name of actor Matt Dillon. Variations include **Dyllon, Dylon, Dillan,** and **Dilon.**

Dimitri: A Russian borrowing of a Greek name; "lover of the earth." From Demeter, the Greek goddess of corn and the harvest. Also a variant of Demetriu, who, in Catholic writings, was the oxymoronic "compassionate thief" who died with Jesus. Although this name has never been common among the general population, it's a popular name among Greek-American parents who want to preserve their ethnic heritage. The granddaddy of all Dimitris must be Dimitri Mendeleev, who was the founder of the Periodic Table of Elements. A common cousin is the Russian form of **Dmitri.**

Dominic, Dominick: Latin; "belonging to God," "of the lord." This name, after St. Dominic, the founder of the order of preachers, has been used pretty regularly since the 13th century. It was a popular Roman Catholic name until the 1950s, when it became more common everywhere. It remains more popular in Britain than in the United States and, because of its meaning, is a handy name for a child born on a Sunday. The hottest Dominic on the scene today is British actor Dominic Monaghan, who costars in the wildly popular *Lord of the Rings* trilogy. Comedic actor and chef Dom Deluise starred in *Cannonball Run.* Popular nicknames are **Dom** and (you guessed it) **Nick.** The variant **Dominique** is occasionally used for boys (think of NBA basketball standout Dominique Wilkins, who's known as "the Human Highlight Film"), although it's much more common as a girl's name.

Donald: Gaelic; an Anglicization of Gaelic *Domhnall,* meaning "world leader." It's probably the most common Scottish name of Highland origin. Although an occasional Donald appeared in the 18th century, its generally late entrance into the United States (about 1850) suggests that it was the result of Scottish immigration. The writers of the Romantic revival, such as Sir Walter Scott, were fond of using such exotic names. In the mid-20th century, Donald became highly popular, reaching the top ten — probably because Scottish names offered a relief from the conventional John, William, and so on and, at the same time, had a certain stability. Two well-known Donalds are Donald Rumsfeld, Secretary of Defense under George W. Bush, and actor Donald Sutherland (father of Kiefer, a name to consider if you're looking for something different), who has appeared in such films as *Backdraft* and *Animal House.*

Douglas: Scottish Gaelic; a river name meaning "black-blue," "dark blue." Amusingly, when Douglas first made a transition to a given name in the 16th century, girls and boys both used it. In the United States, the name has generally been less popular than DONALD but has followed a similar course. Douglas MacArthur is one of America's most storied generals, leading the Allies to victory in World War II before being relieved of his duties by President Eisenhower. Douglas Adams wrote the cult sci-fi classic *A Hitchhiker's Guide to the Galaxy.* **Doug** is a common nickname.

Drake: Old English; "dragon." Drake's origins are animal-related: It comes from the word *draca*, which was the term for dragon, and it's also an English male duck. The name has inched up the charts in the past decade and currently sits near the middle of the top 500 names in use in the United States. Like many others, it's also common as a surname, and most famous Drakes employ the name as a last name rather than a first name. For example, British explorer Sir Francis Drake was the first man to circumnavigate the globe. Mod singer/songwriter Nick Drake, who was known for being extremely reclusive and died when his promising career had barely begun, is another famous British Drake. Chicago's Drake Hotel, which sits on the shore of Lake Michigan, has a long and proud history of hosting dignitaries visiting the Windy City. One variant of Drake is the somewhat more exotic **Draken.**

Drew: Old French; from the given name *Drogo*, meaning "to carry, to bear." Since the 1960s, Drew has increasingly stood on its own rather than being a nickname of ANDREW, although it's never been a wildly popular name. Although its meaning suggests masculinity, Drew is a girl's name as well; actress Drew Barrymore is one popular example. Actor and comedian Drew Carey and NFL quarterback Drew Bledsoe are other well-known Drews. It's occasionally spelled **Dru** or **Drue.**

Duane: Irish; from the surname O'Dubhain, meaning "black." As a given name, Duane is pretty rare. Duane Allman of the Southern rock band The Allman Brothers is known for having been married to Cher. Duane Reade is a chain of drugstores in New York City. The alternate spelling **Dwayne** is more popular in the African-American community.

Duncan: Gaelic; "brown warrior." This well-established Scottish name is found occasionally in American usage but has failed to attain the popularity

Chapter 2: Bailey, Brian, or Brent? Names for Boys

☺ 😐 ☹ ☺ 😐 ☹ ☺ 😐 ☹ ☺ 😐 ☹ ☺ 😐 ☹ ☺ ☺ 😐 ☹ ☺

of DONALD, DOUGLAS, and other names with which it's associated. Currently, it barely cracks the top 500. Shakespeare's play *Macbeth* describes the murder of Scotland's King Duncan, its most famous line probably being "Out, out, damned spot." Singer and Brown University graduate Duncan Sheik achieve a moderate amount of fame with his tuneful song "Barely Breathing."

Dustin: English; from any of several locative surnames with the meaning "dusty town." Former baseball player Dusty Baker now manages the Chicago Cubs. Dustin Hoffman has proven his acting prowess in films such as *All the President's Men, Midnight Cowboy,* and *Tootsie.* **Dusty,** an English surname, comes from the literal meaning "dusty," although modern use links it to a shortening of Dustin. The nickname can also be spelled **Dustee, Dustie,** and **Dustey.**

Dwight: Old English; from a given name, Diot, a diminutive of Dye, which in turn was a pet name for Dionisia (the equivalent of the modern-day Denise). The name itself is attractively direct and short. It had a period of some popularity about 1870 but has failed to capture many parents' interest since. Dwight D. Eisenhower, commonly known as Ike (his memorable campaign slogan was "I like Ike"), was a World War II general and served as President during part of the Korean War. Country singer Dwight Yoakam is another well-known Dwight.

Dylan: Welsh; "ocean, wave." In Welsh mythology, Dylan was a god of the sea who died when his uncle accidentally killed him. Welsh-born poet Dylan Thomas is known for his fluid and powerful poetry. American singer/songwriter Bob Dylan was born Robert Zimmerman but took the poet's name as his own as a tribute. He writes and sings folksy songs that have an elemental attraction as strong as the tide. Actor Dylan McDermott starred on TV's legal drama *The Practice.* Dylan was in the top 50 most popular names for boys in the late 1990s and is making headway as a name for girls as well.

E

Edgar: Old English; from *ead,* meaning "rich," and *gar,* meaning "spear." Important in the Anglo-Saxon period, the name Edgar declined in popularity and probably wasn't in use during the period of the settling of the American colonies. The name revived in the later 18th century under Romantic influences, and it appears in the title of Charles Brockden Brown's *Edgar Huntly* (1800), one of the earliest American novels. Though never common, Edgar has continued in use. Writer Edgar Allan Poe is a master of telling frightful tales in verse, his most popular works including the poems "The Raven" and "Annabelle Lee" and the short story "The Fall of the House of Usher." **Ed** is a possible nickname, although it's likely to be mistaken to be short for EDWARD.

Ten names from Shakespeare

If great literature inspires you, a name from one of the Bard's many plays just might fit the bill for your baby. Here are some names from Shakespearean classics that still sound modern today:

- **Adrian:** *The Tempest*
- **Curtis:** *The Taming of the Shrew*
- **Duncan:** *Macbeth*
- **Edmund:** *King Lear*
- **Francisco:** *Hamlet, The Tempest*
- **Frederick:** *As You Like It*
- **Leonardo:** *The Merchant of Venice*
- **Orlando:** *As You Like It*
- **Philip:** *The Taming of the Shrew*
- **Ross:** *Macbeth*
- **Toby:** *Twelfth Night*

Edward: Old English; formed from the conventional name elements *ead*, "fortunate, happy," and *weard*, "guardian." Edward was the name of two Anglo-Saxon kings, the second canonized as St. Edward the Confessor. The name survived the Norman Conquest and acquired new vitality in the later part of the 12th century because of King Henry III's devotion to St. Edward. He gave the name to one of his sons, who succeeded him as Edward I. Other Edwards reigned in the 14th and 15th centuries, and thus the name became firmly entrenched throughout England. The early American colonists included many men of the name. Among the colonists themselves, however, Edward was not a popular name for their children; its thoroughly English quality had no special appeal to the many Dutch, German, and Scotch-Irish settlers of the middle and southern colonies. In the 18th century, however, Edward became fully established throughout America. Although not a favorite among modernists, it continues to be a viable name. In the United States, the nicknames are **Ed** and **Eddie.** How **Ted** and **Teddy** developed from Edward is something of a mystery; these nicknames, often used in decades past, are seldom used today. **Eduardo** is the Spanish variant and ranks just below Edward in the Social Security Administration's list — they're ten spots apart at Nos. 128 and 118, respectively. Notable bearers of this name include Senator Edward "Ted" Kennedy, actor Edward Norton, and painter Edward Hopper.

Chapter 2: Bailey, Brian, or Brent? Names for Boys

☺ ☺ ☹ ☺ ☺ ☹ ☺ ☺ ☹ ☺ ☺ ☹ ☺ ☺ ☹ ☺ ☺ ☹ ☺ ☺

Edwin: Old English; from *ead*, meaning "rich," and *wine*, meaning "friend." This name was common before the Norman Conquest and immediately after, but faded out. It probably wasn't in use at the time the American colonies were being settled. Around 1800, though, it began to make an impression on American naming, being revived, like many obsolete names, under Romantic influences. It gained in popularity through the 19th and 20th centuries, and in 1920 surpassed all other Anglo-Saxon names. After that time, it fell off sharply, but it's regained strength of late, reaching number 166 in 2002. We have astronomer Edwin Hubble to thank for the knowledge that the Milky Way is but one of millions of galaxies in the universe. Edwin McCain is a folksy singer-songwriter.

Eli: Hebrew; "height." During the period when biblical names were popular, this name appeared occasionally, probably because of its brevity. Moreover, Eli was the father of Samuel, who bore one of the most widely used names of the time. Today, this name is rising in popularity, having broken into the top 200 in 2002. Eli Whitney was the inventor of the cotton gin, which played a part in America's Industrial Revolution and greatly reduced the perceived need for slavery on cotton plantations in the South. Eli is also a nickname for ELIAS and ELIJAH, as well as for a person who attended Yale University.

Elijah: Hebrew; "Jehovah is God." **Elias** is the form of the name in the New Testament, under Greek influence. As a notable major prophet, Elijah achieved some popularity as a name in colonial New England, and the name was also viable in other regions. It died out in the general 19th-century decline of biblical names, but has since made a comeback. Today, it's among the top 50 most popular names for boys. Actor Elijah Wood brought the hobbit Bilbo Baggins to life in the film version of Tolkien's *The Lord of the Rings* trilogy, while Elias Howe was an American inventor.

Emerson: Old English; "son of Emery." Emerson is a surname — as in essayist and poet Ralph Waldo Emerson — but it's occasionally used as a first name. Race car driver Emerson Fittipaldi won the Indianapolis 500 in 1989 and 1993.

Emilio: Spanish or Italian; "eager to please," "industrious." The French form, Émil, became popular in English-speaking countries in the mid-19th century. It's also the masculine form of Emily, which was the most popular name in the United States in 2002. Italian designer Emilio Pucci, Mexican independence revolutionary Emilio Zapata, and actor Emilio Estevez are notable bearers of the name. Variants include **Emiliano** and **Emilion.**

Eric: Old Norse; probably "ruler." The meaning of the *e* part is uncertain, but the element *-ric* appears in Germanic languages with the meaning "government, powerful." In the United States, Eric is closely connected with Scandinavian immigration, and it began to show up in lists of popular names toward the middle of the 19th century. Although many Scandinavian names failed to take hold, Eric clicked, and around 1975 approached the

☺ ☺ ☹ ☺ ☺ ☹ ☺ ☺ ☹ ☺ ☺ ☹ ☺ ☺ ☹ ☺ ☺ ☺ ☹ ☹ ☺

top ten. Among famous Erics, Eric Clapton stands out for his guitar-playing prowess. As a member of Monty Python's Flying Circus, Eric Idle made fans laugh. To make this fairly common name more unique, try spelling it **Erick** or **Erik,** as Erik Estrada, half of the motorcycle-riding cop duo of *CHiPs,* does.

Ernest: German; "earnest." As a name, it probably didn't occur in English usage until the late 18th century, when the Hanoverian dynasty introduced it as a name in the royal family — for example, for the Duke of Cumberland (born in 1771). Today, Ernest seems old-fashioned, but the Spanish form ERNESTO is among the top 325 boys' names in the United States. The adjective *earnest* is immortalized in Oscar Wilde's play *The Importance of Being Earnest.* Much-lauded novelist Ernest Hemingway, known for his spare writing style, penned such 20th-century classics as *A Farewell to Arms* and *The Sun Also Rises.*

Ernesto: The Italian, Portuguese, and Spanish version of ERNEST; "serious minded." Probably the most famous Ernesto (and possibly the most serious minded) is Ernesto (Che) Guevara, the revolutionary who aided Fidel Castro's efforts to overthrow Cuba's Batista regime in the late 1950s. Guevara served in Castro's cabinet for a few years before heading to Bolivia to lead a revolution there. That engagement wasn't as successful for Guevara, who was shot there. Daytime soap operas *Days of Our Lives* and *The Young and the Restless* both have boasted characters named Ernesto: Ernesto Toscano and Maestro Ernesto Faustche, respectively. **Nesto** is a diminutive used as a nickname.

Ethan: Hebrew; "perennial, constant." Originally, this may have been an honorary name bestowed on an old man. It was used occasionally during the period of biblical names, probably aided by the popularity of American Revolutionary hero Ethan Allen. Today, Ethan is a very common name, taking the fifth spot in the latest Social Security Administration list. Actor and novelist Ethan Hawke has starred in many films, from *Reality Bites* to *Hamlet.*

Evan: Welsh; Believe it or not, Evan is a form of JOHN ("God is gracious"). The name is most popular in Wales and is becoming more widely used in the United States. Today it ranks among the top 100 names for boys. Novelist Evan Hunter (who writes as Ed McBain), musician Evan Dando, and Indiana Senator Evan Bayh are notable bearers of the name Evan.

Ewan, Ewen: See OWEN.

Ezekiel: Hebrew; "May God strengthen." Ezekiel is the name of a major prophet and a book of the Bible. Though not popular, it occurred regularly in the lists of names used in New England and less commonly in other regions, dying out with the general decline of biblical names. It remains in use, however, reaching No. 351 in 2002, up from No. 629 in 1993. Its well-established shortened form is **Zeke.**

Ezra: Hebrew; "help." From the biblical character whose name is given to one of the books of the Bible. Use of the name Ezra began around 1700, and it began to fade out around 1800. Chiefly used in New England, it was never a popular name. The acclaimed poet Ezra Pound penned his most famous poems in the first half of the 20th century. In the 1990s, the alternative rock band Better Than Ezra brought the name back into the public consciousness.

F

Felipe: Spanish; "fond of horses." Felipe is a Spanish borrowing of the Greek-origin PHILIP, who was one of the 12 apostles in the Bible. Both Philip and PHILLIP remain more popular, but Felipe is certainly a viable name today. Felipe Rodriguez was a popular musician and was the first Puerto Rican to sing the national anthem at a nationally televised sporting event. Crown Prince Felipe of Spain is another notable Felipe. **Filip, Fillip,** and **Fillipo** are variations of this Spanish form.

Finn: Gaelic; "white," "fair." Used for both boys and girls, though mostly for boys. Finn is a form of the Anglicized Irish Fionn. An early Irishman with the name was Fionn Mac Cumhail, a third-century hero along the lines of Robin Hood, who reportedly gained wisdom when he ate an enchanted fish. Another fair fighter from the American Old West was Finn Clanton, one of the Clanton Boys, who, legend has it, fought it out with the Earp brothers and Doc Holliday at the O.K. Corral. The most famous fictional Finn is found in tales by Mark Twain — Huckleberry Finn. **Fin** is another possible spelling (although it's more closely tied to fish, which may be a negative), while **Findlay, Finlay, Findley,** and **Finley** are similar, longer names.

Fletcher: English; "arrow maker." In ancient European countries, a fletcher made and feathered arrows, and the name has come down the centuries with its meaning intact. Today, it's rarely used. In the United States in the 1920s and '30s, the Fletcher Henderson Orchestra played jazz for patrons of the Roseland Ballroom and other venues. Bandleader and pianist Fletcher Henderson hired Louis Armstrong for his band and became the first African-American musician hired by a Caucasian bandleader when Benny Goodman asked Henderson to join his band in 1939. The most famous fictional Fletcher served on the ship *Bounty*, headed by the infamous Captain Bligh. Chevy Chase played nosy reporter Irwin Fletcher in the beloved comedy *Fletch* — a common nickname.

Francis, Francisco: Multiple origins; French (person). Filmmaker Francis Ford Coppola created acclaimed works such as *Patton, The Godfather* trilogy, and *Apocalypse Now*. Francisco is a popular Spanish version of the name — currently more popular than Francis itself — that evokes the beloved West Coast city of San Francisco, although this version has negative associations as well: Francisco Franco was the leader of the Spanish Revolution in the mid-1930s and served as the dictator of Spain until 1975.

Frank: A derivative of FRANCIS. Its rapid buildup in the latter half of the 19th century may be a result of the feminist raid on the name Francis — mothers didn't want to give their sons a name that beginning to be perceived as a girl's name. Into the 20th century, Frank maintained some of its popularity, occasionally breaking into the top ten. Today, it sits just above the 200 mark. Crooner and Rat Pack member Frank Sinatra stole hearts with his bright blue eyes and velvety vocal stylings. Alternative rockers know Frank Black (also called Black Francis), who fronted the critically acclaimed band The Pixies. See also FRANCIS, FRANKLIN.

Franklin: From a family name, which in medieval England indicated a free landholder. In the late 18th century, Franklin began to be used as a given name, largely because of the popularity of Benjamin Franklin. The name fell off during the latter part of the 19th century — a decline that may be attributed to the comparative decline of Benjamin Franklin as a hero, especially because a bumper crop of heroes was harvested from the Civil War. Populist president Franklin Delano Roosevelt brought renewed popularity to the name in the mid-20th century, and it has remained in use since, although today it barely cracks the top 500 list. Boys with this name are commonly called **Frank.**

Frederick: German; from *frithu*, "peace," and *ricju*, "rule." Although this name lingered in post-Conquest times, Frederick really entered English usage in the 18th century, being brought over from Germany (as Friedrich) with the Hanoverian dynasty. Enough tradition lingered for the name to take on a characteristic English spelling. In the American colonies, the Hanoverian kings and their names made little impression, but for unknown reasons, the name leapt into popularity in the United States during the early 1800s, largely fostered by the heavy immigration from Germany in the years following the Revolution of 1848. It reached its height of popularity about 1900. Occasional use of the nickname **Fritz** reveals the German connection, but the almost universal variant in the United States is **Fred.** Because of its German associations, Frederick suffered during the two world wars. Notable Freds and Fredericks include PBS staple Fred Rogers, whose neighbor millions of children wanted to be; silver-screen legend Fred Astaire; and abolitionist Frederick Douglass.

G

Gabriel: Hebrew; "mighty God." Although the angel Gabriel is well known for his assignment to blow the last trumpet, Gabriel has been a rare name, even during the periods when biblical names have been popular. It had some usage among the French colonists, with Gabrielle supplying a feminine. Today, however, both Gabriel and the female equivalent have surged in popularity, both cracking the top 100, with Gabriel at number 32. **Gabe** is a possible nickname.

Garrett: English; from a French borrowing of Old German Gairhard, meaning "spear + hard." This powerful name has consistently been among the

Chapter 2: Bailey, Brian, or Brent? Names for Boys

☺ ☺ ☹ ☺ ☺ ☹ ☺ ☺ ☹ ☺ ☺ ☹ ☺ ☺ ☹ ☺ ☺ ☺ ☹ ☺

top 100 for more than a decade. Several famous Garretts can be found among fictional characters and real-life celebrities. For example, take Jack Nicholson's character Garrett Breedlove in the movies *Terms of Endearment* and *The Evening Star*. This fictional Garrett — in both the movies and the James L. Brooks books they're based on — starts out as a disinterested observer but soon becomes mightily involved with Shirley MacLaine's Aurora Greenway character. Actor/comedian Garrett Morris served up wry observations during his tenure on *Saturday Night Live*. A couple of strong men with Garrett as a last name are Pat Garrett, the Old West sheriff who tracked down and killed outlaw Billy the Kid, and 1970s teen heartthrob Leif Garrett, who pursued both acting and singing careers well into the 1990s. **Garret** is an alternate spelling, and **Gary** and **Garry** are common nicknames.

Gary: From a Scottish place name — for example, Glengarry. It arose from a family name that came to be used as a given name. In the mid-20th century, it sometimes made the top ten, its popularity based on its brevity and euphony but even more on its use on stage and screen. Famous Garys include dancer and actor Gary Cooper, diminutive Gary Coleman, and former presidential hopeful Gary Hart. For added flair, add an extra *r* and make it **Garry.** Garry Trudeau, the cartoonist who brings *Doonesbury* to your morning paper, uses this form of the name. See GARRETT.

Gavin: Origin and meaning unknown; it has been popularly associated with Old German name Gawain, meaning "a district of land." Despite its murky beginnings, Gavin has seen a great increase in popularity in recent years, rising to 61st place in 2002, up from 300th ten years earlier. Actor John Gavin had to exhibit the instincts of a hawk in his role as Sam Loomis, Marion Crane's boyfriend and the man who tracked Marion to the Bates Motel in the Hitchcock thriller *Psycho*. Singer Gavin Rossdale fronted the band Bush and achieved additional fame by marrying Gwen Stefani of the group No Doubt. **Gavan** and **Gaven** are alternate spellings.

Genesis: Latin; "birth." Genesis, the first book of the Bible, describes the creation of the world and the first humans. It's a strong name suitable for either a boy or girl. Naming a child Genesis ensures that he comes into the world with history and tradition on his side.

George: Greek; "earth man, farmer." The crusaders of the 11th century found themselves moved by some of the Eastern Church's colorful saints, one of them being St. George, the dragon slayer. The Norman crusaders took him as their patron. As a result, many English churches were dedicated to the dragon slayer, and some English children bore his name. More important, King Edward III had a special devotion to St. George, dedicated to him the Order of the Garter in 1349, and thus really established him as the patron saint of England. Even so, the name didn't become common. Even with the Reformation (and its hostility to nonbiblical saints), though, George held on — probably because of its patriotic connections. Among the early emigrants to Massachusetts, the name George stood high, one count showing it in eighth place. But, as frequently happened, the new

☺ ☺ ☹ ☺ ☺ ☹ ☺ ☺ ☹ ☺ ☺ ☹ ☺ ☺ ☹ ☺ ☺ ☺ ☹ ☺

settlers didn't follow their fathers' ways, and the use of the name waned. About 1730, however, there came a stirring of change because of something that happened far away: the coronation of King George in 1714. Moreover, four Georges in succession were kings. The New Englanders generally dislike kings, so George may have been more popular in the middle and especially in the southern colonies. At least we know of one Virginia baby named George born in 1732; his family name was Washington. Although his name echoed the royal name, he affected American naming more than any king, becoming nationally well known and popular in the 1770s. In the later 20th century, George finally slumped, failing to make the top ten but remaining somewhat common. Today, famous Georges are numerous, with the list including both Presidents George Bush, actor George Clooney, New York Yankees owner George Steinbrenner, and boxer and indoor grillmaster George Foreman (and his sons, all named George as well).

Gerald: German; "spear + rule." Although the English form Gerald still exists as an American name, it teamed up with JEREMIAH to spin off JERRY, now considered an independent name. It's unusual that two formal names become almost extinct, as these two did, but their familiar form remains common. President Gerald Ford is a distinguished holder of this name.

Gerard: German; from *gairu*, "spear," and *hardu*, "hard." It has historically been rare in America but, along with GERALD, can be considered a source for JERRY. The most famous bearer of this name may be French actor Gérard Depardieu. **Gerardo** is a popular Spanish form of this name; in fact, the Spanish version has surpassed Gerard in popularity.

Graham: English; "gravelly homestead." Despite the humble meaning of their name, Grahams are known for their inventiveness and creativity. For example, Alexander Graham Bell was long thought of as the inventor of the telephone, although history now records that he merely perfected the designs of Italian inventor Antonio Meucci. Another creative Graham is musician Graham Nash, one of the members of the rock-folk group Crosby, Stills, Nash & Young. He wrote several of the group's hit songs, including "Teach Your Children," "Marrakesh Express," and "Just a Song Before I Go." From the literary realm, author Graham Greene became one of the most read novelists of the 20th century with his works *The Power and the Glory, The End of the Affair, The Third Man,* and *The Quiet American.* This name isn't especially popular in the United States today but has the same feel as other trendy names, so it may be worth considering if you like less traditional names but don't want to choose something that every other parent is thinking about.

Grant: French; "grand." This solid and substantial boy's name's popularity ebbs and flows with the times. Famous Grants include painter Grant Wood, termed an American Regionalist painter, whose best-known work is "American Gothic," a painting of a farm couple (think pitchfork). Basketball

☺ ☺ ☹ ☺ ☺ ☹ ☺ ☺ ☹ ☺ ☺ ☹ ☺ ☺ ☹ ☺ ☺ ☹ ☺

star Grant Hill plays with exceptional grace. A couple of debonair British last-name Grants are Cary (born Archibald Alec Leach) and Hugh, both of whom can generate affection in their audiences. Variations include **Grand, Grantham,** and **Grantley.**

Grayson: English; "reeve's son," from an archaic form of the occupational form, "grieve." Although this name is still pretty rare, its popularity has climbed more than 300 spots since the 1990s. Soap opera fans are familiar with Grayson McCouch, veteran actor from *Another World* and *As the World Turns.* Comic book fans admire Dick Grayson, the young ward who eventually became Robin, the sidekick to Batman.

Gregory: Greek; "watchful." Unlike GRAYSON, the popularity of this name is waning; it has slipped from 57th in 1991 to 167th in 2002. Famous Gregorys include dancer Gregory Hines and actor Gregory Peck, who played Atticus Finch in the classic film adaptation of Harper Lee's novel *To Kill a Mockingbird.*

Griffin: Welsh; a variant of Gruffudd, which may derive from elements meaning "strong lord." Although there were many Welsh people among the American colonists, they apparently gave this name little support, and it remained rare. Today, though, Griffin has become a hip and distinctive name, breaking into the top 250 names on the Social Security Administration's list. Son of writer Dominick Dunne, actor Griffin Dunne has starred in such films as *An American Werewolf in London* and *My Girl.*

Gus: See AUGUSTUS.

H

Haley: English; "hay meadow." An uncommon yet distinctive name for either a boy or a girl, Haley is adaptable to many different spellings, including **Haleigh, Hailee,** and **Hayley** (although most people would argue that these spellings are more appropriate for girls than for boys). The twin sisters that actress Haley Mills played in the 1960s movie *The Parent Trap* exhibited ingeniousness in getting their parents back together. Actor Haley Joel Osment garnered numerous awards and an Oscar nomination well before his 15th birthday.

Hank: See HENRY.

Harlan: Origin uncertain; "from the army." Harlan lends itself to many spellings and is a fairly unusual name no matter how it's spelled. Writer Harlan Ellison was gifted in a number of media and won praise and awards for his books, screenplays, teleplays, and journalistic writing. He wrote scripts for television shows ranging from *The Outer Limits* to *Star Trek.* **Harlin** and **Harlon** are alternate spellings.

49

☺ ☺ ☹ ☺ ☺ ☹ ☺ ☺ ☹ ☺ ☺ ☹ ☺ ☺ ☹ ☺ ☺ ☺ ☺ ☹ ☺

Harley: English; "hare + brave" or possibly "hare + meadow." An unusual name, Harley has a variety of spellings — **Harlee, Harleigh** and **Harly,** to name just a few. Probably the most famous Harley is a man whose last name it was: William S. Harley was one of the engineers who lent his name to the Harley-Davidson Motorcycle Company. Harley and his partners, brothers Arthur and Walter Davidson, sold their first racing cycle in 1903 and went on to found a dynasty that still thrives today.

Harold: Old English; from *here,* "army," and *weold,* "power." Its use lapsed after the Norman Conquest, but it revived in the early 19th century, probably because of its Romantic feel. Today, the name seems kind of old-fashioned; it no longer is among the top 500 names in use. Author Harold Robbins is known for having the confidence of a military leader, as he became one of the most provocative and popular writers of the 20th century. Of a different literary ilk is critic and historian Harold Bloom, the Yale-educated author of 20 books of literary criticism and philosophy. Another famous Harold is actor and director Harold Ramis, who is best known for teaming up with actor Bill Murray in the *Ghostbusters* films and in the Army comedy *Stripes.* He is also one of Hollywood's finest comedic writers, having written or collaborated on such hits as *Animal House, Groundhog Day,* and *Analyze This.* **Hal** (brought to the limelight in recent years by the movie *Shallow Hal*) is a common nickname.

Harrison: English; "son of Harry/Harold." Like many names that end in "son," Harrison signifies "son of," which in this case is "son of Harry" or "son of Harold." It's gained prominence as a first name in recent years, although it still barely breaks into the top 200. Movie star Harrison Ford is second to no one when it comes to portraying an action hero. His roles as Han Solo in *Star Wars* and as Indiana Jones have cemented his reputation as a wry, self-deprecating hero. Among the well-known people with the surname Harrison, 9th president William Henry Harrison and his grandson, 23rd president Benjamin Harrison, stand out.

Hart: English; "deer." Although it's more common as a last name (remember the TV show *Hart to Hart*?), Hart can be a distinguished first or middle name for a boy or a girl. Hart Crane was a 20th-century American poet who fused European influences with a unique American-ness. Playwright Moss Hart teamed up with George Kaufman to write plays in the 1930s and '40s that took Broadway by storm, such as *You Can't Take It with You* and *The Man Who Came to Dinner.* On his own, Hart continued to write outstanding dramas, including *Winged Victory.*

Harvey: Probably from the old Breton *haerveu,* meaning "battle worthy." This name likely was introduced by Bretons who accompanied the Normans in the Conquest. (To have a Breton name become English is highly unusual.) It was also the name of a saint who generally appears in the French form as St. Hervé. Though fairly common in the Middle Ages, Harvey went out of use for several centuries as a given name, and its reappearance in the early 19th century probably owes nothing to the Bretons

Chapter 2: Bailey, Brian, or Brent? Names for Boys

☺ ☺ ☹ ☺ ☺ ☹ ☺ ☺ ☹ ☺ ☺ ☹ ☺ ☺ ☹ ☺ ☺ ☺ ☹ ☺

or the saint, but was merely the adoption of a family name. Movie producer Harvey Weinstein wields a great deal of power in Hollywood, whereas actor Harvey Fierstein appeals to a more artsy crowd.

Hayden: English; "from the hedged-in valley." Hayden is a variation of **Haydn,** which was once popularized by a well-respected bearer of the surname, Austrian composer Franz Joseph Haydn. Robert Hayden, Poet Laureate to the U.S. Library of Congress from 1976 to 1978, is perhaps best known for his poem *Those Sunday Mornings*. Today, the most famous bearer of the name is handsome young actor Hayden Christensen, who portrays Anakin Skywalker (who later becomes known as Darth Vader) in *Star Wars* Episodes One, Two, and Three. The name broke into the top 100 for the first time in 2002.

Hector: Greek; the meaning is uncertain, but it may be something along the lines of "holding fast" or "prop." The name of the illustrious Trojan of the *Iliad* appeared as an occasional name for slaves, in accord with the custom of giving slaves classical names, and also has been used by the general populace. Today, Hector is a popular name in the Latino community.

Henry: German; "home rule." Henry was a favorite name among the Norman conquerors. The speech of the Normans was French, and the name developed in that language into what was spelled Henri. Through further development in ordinary speech, the *n* disappeared, and the pronunciation became that which was represented in the English spelling as Harry. On the other hand, most of the writing of the time was in Latin, and the clerks Latinized the name as Henricus. Because all official documents were in Latin, people naturally came to feel that the proper (that is, official) name was Henricus, and a second pronunciation, commonly spelled Henry, developed from the Latin form. Through the Middle Ages, these two spellings and the two pronunciations continued to be used. The name was both common and notable, being that of eight English kings. In 17th-century England and in early New England, however, Henry fell from common use, only to return gradually in the first half of the 18th century. This return coincides with the falling off of the biblical names. In the mid-20th century, Henry again slumped, but, like many names, it has made a comeback in recent years and currently just misses the top 100 list. The development of **Hank,** the ordinary, grass-roots abbreviation or nickname for Henry in the United States — and now a given name in its own right — is a mystery. There are many notable bearers of this name, including baseball's Hank Aaron, carmaker Henry Ford, poet Henry Wadsworth Longfellow, writer Henry Miller, and African-American scholar Henry Louis Gates, Jr.

Holden: English; "hollow, valley." Traditionally a boy's name, Holden is also a distinctive name for a girl. It isn't very common these days, but if you're a fan of J. D. Salinger's novel *The Catcher in the Rye*, it might appeal to you. Although the protagonist, Holden Caulfield, is a troubled and ultimately tragic figure, his engrossing account of himself has become shorthand to express teen angst. Alternate spellings include **Holdan** and **Holdun.**

☺ ☻ ☹ ☺ ☻ ☹ ☺ ☻ ☹ ☺ ☻ ☹ ☺ ☻ ☹ ☺ ☺ ☻ ☹ ☺

Howard: From an English surname of multiple origins. The Howards were one of the foremost English noble families. Pre-1800 uses of the name may be for actual Howard families in America. In the mid-19th century, however, the name built up quickly, indicating that it's another a feudal name by which certain citizens of a democracy mimic the aristocracy. Howard is the most successful of these names. By becoming so common, it lost its snobbish suggestions and became just another solid American name. It still remains moderately common, although today it can sound a bit old-fashioned. Mega-millionaire Howard Hughes and risqué DJ Howard Stern are two well-known Howards.

Hugh: German; a short form of a name containing the root *hugu*, which means "mind, heart." This name was popular in the Middle Ages, partly because of the two saint Hugos who were associated with the city of Lincoln. Along with the names of other nonbiblical saints, Hugh went out of favor with the growth of Protestantism. It gradually returned to modest usage and has remained a viable, though certainly not wildly popular, name in modern times. The form **Hugo** appears occasionally — probably because of direct German influence. English actor Hugh Grant makes moviegoers swoon with his boyish charm, while Hugh Downs anchored the desk of television's *20/20* for many year

Hunter: English; "one who hunts" (surprise!). A common surname that became a popular boy's name in the 1990s, Hunter denotes courage and strength. Journalist Hunter S. Thompson is probably the best-known Hunter of modern times. Thompson founded the school of gonzo journalism, which relinquishes objectivity for in-depth, experiential accounting. His book *Fear and Loathing in Las Vegas*, which was made into a film starring Johnny Depp and Benicio Del Toro, relays his adventures on a trip in the American West. The name can be shortened to **Hunt,** although this nickname isn't particularly popular.

I

Ian, Ion: The Scottish forms of JOHN. They're usually treated as independent names, but they've seldom been common in the United States. Today, however, Ian has climbed to a respectable 67th on the Social Security Administration's list of names, although the form Ion doesn't make the cut. Rock musician Ian Anderson of Jethro Tull is one prominent Ian.

Isaac: Hebrew; "laughter." Genesis 21 tells the story of the reason for the naming. The story of the laughter, however, is probably an attempt by Hebrew speakers to give Hebrew meaning to an unintelligible name. Like many other names in Genesis, this one is probably from a language other than Hebrew, and we just can't be sure of its meaning. Isaac was a well-established name in England during the Middle Ages. Being biblical, it didn't suffer during the Reformation and may even have been stimulated

Chapter 2: Bailey, Brian, or Brent? Names for Boys

☺ ☺ ☹ ☺ ☺ ☹ ☺ ☺ ☹ ☺ ☺ ☹ ☺ ☺ ☹ ☺ ☺ ☺ ☹ ☺

by the vacuum left by the abandonment of the names of nonbiblical saints. Early immigrants to America brought the name with them. Among baptisms in Boston from 1630 to 1669, for example, Isaac appears 14th, and among Plymouth baptisms was ninth. Because Isaac was a well-known figure of the Old Testament, the reason for the use of his name is obvious. Toward the end of the 19th century, the name slumped, but it has seen a comeback and now sits in the No. 50 slot. Among the notable Isaacs are scientist and mathematician Isaac Newton, science fiction writer Isaac Asimov, and soul singer Isaac Hayes.

Isaiah: Hebrew; "salvation by God." In spite of its importance as the name of a major prophet and a book of the Bible, Isaiah has never been more than a mildly popular name. Basketball star Isiah Thomas, who uses an alternative spelling of the name, led the Indiana Hoosiers to a national title and later helped the Detroit Pistons win back-to-back NBA championships.

Ismael, Ishmael: Possibly Hebrew; "God hears." Like many names that appear in Genesis, though, it may not be Hebrew. The most famous use of this name is probably in Melville's novel *Moby-Dick*, in which the protagonist begins the story by saying, "Call me Ishmael." The Ish- form is absent from the 500 most popular names list, but the version Ismael does appear. Among American names, it has consistently ranked in the mid-300s for more than ten years.

Ivan: The Russian form of JOHN. It began to appear after 1870 and can be considered a literary name, developed from the reading of novels by Tolstoy, Turgenev, and so on. You may be surprised to discover that this name has been among the top 150 or so for more than ten years running. Tennis great Ivan (ee-VHAN) Lendl is a well-known Ivan.

J

Jack: This name clearly developed from JOHN. (The resemblance to the French form Jacques, meaning JAMES, is coincidental.) The development of the name began in the later Middle Ages, when the common diminutive suffix -*kin* was added to John, creating Johnkin, which soon came to be spelled Jankin, as in Chaucer's *The Canterbury Tales*. The dropping of the first *n* soon followed, and the -*in* was clipped off with the resulting Jak, commonly spelled Jakke, and, as the spelling normalized, finally producing Jack. As early as Shakespeare's time (and probably a century or so earlier), anyone named John could expect to be called Jack when addressed by friends, as with Sir John Falstaff, whom his comrades regularly call Jack. There are many well-known Jacks today, from legendary golfer Jack Nicklaus to Academy Award-winning actor Jack Nicholson to Beat writer Jack Kerouac, best known for *On the Road*. Parents try to forget serial killer Jack the Ripper when choosing this name. If you just can't get past that association, try JACKSON or JAKE.

Ten popular Spanish names

As the Latino population in the United States explodes, the use of Spanish names is increasing rapidly as well. This section lists ten common Spanish names for boys, in order of popularity.

1. Jose
2. Angel
3. Luis
4. Juan
5. Carlos
6. Jesus
7. Miguel
8. Antonio
9. Xavier
10. Alejandro

Jackson: A common surname meaning "Jack's son," Jackson is also fairly common as a given name, partly because of the hero status of Andrew Jackson and of General "Stonewall" Jackson. In modern times, modernist painter Jackson Pollack and singer Jackson Browne have brought fame to this name. Like JACK, its popularity has risen considerably in recent years, and it's poised to break into the top 50 American boys' names.

Jacob: The Bible attributes this name to the Hebrew, "heel," and gives a highly implausible story of its origin (Genesis 26). As with many other early names, it's probably better to consider it to be borrowed from some unknown language, and thus to be of unknown meaning. Although the story of Jacob is more fully developed in the Bible than that of ISAAC, the name Jacob was less popular in the American colonies, possibly because the patriarchal Jacob lacked heroic qualities. From early colonial times, the name was associated with two quite distinct groups: the Jews and the Germans. The latter, much more numerous than the former, settled chiefly in southeastern Pennsylvania. Since these "Pennsylvania Dutch" continued to speak German, their retention of Jacob in place of the related JAMES was natural. As a general rule, the association of a particular name with a particular group tends to make the name avoided by other groups, even when no prejudice is involved. So the moderate use of Jacob may be partly the result of a feeling that the bearer of the name would be judged as belonging to a minority. By the mid-19th century, heavy German

Chapter 2: Bailey, Brian, or Brent? Names for Boys

☺ ☻ ☹ ☺ ☻ ☹ ☺ ☻ ☹ ☺ ☻ ☹ ☺ ☻ ☹ ☺ ☺ ☻ ☹ ☺

immigration and the beginnings of anti-Semitism worked toward a near
extinction of the name among the general public. In the 20th century, the
anti-German feeling, inevitable during the two world wars, kept Jacob at
the verge of extinction. In recent years, however, this name has made a
remarkable comeback; in fact, it captured the No. 1 spot on the most
recent Social Security Administration list. The short form **Jake** (see also) is
popular as either a nickname for Jacob or a given name itself. **Jakob** is an
alternate spelling; you'll probably recognize this name as the name of
singer Bob Dylan's son.

Jaden: Hebrew; "God has heard." A relatively recent addition to the list of
America's more popular names, Jaden probably evolved from Jadon, a
character mentioned in the Bible. Actors Will Smith and Jada Pinkett Smith
named their second son Jaden Christopher Syre Smith. A nickname is **Jay,**
and alternate spellings include **Jayden, Jadon, Jaiden,** and **Jaydyn.**

Jaime: Spanish. See JAMIE.

Jake: English. Jake is an abbreviation of the Hebrew name JACOB, which
means "follower" or "supplanter." Fans of literature know Jake Barnes,
Ernest Hemingway's narrator and protagonist in *The Sun Also Rises*. Boxer
Jake LaMotta was immortalized in the 1980 Martin Scorsese film *Raging
Bull*; Robert DeNiro put on 50 pounds to play the role. Actor Jake
Gyllenhaal makes audiences laugh and swoon, taking roles in films such
as *The Good Girl* and *Lovely and Amazing*. Still another famous Jake is
Jake Steinfeld, the first nationally recognized fitness trainer and a motivat-
ing force behind America's quest for fitness; he may be more famous for
his branding, "Body by Jake."

Jalen: English. Jalen is a variant of **Galen,** which means "calm" in Greek.
Professional basketball's Jalen Rose, who has played for both the Indiana
Pacers and the Chicago Bulls, has popularized the name in recent years.
For variety, try a different spelling, such as **Jaylin, Jaylon,** or **Jaylen.**

Jamal: Arabic; "handsome." An ancient name, Jamal can also be spelled
Jamil or **Jamaal.** Actor Malcolm-Jamal Warner is probably best known for
his role as Theo Huxtable in *The Cosby Show*. Basketball player Jamal
Mashburn has been a professional basketball star since being the fourth
pick in the 1993 NBA draft.

James: Hebrew; "following after," "the supplanter." The history of this
name is a little peculiar. In the Hebrew text of the Bible, James and JACOB
are actually the same name. The Latin form was Jacobus, with a long *o*. At
some point, however, a colloquial version developed with a short *o* and an
m instead of a *b* — Jacomus. This form took hold in Spain (as JAIME) and
Great Britain (as James). The popularity of James in the English tradition
came about due to several circumstances. It was the name of two apostles
and three other prominent people in the New Testament. The great pilgrim-
age to St. James (Santiago) at Compostela in Spain was a major event in

☺ ☻ ☹ ☺ ☻ ☹ ☺ ☻ ☹ ☺ ☻ ☹ ☺ ☻ ☹ ☺ ☺ ☻ ☹ ☺

the Middle Ages. Among New Testament names for men, James is usually bested only by JOHN and THOMAS in most English lists. In Scotland, the name was even more popular, since it was the royal name for over a century. This Scottish influence helped bring the name some popularity in America, and it remained popular throughout the 19th century and the earlier part of the 20th. The colloquial variations are **Jim, Jimmy,** and **Jamie.** Notable Jameses, Jims, and Jimmys abound: Presidents James Madison and Jimmy Carter, Irish writer James Joyce, musicians Jim Morrison and James Brown, actors James Dean and Jimmy Stewart, comedic actor Jim Carrey, and football legend Jim Brown. See also JAMIE.

Jamie: Hebrew; "follower." Alternate spellings include **Jamey** and **Jaymee.** In **Jaime,** the Hebrew version used extensively in the Spanish-speaking world, the pronunciation is HI-may. Though most often a boy's name, the television show's heroic "Bionic Woman" was named Jamie Summers. Celebrity "Naked Chef" Jamie Oliver is a popular male Jamie. The popularity of this name has slacked off in recent years, but it's still among the top 300 names in use for boys (and even more popular for girls). If you like this name but would prefer to use a more formal given name, you can opt for JAMES, with Jamie as a nickname.

Jamil: See JAMAL.

Jared: Hebrew; either "rose" or "descend." A figure in Genesis, Jared is chiefly notable for having lived to the ripe old age of 962 — a good second to Methuselah's 969. The name Jared may have been used for its suggestion of long life, or it may be another name chosen by luck. Jared Ingersoll and his son of the same name were prominent in public affairs in the late 18th century, and the name lingers still in that family. Today, Jared maintains modest popularity, with the most popular bearer of the name being Jared Fogle, the spokesperson for the sandwich chain Subway.

Jason: Greek: "healer." A biblical name (Acts 17:5). In the Greek text the name is Eason, and the rendering in English may have been influenced by the name of the Greek mythological hero. Historically, it's been rare as an American name, although its use in Faulkner's novels gave it some currency. In the mid-20th century, it enjoyed a mild boom, and in the last ten years, it has consistently ranked among the top 50 most popular names for boys. The alternate spelling **Jayson** gives it a more contemporary feel. Two acting Jasons include Robards and Lee, the latter starring in 1997's *Chasing Amy* and 2000's *Almost Famous.*

Javier: Arabic; see JAVIER. Well established as a Spanish adaptation of the Basque place name Etcheberri ("new house"). A traditional and distinctly masculine name, Javier isn't open to many permutations, except, perhaps, for a phonetic spelling along the lines of Haviere. Famous Javiers include Javier Bardem, the award-winning and Oscar-nominated (for *Before Night Falls*) Spanish actor and Javier Pérez de Cuéllar, former Secretary General of the United Nations.

☺ ☹ ☹ ☺ ☹ ☹ ☺ ☹ ☹ ☺ ☹ ☹ ☺ ☹ ☹ ☺ ☺ ☹ ☹ ☺

Javon: English; most likely a variant of the Biblical name **Javan.** (This seems to be a created name that spread by word of mouth.) The name has gained attention in recent years because of Green Bay Packers wide receiver Javon Walker and jazz saxophonist Javon Jackson. Also spelled **Jevon,** as in Jevon "The Freak" Kearse, defensive end for the Tennessee Titans.

Jaxon: See JACKSON.

Jay: French; "a bird." Jay — or **Jaye** or **Jai** — is a popular middle name for both sexes as well as a boy's first name that spans the generations. Early 20th-century businessman and financier Jay Gould carried the name. Actor Jay Silverheels, better known as Tonto to a generation of 1960s Lone Ranger fans, made the name known in the 1950s. Around the same time, composer Jay Livingston, along with his partner Ray Evans, was composing songs such as "Que Sera Sera" for the movies and television theme songs for shows such as *Mr. Ed.* Today, television personality Jay Leno hosts *The Tonight Show.*

Jayden: See JADEN.

Jaydyn: See JADEN.

Jaymee: See JAIME.

Jefferson: English; "son of Geoffrey." The name had some currency in the early 20th century because of the hero status of Thomas Jefferson. Its short form is **Jeff,** the handiness of which somewhat compensates for the awkward length of the whole. Jefferson is, however, scarcely viable today. Its most eminent bearer as a first name has been Jefferson Davis, president of the Confederacy. Jefferson Holt managed the alternative rock band REM for many years, and he was often referred to as the band's "fifth member." And Democrat William Jefferson Clinton served as President of the United States for two terms.

Jeffrey: Old German; based on several words, including Gaufrid ("district + peace"), Walahfrid ("traveler + peace"), and Gisfrid ("pledge + peace). The modern American spelling has become dominant in the United States, but the older spelling, **Geoffrey,** sustains itself in Great Britain. Another spelling is **Jeffery.** Aside from its being Germanic, little is known about the etymology of Jeffrey. Several names may have become mingled during the Middle Ages. The element *-frey* is quite possibly from the Germanic *frithu,* meaning "peace." Historically, Jeffrey has been fairly rare; its shortening, **Jeff,** has been more common. (And actually, Jeff may be from Jeffers, Jefferson, or some other family name.) As recently as ten years ago, however, Jeffrey was among the 50 most popular names for baby boys in the United States. Well-known Jeffreys and Jeffs include actor Jeff Bridges, who starred in *Seabiscuit* and *Tucker,* among many other movies, and Jeff Bezos, the founder of Amazon.com.

☺ ☺ ☹ ☺ ☺ ☹ ☺ ☺ ☹ ☺ ☺ ☹ ☺ ☺ ☹ ☺ ☺ ☹ ☺ ☺ ☹ ☺

Jeremy: Hebrew; "God will uplift." A popular boy's name in the 1990s, Jeremy is also starting to appear as a unique name for girls. It has a variety of spellings, including **Jeramy, Jeramey, Jeremie,** and **Jeromy.** Often thought of as a derivation of Jeremiah, **Jem** is a common nickname. Jeremy Irons, a British actor who won an Oscar for his work in *Reversal of Fortune,* wears the name with distinction. American actor Jeremy Sisto has played historical figures from Julius Caesar to Jesus of Nazareth on television and a variety of roles in feature films. Derivatives include **Jeremiah** and **Jeremias.**

Jermaine: French, Latin; "from Germany," "brother." A boy's name that is more popular now than it was in the past, Jermaine is a variation of the French **Germain,** which, along with **Jermain** and **Germaine,** is an alternate spelling. Jermaine O'Neal showed his talent at a young age and entered the world of professional basketball when he was just 18 years old — the youngest player in NBA (National Basketball Association) history at the time. Jermaine Jackson was one of the singing brothers known as the Jackson 5 (along with his brother Michael) and launched a solo career after the group split up.

Jerome: Greek; based on the form of Hieronymus, from which the English form has evolved. The name is chiefly associated with St. Jerome (fifth century). As a nonbiblical saint, he was not cherished by the Protestants, and his name has been fairly rare in the United States. Jerome Bettis starred as a running back at Notre Dame, before embarking upon a pro career with the St. Louis Rams and Pittsburgh Steelers.

Jerry: See GERALD, JEREMIAH, GERARD.

Jesse: Hebrew, "God is." Being the father of David, Jesse was a well-known biblical character, and his name was steadily used, though never attaining great popularity. Its usage seems to have arisen late, after 1750. As if in compensation, it remained in use at a later date than most of the biblical names, being still current as late as 1875. An alternate spelling is **Jessie,** which is also occasionally used for girls. Notable bearers of this name include Jesse Jackson and Jesse Owens.

Jesus: Hebrew; see JOSHUA; "God is generous," "God helps." In the Anglo-American tradition of naming, Jesus isn't used. Its occurrence may confidently be put down to the use of some other language, most commonly Spanish. Still, the name managed to rank as the 66th most popular boys' name in 2002 according to the Social Security Administration.

Joaquin: Hebrew; "God will establish." A variant of Joachim. This name occurs in a Spanish context and was adopted as a pseudonym by the 19th-century poet Joaquin Miller. Joaquin Phoenix received an Academy Award nomination for his work in *Gladiator.* This name is pretty rare, but you might like it if you're drawn to exotic-sounding names.

Joe: See JOSEPH.

Chapter 2: Bailey, Brian, or Brent? Names for Boys

☺ ☺ ☹ ☺ ☺ ☹ ☺ ☺ ☹ ☺ ☺ ☹ ☺ ☺ ☹ ☺ ☺ ☹ ☺

Joel: Hebrew; "Jehovah is God." Joel was viable in the period of biblical names and it still survives, probably because its brevity and euphony count in its favor. Joel is generally not abbreviated, probably so as to avoid confusion with JOSEPH in the form JOE. Joel Schumacher has directed such films as *The Lost Boys, Dying Young,* and *Phone Booth.*

John: Hebrew; "God is gracious." In the Hebrew form Johanan (Old Testament) and the Greek form Ioannes (New Testament), it's the name of 14 men mentioned in the Bible. With the advance of Christianity, the name spread to many different languages. John passed readily into Christian use, but was much less popular in the Western Church than in the Eastern. The Anglo-Saxons, even after their conversion, retained their old names, though an occasional churchman took the name John. The early Crusades reestablished contacts with the East, and thus may have brought John back into usage. More likely, the more highly organized Church of the Norman period, by steady pressure, succeeded in building up the biblical names in contrast to the Anglo-Saxon names, with their partially pagan suggestion. By 1200, John had become a much used name. This popularity sprang largely from the circumstance that two prominent saints (the Baptist and the Evangelist) bore the name, and that each of them also had a day of special festival. A child therefore had twice the ordinary chance, on a purely numerical basis, of being born on or near a festival of St. John. Thus, of 427 baptisms of males in London during the decade 1540 to 1549, John is decisively in the lead with a quarter of the total. Since the English Puritans accepted biblical saints in some fashion, the Reformation really aided the hegemony of John, as it cut down the competition. Consequently, John is the usual leader of any English or American list. In the early period, as many as a fifth of all American men may have borne this name. In the last century, John has generally maintained leadership, though the percentage has declined, since there has been a tendency, because of larger population units, to keep away from very popular names. Variants and nicknames include **Jon, Jonny,** and **Johnny.** Famous bearers of this name include President John F. Kennedy, tennis great John McEnroe, writer John Updike, talk-show host Johnny Carson, musician Johnny Cash, and legendary quarterback Johnny Unitas.

Jonah: Hebrew; "dove (as in the bird)." Though a well-known biblical character, Jonah was inevitably linked to the whale and was a somewhat humorous, unlikely, and grotesque figure. Understandably, namings for him were rare. When occurring, parents were likely to use the New Testament (Greek) form, **Jonas.**

Jonathan: Hebrew; "God gave." Known from the gallant prince, the son of King Saul, and as the friend of David, Jonathan entered English nomenclature shortly after the Reformation. In New England, it became much more popular, and in the summations that are available for the 17th century, the name stands in the top ten. Its popularity continued to rise in the 18th century. In the Fourth Regiment of the Connecticut Line (1781), Jonathan is in third place, exceeded only by John and William in the list of enlisted men and privates. Among officers, however, the name failed to make the top ten, a possible indication that it was already being considered as socially on the down side. From contact with this regiment or others like it (which may even have harbored still larger proportions of Jonathans), the British at the siege of Boston applied the nickname "Brother Jonathan." The term "Brother" doubtless originated from the ideas of the basic brotherhood of the two English-speaking entities. There was nothing especially derogatory about the nickname, and it may even have been half affectionate, but any such term applied by the enemy in wartime is sure to be resented. Apparently, the Americans showed their resentment, in one way, by ceasing to name their sons Jonathan. The use of the name fell off, along with the general decline of the Old Testament names, and by 1840, it was almost extinct. It has enjoyed a rise in popularity in more recent times, and in 2002, it was No. 21 on the list of the most popular boys' names. Some of Jonathan's popularity may spring from its resemblance to JOHN, to which it can readily be shortened. Alternate spellings include **Jonathon, Johnathon,** and **Johnathan.**

Jordan: Hebrew; "something that descends, flows down." The river Jordan figures significantly in the Bible and in the history of the Middle East. As far as names go, there's an interesting split in whether Jordan is given to a boy or to a girl. African-American parents are more likely to name their sons Jordan, perhaps in honor of basketball great Michael Jordan, while Caucasians name daughters Jordan more often than they give the name to their male offspring. Whether given to a boy or a girl, Jordan, and it variations **Jordyn, Jory, Jordann,** and **Jourdan,** was a very popular choice in the 1990s and continues to be the choice of many parents.

Jorge: Spanish/Portuguese; variant of Greek Georgios ("farmer"). In medieval legend, St. George (the knight who became the patron saint of England) struggled with a fire-breathing dragon symbolizing the devil. Argentine writer Jorge Luis Borges wrote fantastic tales of how metaphysical elements interact with human existence that made him a foremost figure of 20th-century literature.

Jose: Spanish; "God will increase." The Spanish version of Joseph and a rough equivalent of the English JOE, Jose has been gaining in popularity, breaking into the top 50 boys' names in the late 1990s. Sometimes a short form of Josefe, nicknames and variations include **Che, Pepe,** and **Pepito.** Musician Jose Feliciano has won scores of awards including six Grammys and was perhaps the first Latin musician to cross over to popular music. Baseball slugger Jose Canseco was a perennial player on all-star teams, and despite injuries and personal setbacks, remains a player with impressive talent.

Joseph: Hebrew; "God will increase." The name is borne by multiple biblical characters, notable among them the husband of Mary. Since this latter Joseph was not especially of interest to the Puritans, we can assume that the numerous namings before 1900 have the patriarchal figure in mind. Afterward, as Joseph was falling in popularity among the Protestants, it

☺ ☺ ☹ ☺ ☺ ☹ ☺ ☺ ☹ ☺ ☺ ☹ ☺ ☺ ☹ ☺ ☺ ☺ ☺ ☹ ☺

began to receive Catholic support, especially from the important segment of population with Italian background — Giuseppe being readily shifted to Joseph. There is no simple explanation for the popularity of Joseph among the colonists, eclipsing, as he does, the other patriarchal figures. Today, Joseph maintains considerable popularity, ranking sixth in the 2002 list of boys' names compiled by the Social Security Administration. The regular short form of the name is **Joe,** with the less common **Joey** being the diminutive. An interesting testimony to the continuing popularity of Joseph is the use, in World War II, of G.I. Joe as the name of the ordinary American soldier. Notable Josephs and Joes include writer Joseph Heller, controversial politician Joseph McCarthy, boxer Joe Louis, and baseball player "Shoeless" Joe Jackson.

Joshua: Hebrew; "God saves." As the conqueror of Canaan (and a book of the Bible), Joshua was well known to the colonists, and the name was in use from the beginnings. Like most of the biblical names, its chief flourishing was in the hundred years from 1750 to 1850. It lingered in use, before surging in popularity during the latter part of the 20th century. For the last ten years, Joshua has consistently ranked among the top five most popular names in the United States. It's often shortened to **Josh,** as in the actor Josh Hartnett, who has appeared in such films as *Black Hawk Down* and *The Virgin Suicides.*

Juan: Spanish; a form of the English name JOHN, which means "gift from God." The biblical John the Baptist baptized Christ in the Jordan River. The Spanish version of the name was borne by Don Juan, a character from Spanish legend who killed his lover's father but was dragged to hell by him. In 1956, poet Juan Ramon Jiminez won the Nobel Prize, and during the last decade, Texas Rangers fans have adored right fielder Juan Gonzalez. The name is very popular in the Spanish-speaking community and has placed near 50th for more than ten years running.

Jude: Hebrew; "one who is praised." Jude and his brother James were apostles of Jesus Christ, and Jude is credited with authorship of several epistles, or letters. On the secular front, actor Jude Law has earned well-deserved praise and awards for his talents as exhibited in movies such as *The Talented Mr. Ripley* and *Artificial Intelligence: AI.* And who can forget the classic Beatles tune *Hey, Jude*? Despite its various positive associations, this name is uncommon in the United States today. Similar names include **Judah** and **Jud** (or **Judd**).

Julian: Greek; "youthful." As the name of a number of saints, Julian was well used in English during the Middle Ages. The more classical **Julius** appeared in the Elizabethan period. In the American colonies, these names made little showing before the later 18th century, at which time the classical influence worked in their favor, and they became current. Today, this name is again rising in popularity — it ranked 79th on the most recent list. Julian Lennon, the son of John Lennon and Yoko Ono, scored a hit of his own with "Too Late for Goodbyes."

Justin: Latin; "just." This is a late Latin name, based on St. Justina. It's become a very common in the United States, having been in the top 25 since the 1980s. As a member of 'N Sync and as a solo performer, Justin Timberlake has caused many a pre-teen heart to beat faster.

K

Kaleb: See CALEB.

Kameron: See CAMERON.

Karl: See CARL.

Keaton: English; a place name, derived from a Brittonic origin meaning "forest stream." Keaton is a name that's part of the growing trend to use traditional surnames as first names. Notable last-name Keatons include actor Michael, who played the title character in the first two live-action *Batman* movies directed by Tim Burton. Born Joseph Francis, Jr., the talented comic writer, director, and actor Buster Keaton was a pioneer of early filmmaking. Talented actress Diane Keaton has numerous award nominations to her credit as well as actual Golden Globe and Oscar statuettes. Alternate spellings of Keaton include **Keyton, Keeton,** and **Keatyn.**

Keegan: Irish; a shortening of the Irish surname Mac Aodhagáin, from a root meaning "fire." Part of the modern trend of assigning last names as first names, Keegan is still a distinctive enough name that you probably won't find two Keegans in the same class. Alternate spellings include **Keagan, Kegan,** and **Keigan.**

Keith: Scottish; from a Scottish place name of Brythonic origin meaning "wood, forest." Keith is well established as a strong male name. *Kung Fu* actor Keith Carradine portrayed the strong, silent type in the popular 1970s television series. Musician Keith Richards has certainly exemplified the meaning of his first name throughout his career in the Rolling Stones. Jazz-fusion improvisational musician Keith Jarrett forges his own way to get the sound he wants from his piano and himself. And pop and still-popular artist Keith Haring fought to open new vistas for artists and art aficionados. Inventive spellings include **Keeth** and **Keyth.**

Kelly: Irish; from a shortening of MacCeallaigh or O'Ceallaigh; various meanings include "strife," "frequenter of churches," and "bright (haired)." A name that historically has been suitable for either a boy or a girl, Kelly is much more common for girls today.

Kelvin: Scottish Gaelic; "from the narrow river." The meaning of Kelvin originates in the fact that there is a river in Scotland with that name.

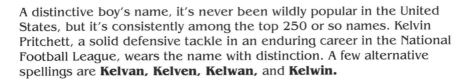

A distinctive boy's name, it's never been wildly popular in the United States, but it's consistently among the top 250 or so names. Kelvin Pritchett, a solid defensive tackle in an enduring career in the National Football League, wears the name with distinction. A few alternative spellings are **Kelvan, Kelven, Kelwan,** and **Kelwin.**

Kendall: English; originates from a place name meaning "valley of the Kent river." Kendall is a name that started out as a boy's name and has gradually become more common for girls. Alternative spellings include **Kendal, Kendel,** and **Kyndall.**

Kendrick: Welsh; based on given name *Cynwrig,* meaning is uncertain, but the first half may mean "hound." Kendrick is more often seen as a last name, but it's not unprecedented as a first name. Former Temptation Eddie Kendrick was fairly fearless as the group's lead singer. One variation is **Kenrick;** natural nicknames are both Ken and Rick.

Kennedy: Gaelic; from another shortened Irish surname, O'Cinneide, meaning "ugly head." Kennedy was almost exclusively a surname until the last half the 20th century, when parents started using it to honor assassinated president John F. Kennedy and his brother Robert Kennedy, who was also murdered. Pulitzer Prize-winning author John Kennedy Toole, despite his name, was not one of those named for the slain president; Toole himself died in 1969, more than a decade before his novel, *A Confederacy of Dunces*, was published to wild acclaim. Bantamweight boxer Kennedy McKinney won a gold medal at the 1988 Olympics in Seoul.

Kenneth: Gaelic; "good-looking, handsome." A popular name in Scotland, it began to appear in America toward the end of the 19th century, enjoying a slight burst of popularity about 1880. It's still something of a favorite, with **Ken** and **Kenny** serving as nicknames. Famous carriers of this name include actor Kenneth Branagh, fashion designer Kenneth Cole, Beat Generation writer Ken Kesey, and singer Kenny "The Gambler" Rogers.

Kent: Brittonic; "border land." Kent is a very old, traditional boy's name in the United Kingdom; there's a county of the same name in England. It isn't often used in the United States today. Prominent Kents include U.S. Senator Kent Conrad, who has served North Dakota in the Senate since 1986. And, of course, the man of steel's secret identity is Clark Kent, and an association with Superman can't be a bad thing. Businessman, philanthropist, and sportsman Jack Kent Cook used the wealth he earned through his business dealings to buy professional sports teams, including the Los Angeles Lakers basketball team and the Washington Redskins football team.

Kevin: Irish; "handsome." Long used in Ireland, this name was introduced into Irish contexts in the United States during the 20th century. The name has been quite popular, consistently ranking in the top 30 on many lists.

Parent's Success Guide to Baby Names

Famous Kevins include the actors Kevin Bacon, known for the movie Footloose as well as for the game based on him, "Six Degrees of Kevin Bacon"; and Kevin Kline, who brought his comedic and dramatic talents to such films as *The Big Chill* and *A Fish Called Wanda*.

Kirk: Scandinavian; "church." Kirk is a strong, steadfast boy's name. Actor Kirk Douglas's varied career spans half a century, and he has the lifetime achievement awards to prove his acting talents. Trekkies' favorite Star Trek captain is none other than James T. Kirk, who helmed the original *Starship Enterprise*.

Kobe: Origin and meaning uncertain; the name may come from the city in Japan. Basketball player Kobe Bryant supplanted all heirs apparent to NBA greats Magic Johnson and Michael Jordan when he joined the pros right out of high school in 1996, becoming the youngest player to ever play in an NBA game. Since then, he helped lead the Los Angeles Lakers to three consecutive NBA championships, and he has become one of the most recognized sports personalities in the world. Probably because of this one celebrity, the name jumped up more than 300 spots from 1997 to 1998 (it wasn't even among the top 1,000 before 1997) and since then has generally broken the top 250 from year to year. **Coby,** the version more likely to be used outside the African-American community, sat at No. 500 in 2002.

Kody: See CODY.

Kolby: See COLBY.

Kristian: See CHRISTIAN.

Kristopher: See CHRISTOPHER.

Kyle: Scottish Gaelic; from a Scottish Gaelic place name meaning "narrow land." Kyle is a name that's always been a solid choice for a boy — never too popular, never totally out of favor — until the 1990s, when its popularity spiked and it hit the top ten most popular boys' names. NASCAR driver Kyle Petty has had a long and successful career on the Winston Cup circuit. Actor Kyle MacLachlin has taken on a variety of quite diverse roles — ruler of an almost waterless planet in the movie *Dune*, FBI agent with a love of cherry pie in the television series *Twin Peaks*, and a colleague who tries to undermine Fred Flintstone in the movie, *The Flintstones*. Alternate spellings for Kyle include **Kile** and **Kial; Kai, Kiley, Kylan,** and **Kylen** are similar.

Kyler: origin and meaning unknown. Kyler has been moderately popular in recent years, rising from 497th to 278th over the last ten years on the Social Security Administration's list of the most popular names. **Kylar** is an alternate spelling.

☺ ☺ ☹ ☺ ☺ ☹ ☺ ☺ ☹ ☺ ☺ ☹ ☺ ☺ ☹ ☺ ☺ ☺ ☺ ☹ ☺

L

Lance: Old German; historically the name comes from the given name *Lanzo*, a diminutive of any of various Old German names beginning with the element "Land-" (meaning "land"). More popular in the late 1950s and early 1960s than in subsequent years, Lance is nonetheless a strong choice for a boy's name. Probably the most well known Lance is bicyclist Lance Armstrong, who overcame cancer and then won the most grueling bike race in the world, the Tour de France, five years in a row. A variation is **Launce.**

Landon: Uncertain origin and meaning. A name traditionally used as a surname, Landon joined the ranks of first names, and gender-neutral names, in the 1990s. It can be spelled **Landan, Landen, Landyn,** or some other configuration according to preference and gender — Landen and Landon are used more often for boys, and Landan and Landyn more often for girls. *Little House on the Prairie* father Michael Landon may be the most remembered Landon.

Lane: English; "narrow road." Lane is fairly ambidextrous in that it can be used for a boy or a girl and as a first, middle, or last name. The so far few famous Lanes are male: Lane Smith is a character actor and children's book illustrator as well as a sometime writer; and Lane Kirkland, who was a labor organizer and president of the AFL-CIO for 16 years.

Langley: English; "long meadow." Traditionally a surname, Langley is part of the growing trend of using last names as first names. Actress Mariel Hemingway named her son Langley. A fictional Langley was Professor Langley Wallingford of *All My Children* fame. On *The X-Files*, one of the three Lone Gunmen who help FBI agents Mulder and Scully with covert computer work, is named Langly, though it's unclear whether it's a first or last name. **Langly** is an alternate spelling.

Larry: Latin; "laurel, bay tree." See LAWRENCE. Often a nickname for Lawrence, Larry is a solid, if somewhat old-fashioned, boy's name. Larry was one of the Three Stooges, and actor Larry Hagman has played roles that live on in popular culture — Captain Tony Nelson in *I Dream of Jeannie* and J.R. Ewing in *the* nighttime soap opera of the 1980s, *Dallas*. Runner Larry Black was figuratively if not literally crowned with laurels when he won both gold and silver medals at the 1972 Munich Olympics. Basketball legend Larry Bird helped the Boston Celtics win three NBA championships during the 1980s.

Lawrence: Latin; "laurel, bay tree," from which the ancient Latin town of Laurentium took its name. The medieval use of the name, however, sprang from St. Laurence of Rome, martyred, by being broiled on a gridiron, in 258 AD. Along with the other nonbiblical saints, Lawrence was shunned by the Puritans, though the name was used a little in the Middle Colonies. In the 20th century, it increased in popularity considerably. Older diminutives maintained the long vowel sound and have resulted in family names such as Laurie and Lowry. In the 20th century, the form, with a short vowel, has become LARRY. Both the name itself and the diminutive Larry have been popular in Ireland, and part of the American usage is the result of Irish influence. An alternate spelling is **Laurence.**

Lee: English; from the family name, which is derived from the Anglo-Saxon *leah,* meaning "meadow, glade, clearing," and signifies a dweller at such a place. In the United States, the given name is from the family name. It began to appear in the early 19th century, but its chief vogue arose after Robert E. Lee had become the heroic symbol of the Confederacy. Because Southern usage allowed a family name to be bestowed on a girl, many women were called Lee. As the memory of the Civil War dulled, the name spread to other parts of the country, used chiefly for men. Lee Majors starred as the bionic Steve Austin on TV's *The Six Million Dollar Man.*

Leo: Latin, "lion." The name scarcely exists in the United States before 1850, but shows some increase in the late 19th century, probably because of Jewish influence. It remains rare today. **Lionel** is from a French diminutive form, but has become an independent name. Another derivative is **Leon.** Pop star Lionel Richie topped the charts as a member of the Commodores and later as a solo artist.

Leonard: German; "lion + bold." The name was established as that of a fifth-century saint. Like the names of other nonbiblical saints, Leonard went out of favor with the Reformation. Around the middle of the 18th century, it began to make a reappearance, and it has continued to be viable. **Leonardo** is a derivative, as in the actor Leonardo DiCaprio. **Leo** is a common nickname that has replaced the now-outdated **Lenny.**

Leslie: Gaelic; meaning unknown, but evidence suggests "court of the holly trees." In the United States, Leslie began to be used as a first name in the later 19th century. It soon became a woman's name, perhaps because the endings suggested a feminine in American usage. It has remained viable, but not common, in the 20th century. Actor Leslie Nielsen has starred in many slapstick comedies, most notably *Airplane* and *Naked Gun.* Alternate spellings include **Lesley** and **Lesly.**

Levi: Hebrew; "united." The name of a son of the patriarch Jacob, and the tribe thus designated. It occurs rarely in the name rosters of early New England. Going out of use with the general decline of Old Testament names, it maintained some special popularity in Jewish use throughout the later 19th century. The tailor Levi Strauss struck it rich by selling canvas pants (jeans) to prospectors during California's 1849 gold rush.

Lewis: German; "famous warrior." As a royal name it enters the record with the Frankish king (466 to 511) whose name commonly appears in English

☺ ☺ ☹ ☺ ☺ ☹ ☺ ☺ ☹ ☺ ☺ ☹ ☺ ☺ ☹ ☺ ☺ ☺ ☺ ☹ ☺

as Clovis. From Clovis, it soon shifted in French to **Louis.** It was brought to England after the Norman Conquest, at first appearing in numerous spellings, but eventually being standardized as Lewis. The American colonists were not especially fond of the name, but a few instances occur, nearly always spelled Lewis. After 1780, however, the name became more common, and the Louis spelling also occurred more noticeably. Naturally, we would tend to ascribe such shifts to the French alliance in the Revolution and the cultural drift away from England after Independence. In recent years, no one has paid much attention to the name, and the question of spelling merely vanishes along with the near-vanishing of the fine old name itself. The most famous bearer of this name would be Lewis Carroll, author of *Alice's Adventures in Wonderland* — though it should be noted that his real name was Charles Lutwidge Dodgson.

Liam: Irish; taken from the name WILLIAM, which means "resolute protector." The name was popularized in the United Kingdom, where for centuries, English boys were given some form of William the Conqueror's name. The name has become popular in the United States of late, capturing the 113th spot in 2002, up from 624 in 1991. One famous bearer of this name is Liam Neeson, the respected star of such films as *Schindler's List* and *Star Wars: Episode One.*

Lincoln: English; "village by the lake." General Benjamin Lincoln was one of the heroes of the Revolutionary War, and a few names may thus have arisen. Of much greater importance as a hero has been Abraham Lincoln. Since Abraham was disappearing in the general decline of biblical names, anyone wishing to name a child after the chief Union hero of the Civil War would be likely to use the name Lincoln. Lincoln remains a viable name, and it may grow in popularity given the trend of using last names as first names. At 6'6" and 335 lb., Oakland Raiders tackle Lincoln Kennedy has no trouble pushing around defensive lineman.

Lindsay: English; "Lincoln island." Lindsay can be used as either a female or male name. A famous example of each is actress Lindsay Wagner and musician Lindsay Buckingham. Lindsay Wagner will forever be known as heroine Jamie Sommers from television's *The Bionic Woman,* for which she won an Emmy Award. Lindsay Buckingham is the guitarist and vocalist for the rock band Fleetwood Mac, and he has performed many of the band's best songs, such as "Go Your Own Way." An alternate spelling is **Lindsey**.

Lionel: See LEO.

Logan: Scottish Gaelic; "little hollow." Logan used to be more commonly known as a surname, but today, it's quite popular as a first name for both boys and girls. A Logan of note is early 20th-century author Logan Pearsall Smith, who is known mainly as a literary critic, although he did produce some works of fiction. Another Logan comes from the world of comic books — Wolverine (whose "real name" is Logan) is the reluctant member of the X-Men who has claws that protrude from his hands. With the recent success of the *X-Men* films, this Logan has become a hero to millions of young moviegoers worldwide. And, of course, who can forget that classic sci-fi movie from the 1970s, *Logan's Run*? In that film, the title character (played by Michael York) leads a rebellion against the computer system that controls his futuristic society.

Louis: See LEWIS.

Lucas: Latin; "light." Like Logan, Lucas is thought of more as a surname than a first name (think George Lucas, creator of the popular *Star Wars* and *Indiana Jones* films), but Lucas does make an interesting choice for a given name. A couple of Lucases of note are Lucas Cranach and Lucas Foss. Lucas Cranach was a minor 16th-century German painter known for his sacred works. Lucas Foss is a contemporary German composer and pianist recognized for his avant-garde creations. He had long tenures as conductor of both the Buffalo Philharmonic and the Brooklyn Philharmonic. The name Lucas pops up often in the soap opera world, as well; on *Days of Our Lives*, Lucas Roberts tends to walk a fine line between being a good guy and a bad guy, but he always manages to do the right thing in the end. Nicknames and derivatives of Lucas include **Lukas** and **Lucius**. See also LUKE.

Luis: The Spanish form of LEWIS, a German name that means "famous warrior." Due to the sizable Spanish-speaking population in the United States, this name has been among the top 50 names for more than a decade. One well-known Luis is Luis Rafael Sanchez, an award-winning Puerto Rican writer whose novel, *Macho Camacho's Beat*, was a bestseller in both Spanish and English. The 20th-century poet Jorge Luis Borges is another famous Luis; his many volumes of poetry, essays, and fiction have won numerous awards and have earned him much respect in the literary world. However, the name Luis isn't just for writers: Luis W. Alvarez was a 20th-century physicist and famed member of the Manhattan Project. His discoveries in radioactive decay allowed for significant advances in atomic research. This Luis was also an originator, with his geologist son, of the theory that the mass extinction of the dinosaurs was caused by a large comet or asteroid hitting the earth — a theory that is still hotly debated today in scientific circles.

Luke: Latin; "light." Although it was universally known to the American colonists as the name of the third Evangelist, Luke was seldom used. After remaining dormant for many decades, the name has experienced a recent upswing in popularity, possibly due to the Luke Skywalker character in *Star Wars*. Luke is also the name of a very popular soap opera character; many viewers may remember the famous "Luke and Laura wedding" from *The Days of Our Lives*. Also see LUCAS.

Lyndon: English; from the name of a village, "linden-hill." Lyndon Johnson served as U.S. President from 1963 to 1969, signing into law the Civil Rights Act of 1964 and later appointing the first African American, Thurgood Marshall, to the Supreme Court.

☺ ☺ ☹ ☺ ☺ ☹ ☺ ☺ ☹ ☺ ☺ ☹ ☺ ☺ ☹ ☺ ☺ ☺ ☹ ☺

M

Malcolm: Gaelic; "a disciple or servant of (St.) Columba." This favorite Scottish name began to be current in the United States around 1800. It has remained in steady use, although it's never reached heights of popularity. Today, it appears to be comparatively out of favor. Among well-known bearers of this name, Malcolm X was a prominent 20th-century civil rights leader. The TV show *Malcolm in the Middle* also keeps this name alive in popular culture. In the past, **Mac** has been a popular nickname, but that short form is unlikely to find many fans today.

Marc: See MARK.

Marcus: Latin; "martial, warlike." The name Marcus is derived from the name of the Roman god Mars and can be found throughout the history of the Roman Empire. And the Romans who held the name more than lived up to its definition. A few well-known Marcuses from ancient times include Marcus Aemilius Lepidus, who was named dictator of Rome by Julius Caesar; Marcus Tillius Cicero (known as Cicero), the Roman statesman and orator famous for his speeches against Antony; and Marcus Aurelius, one of the most respected emperors of Rome. A famous modern-day Marcus (albeit a fictional one) is Marcus Welby, the title character of the popular medical drama of the 1970s portrayed by actor Robert Young. Derivatives of Marcus include **Markus** and **Marcos,** and **Marc** is a possible nickname. Also see MARK.

Mario: Italian; "warlike." If you're named Mario, then you certainly have a fighting spirit. Case in point: Born of Italian immigrants, Mario Cuomo, the former governor of New York, has been a passionate spokesman for the Democratic party. Another Mario took his battles to the racetrack: Mario Andretti, the only driver to have won the Indianapolis 500, the Daytona 500, *and* the Grand Prix. Having fought his way out of Hell's Kitchen in New York, author Mario Puzo knows all about Mafia gangland wars, which he wrote about in his bestselling novel *The Godfather.* This Mario was also a successful screenwriter, having collaborated on the scripts for not only the *Godfather* films but also the screenplays for the first two *Superman* movies. In the past decade, this name has consistently ranked between 100 and 200 in popularity in the United States.

Mark: Latin; probably derived from Mars, the name of the war god. Of the names of the four Evangelists, Mark has traditionally been the least often used as a personal name. It scarcely appeared before 1800. However, it had a sudden run of popularity beginning in the early 20th century. Although the reason for this popularity is unknown, it's possible that many namers viewed favorably the fact that Mark, a name that was well known but little used, could be taken for something new without actually being a decisive break with the past. Famous Marks include author Mark Twain, baseball slugger Mark McGwire, and actor Mark Wahlberg. An alternate spelling is **Marc.**

Parent's Success Guide to Baby Names

☺ ☻ ☹ ☺ ☻ ☹ ☺ ☻ ☹ ☺ ☻ ☹ ☺ ☻ ☹ ☺ ☺ ☻ ☹ ☺

Marshall: French; "horse keeper." This name has never been common, but it remains in use. Singer/songwriter/guitarist Marshall Crenshaw, who has been compared to Buddy Holly and Elvis Costello, broke onto the music scene with his self-titled debut album in 1982. Over the years, he's achieved something of a cult following among music fans with his songs "Someday Someway," "Cynical Girl," and "You're My Favorite Waste of Time." Another well-known Marshall is Marshall Field III, the newspaper publisher who founded *The Chicago Sun* in 1941, and after whom the landmark Chicago department store is named. Two more Marshalls of note are John Marshall Harlan, who was appointed to the U.S Supreme Court for a 33-year tenure, and his grandson, also named John Marshall Harlan, who followed in his grandfather's footsteps by being named to the Supreme Court in 1955 by President Eisenhower, where he served for 16 years.

Martin: From the Latin form Martinus, a diminutive of Martius, meaning "of Mars." Much used in medieval England, the name Martin scarcely survived the period of prejudice against the names of nonbiblical saints. It gradually came into use again, though, with President Martin Van Buren (born in 1782) being one of its prominent bearers. Other famous Martins include filmmaker Martin Scorsese, actor Martin Sheen, and civil rights leader Martin Luther King, Jr. **Marty** is a common nickname.

Marvin: Multiple origins, including Old English; "sea + friend." This name isn't especially common today, but it's still in use and is among the top 350 boys' names in the United States. Marvin Hamlish is one of the most celebrated composers in the world, having composed the music for numerous films and Broadway musicals. He won Academy Awards for *The Way We Were* and *The Sting*, but he is best known for producing the music for the longest-running musical on Broadway: *A Chorus Line*. Another musical Marvin is the Grammy Award-winning Marvin Gaye, who is known for his countless No. 1 hits, including "I Heard It Through the Grapevine," Ain't Nothin' Like the Real Thing," and "Ain't No Mountain High Enough."

Mason: French; "stone worker." You may be surprised to learn that that this name is No. 55 on the most recent list of popular boys' names in the United States. Character actor Mason Adams has long been one of Hollywood's most dependable actors, from his early days in radio to his best-known role of managing editor Charlie Hume on the TV series *Lou Grant*. Another Mason of note is John Mason Neale, the 19th-century writer of books on the history of the Church, as well as many church hymns, including "O Happy Band of Pilgrims" and "Jerusalem the Golden." The football running back Archie Mason Griffin epitomizes the definition of "stone worker," having carved through defensive lines his entire career. He was the only college player to win two consecutive Heisman Trophies (1974 and 1975) while playing for the Ohio State Buckeyes. As a pro, he played for eight years for the Cincinnati Bengals.

Mateo: The Spanish form of MATTHEW, a Hebrew name that means "gift of God." San Mateo is a city in California that was established by a group of

☺ ☺ ☹ ☺ ☺ ☹ ☺ ☺ ☹ ☺ ☺ ☹ ☺ ☺ ☹ ☺ ☺ ☺ ☹ ☺

Spanish explorers from Mexico in 1776 and grew into a thriving city. A literary Mateo of note is the 17th-century Spanish author Mateo Aleman, who is known for his novel *Guzman de Alfarache*.

Matthew: Hebrew; "gift of God." Matthew was universally known among the Puritans as the name of the first evangelist, although the early colonists weren't fond of the name. From 1700 on, however, it steadily grew in popularity. Today, the name is one of the most popular in the United States — in 2002, it was No. 4. A number of famous actors hold the name, including Matthew Broderick, Matthew McConaughey, Matthew Perry, and Matthew Modine. Matthew Brady rose to prominence with his Civil War photographs. An alternate spelling is **Mathew,** and **Matt** is the obvious nickname.

Maurice: Latin; "Moor." The name enjoyed considerable vogue in the Middle Ages because of the cult of Saint Maurice. As the name of a nonbiblical saint, it went out of favor with the Reformation. It's never regained a great deal of popularity in the United States, but the English-American form **Morris** has been commonly used in Jewish contexts. Derivatives include **Mauricio.** Maurice Gibb was one of the Bee Gees, whom we have to thank for the *Saturday Night Fever* soundtrack and other disco classics, while Maurice Cheeks was a star guard for the NBA's Philadelphia 76ers and currently serves as a coach in the league.

Maxwell: Old English; "Macca's spring." There is a string of Maxwells from the world of music. The name appears in the Beatles song "Maxwell's Silver Hammer." Also, two of the most well-known drummers in history were named Maxwell. Maxwell Roach is considered one of the premiere jazz drummers; he played with Dizzy Gillespe, Charlie Parker, and Stan Getz. Max Weinberg played drums in Bruce Springsteen's E Street Band and has served as late-night talk show host Conan O'Brien's music director. And who can forget bumbling secret agent Maxwell Smart, played to the hilt by actor Don Adams on the 1960s TV series *Get Smart*? Nicknames and similar names include **Max** (also an independent name)**, Maximillian,** and **Maximus**. All four forms reside among the top 325 boys' names in use today, with Maxwell the most popular at No. 130.

Merrill: Multiple origins in several Celtic languages; "shining sea." Merrill Osmond (older brother to pop star Donny) helped establish the Osmonds as successful recording artists in the 1960s and 1970s. A famous female Merrill, although she spells her name differently, is actress Meryl Streep, known for her shining performances in such films as *The Deer Hunter, Kramer vs. Kramer,* and *The Bridges of Madison County*. This name is rarely used today.

Michael: Hebrew; "who is like God?" A common name in medieval England, Michael became unpopular with the Reformation, probably because St. Michael, though securely biblical, was also an angel, and angels had a rather uncertain status with the reformers. With the heavy

☺ ☻ ☹ ☺ ☻ ☹ ☺ ☻ ☹ ☺ ☻ ☹ ☺ ☻ ☹ ☺ ☺ ☻ ☹ ☺

growth of Irish immigration in the mid-19th century, Michael became more common. Toward the end of the century, as the Irish increased in wealth and social status, the use of the name Michael increased accordingly. By 1950, the change had become striking. Michael was one of the most popular men's names, making its way well into the top ten. Although the Irish influence was still important, much of the use of Michael must be attributed to the general workings of a fashionable trend. Conforming parents name their boy Michael because they're aware that Michael is often used and therefore should be a "safe" name — as it may well be, although it can scarcely be a distinctive or a distinguished one at the same time. Today, Michael still tops many most popular-name lists. The omnipresent nickname is **Mike.** Noteworthy Michaels and Mikes include basketball legend Michael Jordan, pop star Michael Jackson, actor Michael J. Fox, and actor/comedian Mike Myers. Variants include **Micheal** and **Micah.**

Miguel: The Spanish form of the name MICHAEL, a Hebrew name that means "who is like God?" Likely corresponding to the growth in the Spanish-speaking population in the United States, this name has risen in popularity and currently is among the top 100 boys' names in the country. Miguel de Cervantes was a 16th-century Spanish novelist and poet who seemingly led a life that was just as adventurous (and dangerous) as the title character in his most famous work, *Don Quixote*. Early in his life, he fought in the Spanish army against the Turks, and on the journey back home to Madrid, he was captured and imprisoned by Barbary pirates in Algiers. Later, after being ransomed and released from captivity, he became a tax collector, but went to jail for accounting irregularities. Many think that he conceived of *Don Quixote* while in jail. Two other Miguels of note are Miguel Asturias, the Guatamalan novelist and poet who won the Lenin Peace Prize in 1966 and then the Nobel Prize for Literature a year later, and the actor Miguel Ferrer, son of legendary actor Jose Ferrar and singer Rosemary Clooney, who has made a name for himself playing offbeat characters in *Twin Peaks*, *Robocop*, and *Traffic*.

Miles: Probably German; meaning uncertain. It's sometimes attributed to the Latin word *miles,* which means "soldier." Because of Miles Standish, many people think of this name as typically Puritan. Historically, it has scarcely occurred in American usage, the redoubtable Standish being an oddity. Today, however, it has crept up to within the top 250 names in use. An alternate spelling is **Myles.**

Morgan: Welsh; meaning uncertain. The first half could mean "sea" or "large, great." In the 16th century, Morgan was a popular first name in Wales. It became a family name and was regarded as such in the American colonies — for example, General Daniel Morgan of the Revolution. Appropriate for a girl (actress Morgan Fairchild) or a boy (actor Morgan Freeman), the name has experienced a recent resurgence, especially for girls, rising to 29th on the 2002 list put out by the Social Security Administration.

☺ ☻ ☹ ☺ ☻ ☹ ☺ ☻ ☹ ☺ ☻ ☹ ☺ ☻ ☹ ☺ ☺ ☻ ☹ ☺

N

Nathan: Hebrew; "gift of God." The meaning is presumably to be taken as "God gave," and the name would be the equivalent of a shortening of NATHANIEL. Nathan has been the preferred form in Jewish usage, but it also was popular in colonial usage generally. During the mid-18th century among students at Harvard University, Nathan exceeded Nathaniel (which then varied in its spelling) and stood in eighth place in the 1750s. Today, it's No. 29. The patriot Nathan Hale serves as a notable example of the usage of the name in the Revolutionary period. Actor Nathan Lane has starred in such comedies as *The Birdcage,* as well as in the Broadway smash hit *The Producers.*

Nathaniel: Hebrew; "gift of God." This name was a particular favorite during the period of Old Testament names, often appearing in the top ten in New England lists. Actually, though, Nathaniel is a New Testament name, borne by one of the 12 apostles, generally supposed to be an alternate name for Bartholomew. This unusual linguistic situation (a Hebrew form with Christian associations) may have had something to do with the popularity of the name. In its meaning — an expression of thanks for the birth of a child — is surely the chief reason for the name's popularity. Nathaniel is one of the few Hebrew names to be adopted into English usage before the American settlements were begun. In the colonies, it grew rapidly in popularity. The Civil War roughly marks the period at which Nathaniel ceased to be a current name, and by 1880, it had become dated. Today, however, it's bounced back to No. 65. American author Nathaniel Hawthorne wrote *The Scarlet Letter.* **Nathanael** is an alternate spelling, and both spellings share the nickname **Nate**.

Neil: Irish; "warrior." In America, Neil began to appear in the 19th century, and it's likely of Romantic origin. Although it has been a fairly common name, it is not often used by today's parents. Astronaut Neil Armstrong was the first person to set foot upon the moon. **Neal** is a variant spelling.

Nelson: English; "son of Neil." Admiral Horatio Nelson of the Royal Navy (1758–1805) was a major hero and a beloved figure in Britain. Some of this enthusiasm apparently spread to the United States, and Nelson has been a moderately popular name. Nelson Mandela, a very worthy namesake, received the 1993 Nobel Peace Prize for his courageous and steadfast efforts to quell racism in South Africa.

Nicholas: Greek, "victorious people." The name derives from Nicholas, Bishop of Myra, whose relics were brought west by the Normans of southern Italy. His cult became immensely important throughout western Europe, and his name was highly popular in England during the late medieval period. Like the other names of nonbiblical saints, Nicholas suffered severely during the Reformation. So many Englishmen had already been named Nicholas, however, that the name had established its own tradition and could not easily be wiped out. From 1700 onward, Nicholas continued to be a moderately popular name in the colonies. An important influence must have been the special interest of the Dutch colonists in the name. It was also used freely among the numerous German immigrants. More recently, the name has been especially associated with Greek immigrants, as in the phrase "Nick the Greek." Today, it's quite popular among parents of many different backgrounds, capturing the No. 10 spot in 2002. St. Nicholas has become the patron saint of Christmas, and from Dutch usage, he has become Santa Claus, making use of the latter part of the name instead of the first. Variants and nicknames include **Nicolas, Nickolas, Nikolas,** and **Nick.** Nicolas Cage received a Best Actor Oscar for his work in *Leaving Las Vegas.*

Noah: Hebrew; possibly "rest, peace," "long-lived." As the divinely appointed builder of the ark and the refounder of the human race, Noah seems to have been held in well-justified honor among early Christians. However, in the English tradition, he became something of a buffoon, from being associated with all those pairs of animals, being caricatured as a henpecked husband, and being a man who definitely couldn't hold his liquor. Nevertheless, he wasn't without honor among the Puritans. Today, the name holds its own quite well — it's currently No. 34 on the list of the most popular boys' names. Noah Webster championed the cause of developing a distinctly American language — his is the name that you see on many modern dictionaries. The actor Noah Wylie rose to TV stardom on *ER.*

Noel: French, from the Latin *natalis;* "having to do with birth," such as with Christmas. Though not a common name, Noel is appropriate for a boy or a girl. (As a male name, it's generally pronounced "nole," whereas it's more likely to be pronounced "no-ELL" when used for a girl.) British playwright Noel Coward wrote more than 60 plays, including *Private Lives* and *Blithe Spirit.* **Nolan,** a similar-sounding name, is more popular today.

O

Oliver: Probably Old German, but possibly Latin; "olive tree, peace." Among the traditional 12 peers of Charlemagne, Oliver was highly conspicuous, and his name became commonly used in England during the late Middle Ages. In the period of American colonization, the name Oliver was chiefly associated with Oliver Cromwell, and such an association (after the Restoration in 1660) meant that the name was taboo. The popular Dickens novel *Oliver Twist* (1840) and a 20th-century stage version of it made Americans conscious of the name, but it hasn't found much favor; today, it stands among the top 300 boys' names. Oliver Wendell Holmes, Jr., served on the U.S. Supreme Court for more than 30 years. Oliver Stone directed such films as *Platoon* and *Wall Street,* among others. **Ollie** is sometimes given as a nickname, although it sounds out-of-date today.

☺ ☺ ☹ ☺ ☺ ☹ ☺ ☺ ☹ ☺ ☺ ☹ ☺ ☺ ☹ ☺ ☺ ☺ ☹ ☺

Orlando: The Italian form of ROLAND. It was introduced into England in the 16th century during a period of strong Italian influence. It has occurred rarely in later centuries in the United States, although actor Orlando Bloom's rise to stardom in such films as *The Lord of the Rings* and *Pirates of the Caribbean* may help to increase its prominence.

Orville: Old German; several origins come from various personal names beginning in Aur- or something similar, combined with -ville ("village"). Orvilles have been known to be pioneers. As one half of the Wright Brothers, Orville Wright, with his brother Wilber, pioneered the development of the first propeller-driven aircraft. Another pioneer, Orville Redenbacher, was the co-creator of snowflake popcorn, which would become one of America's favorite snack foods. This name is uncommon today.

Oscar: English; "god + spear." James Macpherson gave the name Oscar to a character in the Ossianic poems, which were widely read, especially in Europe. The name thus came into use in Europe and was scarcely introduced into the United States until it came with Scandinavian and German immigrants in the mid-19th century. It has remained viable, but has never gained widespread popularity in America. The fact that Oscar was the slob on TV's *The Odd Couple*, combined with the existence of the character Oscar the Grouch on *Sesame Street*, probably hasn't helped!

Ten popular Irish names

For many people of Irish ancestry, choosing a baby name of Irish origin is important. Here are ten popular Irish names.

* Aidan
* Brendan
* Connor
* Cory
* Dillon
* Finn
* Liam
* Patrick
* Sean
* Kevin

Oswald: Old English, "god power." In England, the name Oswald had remained in use from the Anglo-Saxon period on. Like most of the names beginning in *Os-*, it has been more popular in England than in the United States. **Osvaldo** is a variant — and today it's more popular than the original, although only at No. 409.

Owen: Welsh; "well-born," "born to nobility." A Latin origin from the name Eugenius has been suggested. Owen Wilson is a rising star in Hollywood, with credits ranging from *The Royal Tenenbaums* to *Shanghai Knights*. Owen is among the top 100 names for baby boys in the United States. Gaelic variants include **Ewen** and **Ewan** (pronounced "EWE-en" rather than "OWE-en"). Scottish actor Ewan McGregor has appeared in numerous movies, including *Trainspotting* and *Moulin Rouge*.

P

Patrick: Latin; "patrician." A certain Sucat took this name, circa 425, when he was consecrated as a missionary to Ireland. Presumably he knew its meaning, although it seems like a curiously snobbish name for a missionary. The bearer of the new name became St. Patrick, and one result of his conversion of Ireland was that his name came to be widely used among the Irish. It was also used in Scotland, but it didn't really penetrate into England. It was thus a rare name among the New England immigrants, and, being the name of a nonbiblical saint, it was under the general suspicion of that type of name. In the United States, the name has been especially associated with Irish immigrants, who became numerous after 1840 and remained a definable class until 1900. In the mid-20th century, this association weakened, and since then Patrick has enjoyed some popularity. The standard short form has been **Pat.** Patriotic politician Patrick Henry became famous for the line that he uttered in 1775, "Give me liberty or give me death!" Actors bearing this name include *Star Trek*'s Patrick Stewart and *Dirty Dancing*'s Patrick Swayze.

Paul: Latin; "small." Paul originates with Saul of Tarsus, who took the name Paul after his conversion to Christianity. The name wasn't used much in England until the 17th century, when it became mildly popular and was carried to the colonies. It remained steadily in use clear down into the 20th century, without any great vogue. Only with the 20th century did Paul become more popular — in one list rising to sixth place. Paul supplies neither a short form nor a diminutive — Paulie is too similar to Polly. With Paul you must be, so to speak, formal — even when addressing a baby in the cradle. Famous Pauls include the musicians Paul McCartney and Paul Simon and the oil magnate J. Paul Getty.

Payton: See PEYTON.

Pedro: The Spanish form of PETER, a Greek name meaning "rock." Pedros have had a strong history in Brazil. Portuguese explorer Pedro Cabral led

Chapter 2: Bailey, Brian, or Brent? Names for Boys

☺ ☺ ☹ ☺ ☺ ☹ ☺ ☺ ☹ ☺ ☺ ☹ ☺ ☺ ☹ ☺ ☺ ☺ ☹ ☺

an expedition bound for the West Indies; however, he found himself in Brazil instead and subsequently claimed the new land for his native country. This Pedro also was the first European explorer to reach Mozambique. The first emperor of Brazil was Pedro I, who declared independence for his country in 1826. Two modern-day Pedros hail from the sports world: Pedro Borbon, the relief pitcher for the Cincinnati Reds who helped lead the Big Red Machine to two consecutive World Series wins in the mid-1970s. All-Star Pedro Guerrero had a career batting average of .300 in his 15-year Major League career with the Los Angeles Dodgers and St. Louis Cardinals. This name is establishing a tradition for itself in the United States as well. For several decades, it has been among the top 200 boys' names chosen by American parents.

Perry: Possibly a short form of the Latin name Peregrine; "wanderer, pilgrim." As a surname, it could come from a place name referring to pear trees. It's a rare name these days. Television character Perry Mason, played by Raymond Burr, was the rock of the long-running courtroom drama, and he was known as a pillar of virtue as he defended those in need. Another famous Perry is singer Perry Como, who chose the name because it sounds like his real surname, Perido. The son of Italian immigrants, he sold more than 100 million records over his six-decade career; some of his most beloved songs include "It's Impossible," "Don't Le the Stars Get in Your Eyes," and "Catch a Falling Star."

Peter: Greek; "a rock." Not only is Peter a biblical name, but it even might be considered the most deeply biblical of all names because of the naming being credited to Christ Himself: "Thou art Simon, the son of Jonah: thou shalt be called Cephas, which is by interpretation, a stone" (John 1:42). The association of St. Peter with the Roman Catholic Church led to the name's being a common one throughout western Europe in the Middle Ages. By the same token, the name suffered during the Reformation. Its use in England fell off sharply in the 16th and 17th centuries, and it scarcely existed among the early immigrants to New England. As this prejudice died out with time, Peter became somewhat more common but failed to attain popularity, partly because of the lack of a large pool of early bearers of the name from which later namers could draw. Outside of New England, Peter was used somewhat more often, in New York and Pennsylvania drawing strength from established use in Dutch and German. But the New Englanders took to the name very slowly. In more modern times — to some extent reflecting the increased Catholic population — Peter has grown stronger, gaining considerably in popularity. **Pete** is the usual nickname. Noteworthy holders of this name include musician Peter Gabriel, baseball's all-time hit leader Pete Rose, and tennis great Pete Sampras, as well as beloved children's characters Peter Pan and Peter Rabbit.

Peyton: Old English; "Pacca's ridge," "Paega's village." This unisex name, slightly more popular for girls than for boys, has achieved great leaps in popularity in recent years and is poised to break into the top 200 male names. Football quarterback Peyton Manning was a standout at the University of Tennessee; he currently takes snaps for the NFL's Indianapolis Colts. An alternate, and only slightly less common, spelling is **Payton.**

Philip: Greek; "lover of horses." Though biblical and borne by one of the apostles, this name's associations were apparently secular, and it was scarcely used in New England during the period of the popularity of biblical names. In the non-Puritan colonies, it was more common, even coming in at ninth in a Virginia regiment of the Continental Army. Its popularity increased during the later Romantic period, from 1850 on, but it never became extremely common, perhaps because it has a slight English or "learned" feel. Variations and nicknames include **Phillip** and **Phil.** Today, psychologist Phillip "Dr. Phil" McGraw is the most likely person to come to mind when this name is mentioned, although modern composer Philip Glass and tobacco company Philip Morris are well-known Philips, too.

Pierce: English; a variant of PETER. On the big screen, dashing actor Pierce Brosnan has portrayed the ageless agent 007, James Bond, since 1995. This name is rare today.

Preston: English; "priest's town." Although the name remains fairly uncommon, it has gained popularity in recent years and has ranked as high as 144th. Preston Sturges was a playwright, screenwriter, and film director in the first half of the 20th century, known for his successful Broadway play, *Strictly Dishonorable,* and his film *The Great McGinty,* for which he won the Academy Award. Musician Billy Preston has played with such heavy-hitters as Ray Charles, the Beatles, and the Rolling Stones.

Q

Quentin: Latin; "the fifth." Namings in medieval England are from St. Quentin, martyred in A.D. 290. In America, the name was close to being extinct in the 18th century, but then it was used a little in the 19th century along with the Romantic revival. Sir Walter Scott's *Quentin Durward,* a popular book, was published in 1823 and exerted some influence. Today, the name is used occasionally — parents might be somewhat turned off by the unusual initial Q. Filmmaker Quentin Tarantino burst onto the scene in the 1990s with *Reservoir Dogs* and *Pulp Fiction.*

Quincy: French; from a family name, which is derived from various French villages of that name. Because those villages were named after a man named Quintus, "fifth," we can establish a whole process — from given name back to given name. Quincy is chiefly known as the middle name of President John Quincy Adams, and it has been rarely used as a personal name. Motown's Quincy Jones produced Michael Jackson's blockbuster LP *Thriller* along with a great deal of other popular music.

☺ ☺ ☹ ☺ ☺ ☹ ☺ ☺ ☹ ☺ ☺ ☹ ☺ ☺ ☹ ☺ ☺ ☺ ☹ ☺

Quinn: An anglicized shortening of an Irish surname — either Mac Cuinn or O'Cuinn — based on the given name Conn, "wise." It's still more common as a last name, but it makes for an intriguing and distinctly Irish-sounding first name. Producer Quinn Martin is considered one of the wise men of television; in fact, if you watched any television during the 1960s and 1970s, the phrase "A Quinn Martin Production" may bring back fond memories. His production company was responsible for some of the most popular television series during those two decades, including *The Untouchables*, *The Fugitive*, *The Streets of San Francisco,* and *Barnaby Jones*. In the world of sports, Quinn Buckner was a standout at Indiana University, serving as the captain on college basketball's last unbeaten team (1976), and played ten seasons in the NBA.

R

Randall: Old English; *rand,* "shield," + *wulf,* "wolf." Randall remained viable during the Norman period and probably never went completely out of use. **Randolph** is one of its variants, and **Randy** is a diminutive. Two popular Randys include the musicians Randy Newman, known in recent years for his scores of Disney animated films like *Monsters Inc.,* and country singer Randy Travis.

Raphael: Hebrew; "God has healed." According to the Bible, St. Raphael was one of the seven archangels who healed Tobias of his blindness and delivered Sara from the devil. Perhaps the most famous Raphael was the 16th-century Italian Renaissance painter Raffaello Sanzio, who was known simply as Raphael. This Raphael painted mainly sacred works in Florence and Rome and was known for his classical compositions based on the Greek philosophy of idealism. In the early 1500s, while Michelangelo was working on the Sistine Chapel, Pope Julius II commissioned Raphael for what would become his greatest works: the frescos at Stanza della Segnatura, which include his masterpiece, *School of Athens.* An alternate spelling is **Rafael** — now more popular than the original, probably due to its use in the Spanish-speaking community.

Raymond: German; *raed,* "counsel," + *mund,* "protection." Although it was brought into England with the Normans, its use then declined, and the name scarcely occurred in the colonial period. About 1800, it reappeared. Historians speculate that the personal name died out entirely but was replaced (after a lapse) by the family name used as a given name. In the 20th century, it was generally considered to be primarily a family name; today, it ranks 176th on the list of the most common boys' names in the United States. **Ray** has developed as the short form. Two famous writers, Raymond Carver and Ray Bradbury, have carried this name. The popular television show *Everybody Loves Raymond* stars comedian Ray Romano.

Reese: Welsh; "splendor, abundance, onslaught." This name evolved from the name **Rhys,** a spelling that continues to be popular in Wales.

☺ ☺ ☹ ☺ ☺ ☹ ☺ ☺ ☹ ☺ ☺ ☹ ☺ ☺ ☹ ☺ ☺ ☺ ☺ ☹ ☺

Appropriate for a boy or a girl, Reese has surged in popularity in the United States in recent years, although it continues to be fairly uncommon. **Reece** is an alternate (and slightly more popular) spelling. The sportscaster Reece Davis covers football for the cable sports channel ESPN.

Reginald: English, German; "power, might." The Anglo-Saxon Regenwald developed in various ways after the Norman Conquest, amalgamation with a similar Norman name, Reginald, being the most common result. This name went out of use in the 16th century but was revived in the mid-19th, becoming somewhat popular in England, commonly in the familiar form as **Reggie.** The revival did not take hold in America — in fact, Reggie became the prime example of an overly pretentious, decadent, un-American name. In the 20th century, however, it experienced a resurgence, due in part to the popularity of baseball hero Reggie Jackson, as well as basketball sharpshooter Reggie Miller.

Reid: English; "red-headed." Even if you're child doesn't have red hair, the name Reid would be a fine choice for either a boy or a girl. A Reid of note is Reid Allen Bryson, a well-known climatologist who founded the Center of Climate Research at the University of Wisconsin, where he developed new methods for studying the earth's climate by analyzing airstreams and recreating data on past climates.

Rene: French; "reborn." In French, the form is commonly Réné, while the English language prefers René. It was originally a Germanic name, brought into France by the Normans as Rayner or Rainer. The present forms were taken over in modern times from the French. The name is rare and may even be rejected as an English name since it maintains a French spelling and pronunciation (although in modern times, the accent mark is usually dropped). René Descartes (1596 to 1650) was a French philosopher and mathematician.

Reuben: See RUBEN.

Richard: German; with the elements *ricja*, "rule," and *heard*, "hard." The elements (and possibly their combination into a name) occurred in Anglo-Saxon. The popularity of Richard, however, springs from the Normans, who used it often. Three kings of England bore the name. In Elizabethan England, the typical stand of Richard (yielding to the three great leaders, John, William, and Thomas) was fourth place. The same situation displays itself among the early immigrants to New England, but among the children of those immigrants (675 males born in Boston in the 1630s through the 1660s), Richard fell to tenth place. In Plymouth Colony during the same period, a list of 1,288 males shows only a tiny remnant — five Richards. Richard may have been simply unable to survive against the enthusiasm for biblical names. A definite change came about with namings in the 1890s. Richard began to appear in the top ten of some lists, reaching as high as fifth. Throughout the 20th and 21st centuries, it remained a popular name, although its position has slipped somewhat in recent decades.

☺ ☺ ☹ ☺ ☺ ☹ ☺ ☺ ☹ ☺ ☺ ☹ ☺ ☺ ☹ ☺ ☺ ☹ ☺

The regular short form is **Dick,** although **Rick** and **Rich** also occur — and are much more accepted today, especially among younger men, than the old-fashioned sounding *D* form. The name supplied Benjamin Franklin with his pseudonym, "Poor Richard." It also furnished the bit of rhyming slang used to describe Richard Nixon, "Tricky Dick." A few prominent Americans happen to have borne the name. We may mention the Confederate General "Dick" Ewell, President Nixon, and actors Richard Gere and Richard Burton. Variants include **Ricardo.**

Riley: English; "rye clearing." Riley is also an anglicized shortening of the Irish surname O'Raghallaigh. Traditionally, Riley is a male name, but it's quickly gaining acceptance as a feminine name as well. Today, it's even more popular for girls, sitting at No. 77 for females and No. 100 for males. Given that the phrase "life of Riley" has come to mean "the good life," this name is an optimistic and hopeful choice. Variants include **Ryley** and **Ryleigh.** See also RYLAN.

Robert: German; "bright fame." One of the half-dozen favorite names among the Normans, the name Robert continued in favor as the English language reasserted itself. In fact, Robert has shown remarkable stability in the Anglo-American tradition. Because of the heroic King Robert the Bruce, the name could count on Scottish support. Also providing a name-hero was Confederate General Robert E. Lee. Largely from this special sup-port, Robert survived the general breakdown of traditional names that occurred in the mid-20th century and maintained its traditional popularity. The variations of Robert are numerous, and some of them are difficult to explain. The Spanish **Roberto** is obvious enough. From the shortened form **Rob,** a common Middle English diminutive, -in, was added to produce ROBIN. The origin of **Bob** is obscure — the shift of an *r*-sound to a *b*-sound is unusual. Noteworthy bearers of this name include politician Robert F. Kennedy, actors Robert Redford and Roberto Benigni, and film director Rob Reiner.

Robin: English; "famous brilliance." This name consists of the shortening of ROBERT with the addition of the common diminutive *-in.* Robin was much used in the Middle Ages, as is shown by its use for a folk hero in Robin Hood and by the commonness of the family name Robinson. In the 17th and 18th centuries, it wasn't used much as a given name. In America, the name was applied to a bird, although not the same bird that was called a robin in Britain. At some point, probably in the early 19th cen-tury, the name was conceived as being feminine. It was then applied to men and women alike, and a small movement toward birds' names was thus inaugurated. Today, the name isn't especially popular for either sex. Robin Williams won an Academy Award for his performance in the film *Good Will Hunting.* The actress Robin Wright Penn has appeared in numer-ous films, including *Forrest Gump* and *The Princess Bride.*

Roger: German; "fame + spear." A common name in medieval England, Roger was well represented among the early immigrants but failed to

establish itself in the colonies, scarcely appearing in the 17th and 18th centuries. In the late 19th century, it enjoyed a slight revival, which was passed on to the 20th century. Today, it's fairly uncommon, but it still appears among the top 400 boys' names. Baseball pitcher Roger Clemens and the lead singer of The Who, Roger Daltrey, are two of the most famous modern-day Rogers.

Roland: German; "fame throughout the land." Among the traditional 12 peers of Charlemagne, Roland became the most famous. Introduced into America at the time of the colonization, the name failed to become popular, but it has lingered as barely viable. The common early spelling was **Rowland.**

Ronald: English, German; "power, might." This name is the Scottish development from Regenwald (see REGINALD). Not much in evidence in America before the 20th century, it came to be moderately popular by 1975 but has since slipped back into obscurity. Famous Ronalds include President Ronald Reagan and McDonald's clown icon Ronald McDonald.

Roscoe: Origin and meaning unknown. There have been a number of famous Roscoes. The actor Roscoe Lee Brown has had a prolific career in television and film, starring as the butler in the sitcom *Soap,* as well as in the films *Topaz, Uptown Saturday Night,* and *The Mambo Kings.* Tennis player Roscoe Tanner was a formidable opponent in the 1970s (winning the Australian Open in 1977), who was ahead of his time with his 120 mph serves — nowadays, of course, big serves like his are commonplace. In the world of journalism, Edward R. Murrow (yes, the R stands for Roscoe) is widely regarded as the standard that journalists try to live up to. His broadcasts from the rooftops of London during the German bombings of World War II brought him into millions of living rooms across America and are responsible for the type of war-time journalism you see today.

Ross: Scottish Gaelic; "peninsula, cape." Like so many other Scottish names (especially the short ones), Ross became a well-established given name in the 20th century. Texas millionaire H. Ross Perot made a name for himself by running for president as a member of the Reform Party. David Schwimmer plays the character Ross on the popular NBC sitcom *Friends.* Despite the show's success (and probably no thanks to Perot), the name is rare today.

Roy: Gaelic; "red." This name was often applied in Scotland to a red-headed man — curiously so, since red hair is common (and therefore not distinctive) among the Gaels. The name can also be considered the archaic form of the French word *roi,* which means "king." As Le Roy ("The King"), it occurs once in a Virginia regiment of the Continental Army. Not until 1870, however, did it become regularly used, even developing a slight boom, which diminished early in the 20th century. Famous Roys include actor/cowboy Roy Rogers and "Pretty Woman" singer Roy Orbison.

Ten popular Scottish names

If your ancestors hailed from the Highlands (or if the thought of droning bagpipes, brightly colored tartans, and lilting accents give you the warm fuzzies), try one of these Scottish names.

* Cameron
* Colin
* Craig
* Duncan
* Graham
* Ian
* Keith
* Kyle
* Logan
* Ross

Ruben: Hebrew; "behold a son." You could say that *American Idol II* gave audiences their next "favorite son" in the rather large form of Ruben Studdard, the Alabama native who wowed audiences and judges to win the competition. This Ruben, an unlikely pop star, managed to beat the rest of the pop star wannabes with a voice that is part Otis Redding, part Smokey Robinson. Ruben Ramos, also known as "El Gato Negro," is a Grammy Award-winning Tejano singer. This name appears to be popular among the Spanish-speaking community. A famous **Reuben** is salsa-singer-turned-actor Reuben Blades, who has appeared in such films as *The Milagro Beanfield War, All the Pretty Horses,* and *Once Upon a Time in Mexico.* Another Reuben of note is Reuben "Rube" Goldberg, the Pulitzer Prize-winning political cartoonist. **Ruban** is another possible spelling variation.

Russell: French; "red head." A common surname, Russell apparently was introduced in the late 19th century as a feudal name, being that of a notable aristocratic family. Today, its popularity has languished, and it sits at No. 332 on the list of the most common names in use. Actor Russell Crowe received an Academy Award for his portrayal of a general-turned-slave in the 2000 film *Gladiator.*

Ryan: Irish; meaning uncertain. This name may come from the name Rían,

☺ ☺ ☹ ☺ ☺ ☹ ☺ ☺ ☹ ☺ ☺ ☹ ☺ ☺ ☹ ☺ ☺ ☹ ☺ ☺ ☹ ☺ ☺

surname O'Riain. This perennially popular choice currently sits at No. 16 on the list of the most common boys' names. In the 1970s, actor Ryan O'Neal was indeed Hollywood royalty, starring in many of the best films of the decade, including *What's Up, Doc?*, *Barry Lyndon*, *Oliver's Story*, and *Paper Moon*. But it was his performance in *Love Story* that won him an Oscar nomination. Television and radio personality Ryan Seacrest is yet another Ryan who has achieved royalty status in show business, especially with his hosting duties on the insanely popular *American Idol*. Perhaps the most beloved Ryan of recent years is Ryan White, who was born with hemophilia and contracted the AIDS virus through a tainted blood transfusion. This admirable Ryan became an activist against the fear and bigotry that surrounded AIDS in the 1980s. After his death, his mother and Phil Donahue established the Ryan White Foundation to continue his work in AIDS awareness.

Rylan: English; from a surname that was derived from "rye land" in Old English. As a first name, Rylan is still pretty rare, but its use has increased tremendously in recent years and continues to rise. A variant is **Ryland**. RILEY and RYAN are similar-sounding names.

S

Samuel: Hebrew; "heard by God," "name of God." The meaning refers to Hannah, wife of Elkanah, who vowed that if God would "give unto thine handmaid a man child," she would dedicate him to God. The birth of Samuel thus showed that Hannah had been heard by God. The story of Samuel's birth and the significance of his name appealed to wives who were under social pressure to populate an empty land. Before the settling of America, Samuel had become a common name in England. In the U.S., the use of Samuel increased, perhaps for the reason already suggested. From a position usually around fifth or seventh, Samuel rose to second place in the Boston birth list of 1630 to 1669, yielding only to John. From 1800, however, Samuel began to share in the general decline of biblical names. Since 1900, Samuel has remained in use; today, it stands at No. 25. Famous individuals bearing the name Samuel — or the variant **Sam** (now also an independent name) — include beer-maker Sam Adams, Texas hero Sam Houston, and code inventor Samuel Morse. And who could forget the ultimate patriot, the fictional hero Uncle Sam?

Saul: Probably Hebrew, "asked for." This unusual origin may be justified by the reality that the tribes of Israel had "asked for" a king (I Samuel 8). Saul was never much used in America. If David was to be a hero (as the frequent use of his name attests), Saul must be considered the opposition, accorded no more popularity than was accorded to other "evil" characters. Moreover, Saul was the original name of St. Paul, and the name-changing suggests that Saul was a particularly unsuitable name. For reasons undetermined, Saul has enjoyed some popularity in the 20th century. Saul

☺ ☺ ☺ ☹ ☺ ☺ ☹ ☺ ☺ ☹ ☺ ☺ ☹ ☺ ☺ ☹ ☺ ☺ ☺ ☹ ☺

Bellow won the National Book Award in 1954 for *The Adventures of Augie March*. In 1976, he was honored with the Nobel Prize in Literature.

Scott: English; "a Scot," "of Scottish origin." It became common as a given name in the 20th century, being another example (like ROSS) of a Scottish family name becoming a frequently used personal name in the United States. Writer F. Scott Fitzgerald is known for his great American novel *The Great Gatsby*.

Sean: Irish Gaelic; "God is gracious." God was certainly gracious when He handed out talent to the many famous Seans of the world. Sir Sean Connery will always be identified with secret agent James Bond, but it was his later films, such as *The Untouchables* and *The Hunt for Red October*, that gained him recognition as one of the world's finest actors. Actor Sean Penn is no slouch when it comes to acting, either. Known for his versatile performances, he gives his all in a broad range of films, from *Dead Man Walking* (for which he was nominated for an Oscar) to *Fast Times at Ridgemont High*. And musician Sean Lennon certainly received the gracious gift of talent from his father, late Beatle John Lennon; the son is making a name for himself in the music world. **Shaun** and **Shawn** are alternate spellings. All three versions are among the top 500 boys' names in use today, with Sean coming out on top at No. 60, and Shaun in third at No. 402.

Sebastian: Latin; "venerable." Those who carry the name Sebastian are known for their achievements. The third-century St. Sebastian had been a Roman soldier who had secretly practiced the Christian faith by performing charitable acts, until he was discovered to be a Christian and subsequently martyred. Sebastian Cabot, who was the son of John Cabot, was a 16th-century European explorer who sailed to the Americas. But any description of the name Sebastian would be incomplete without the mention of Johann Sebastian Bach, the truly venerable German composer of some of the most well-known classical music in history. His long career spanned the first half of the 18th century, and much of his work involved religious themes. He's perhaps most well-known for the *Brandenberg Concertos*. Perhaps because of its lofty associations, this name has gained popularity in recent years; it's been in the top 80 for three years running.

Seth: Hebrew; "compensation, substitute." In spite of the many non-Hebrew names in the early chapters of Genesis, this one must be somewhat tentatively accepted as Hebrew because of its aptness of meaning — that is, another son to Adam and Eve after the catastrophe of Cain and Abel. Seth was a moderately popular name in early New England, no doubt being sometimes given in recognition that the child was a compensation for an earlier son who had died. Also, the name was short, simple, and easy to pronounce. Seth declined in popularity in the mid-19th century, along with other biblical names. Today, however, it's back in the top 75. Teen heartthrob Seth Green made a name for himself in the TV series

Buffy the Vampire Slayer and went on to play roles in two *Austin Powers* movies and a host of forgettable films.

Shane: An English phonetic rendering of the Irish pronunciation of SEAN. Although this name has slipped from the top 100, it's still fairly common in the United States. The classic 1953 Western *Shane* starred Alan Ladd in the title role as a gunfighter who attempts to retire to family life on the homestead, but instead gets drawn into a conflict with ranchers. Another Shane of note is the 20th-century writer Sir Shane Leslie, who achieved some success with his novels and short stories.

Shannon: Irish Gaelic; "ancient." Another possible origin is the river Shannon. Although this name is much more popular for girls than for boys today, it's still given to boys on occasion. Tight end Shannon Sharpe, considered to be one of the finest tight ends to play football, has three Super Bowl wins to his credit, two (so far) with the Denver Broncos and one with the Baltimore Ravens. Shannon Hoon fronted the 1990s band Blind Melon before dying of a drug overdose.

Shaun, Shawn: See SEAN.

Sidney: English; a surname derived from a French place name based on Saint Denis. Another possible English meaning is "(piece of) wide, well-watered land." Mark Twain used Sid Sawyer for the unpleasant younger brother of the typically American older brother named Tom. In spite of Mark Twain, Sidney continued in use. In fact, it shows a marked increase from 1870 to 1890, thus including the year of publication of *Huckleberry Finn.* The heroic figure of Sydney Carton in Dickens's *Tale of Two Cities* (1859) probably stimulated the use of the name. With the passage of time, the aristocratic aura of the name faded out, but Sidney has remained viable. Sidney is occasionally used as a girl's name. The variation between *i* and *y* is a matter of no importance, since early printers used the two letters interchangeably. Variants and nicknames include **Sydney, Syd,** and **Sid.**

Simon: Possibly Hebrew; "hearkening" or "hyena." Simon was a popular name in Biblical times; there were eight Simons in the New Testament. The popularity of the South American liberator Simon Bolivar led to some 19th-century usage. On the other hand, as the name of the villainous Simon Legree in *Uncle Tom's Cabin* (1859), the name must have fallen in esteem. Today, it's among the top 250 names for boys, having risen about 100 spots since 1991.

Skylar: Origin and meaning unknown. Suitable for a girl or boy, Skylar has risen in popularity in recent years. According to statistics from the Social Security Administration, in 1992, Skylar ranked as the 479th most popular name for boys and 595th most popular name for girls; in 2002, the name rose to 389th for boys and 144th for girls.

☺ ☻ ☹ ☺ ☻ ☹ ☺ ☻ ☹ ☺ ☻ ☹ ☺ ☻ ☹ ☺ ☺ ☻ ☹ ☺

Solomon: Hebrew; from the word for "peace," *shalom.* It's suggested that Solomon originally bore some other name and that Solomon itself was a name that was ascribed to him when the unwarlike nature of his reign had become known, and notable. Though lacking the charisma of his father, David, the wise King Solomon is an important biblical character. The American colonists used his name regularly until it began to fade out with the decline of biblical names after 1800. Toni Morrison's groundbreaking novel *Song of Solomon* brought some prominence to this name among the African-American community.

Spencer: English; "dispenser of provisions." Spencer is a common British surname (think Diana Spencer, who became Princess Diana), but it's also becoming more common as a first and middle name. The Oscar-winning actor Spencer Tracy dispensed his talent in many of the finest films in history, including *Captains Courageous, Boys Town, Inherit the Wind,* and *Judgment at Nuremberg.* But it was his films with Katharine Hepburn that made him one of the most beloved actors in history. Another famous Spencer is Sir Winston Leonard Spencer Churchill, the British prime minister who led Britain through its darkest days during World War II. He was also an accomplished statesman, orator, and author. And from the world of music comes guitarist and vocalist Spencer Davis, whose Spencer Davis Group took the British rock scene by storm in the 1960s with hits like "Gimme Some Lovin'" and "I'm a Man." Later, he helped dispense other musical talent into the world, guiding the early musical careers of rocker Robert Palmer and reggae superstar Bob Marley. The 15th-century English poet Edmund Spenser wrote "The Faerie Queene," a notable work. **Spenser** is an alternate spelling.

Stanley: English; a place name meaning "stone glade." In England, it became a common family name and, as such, became a given name in the 19th century. The Stanleys were an eminent English family; the adoption of the name in the United States, therefore, relates to the aristocratic namings of the 19th century. The name began to appear about 1850 and was most common around 1890. Stanley Kubrick was a prominent and revered film director, known for such masterpieces as *2001: A Space Odyssey* and *A Clockwork Orange.* Another well-known Stanley is the character Stanley Kowalski from the Tennessee Williams play *A Streetcar Named Desire.* In the film version of the play, Marlon Brando gave a fiery performance as the conflicted Stanley. **Stan** is the short form of this name, which may seem a bit old-fashioned these days.

Stephen: Greek; "crown." This name was common in the time of Christ; Stephen was the first martyr and became a saint (further immortalized by the Grateful Dead in the song "St. Stephen"). The Greek -ph spelling is more common for middle names, whereas the -v spelling, representing the tradition of the Middle Ages, is the primary form used for a first name. Today, there's no shortage of well-known Stevens, and it seems that they always achieve kinglike status in their professions. The reigning king of film is without a doubt Steven Spielberg, the director who has helmed box office blockbusters including *Jaws, E.T., Raiders of the Lost Ark* (and its sequels), and *Close Encounters of the Third Kind*. However, it wasn't until he made *Schindler's List* that he achieved the kind of respect reserved for Hollywood's truly great filmmakers. Television producer Steven Bochco certainly has the Midas touch when it comes to creating television series of outstanding quality, including *Hill Street Blues, NYPD Blue,* and *LA Law.* Royalty in the music world wouldn't be complete without composer and writer Steven Sondheim, who's known for his musicals, including *West Side Story* and *Gypsy*. Alternate forms include **Steven, Stefan,** and **Stephan. Steve** is the most common nickname.

Stewart: From a family name derived from the Anglo-Saxon word *stiweard* — in modern English, "steward." The exact meaning in early times is somewhat uncertain, but the office of steward in the king's household became highly important. The surname was adopted by the hereditary stewards of Scotland and passed on to the clan. In spite of the uninspiring short form **Stew,** the name has been fairly common as a given name in the past, possibly profiting from the popularity of Scottish names in general. Today, however, it's become rare. **Stuart** (with the nickname **Stu**) is an alternate spelling that's used is the classic E. B. White children's book *Stuart Little.* The talking mouse has been featured in two films in recent years, with Michael J. Fox providing Stuart's voice.

Sydney: See SIDNEY.

T

Tanner: English; "leather worker." Tanner is a common surname that has achieved some popularity as a first name. It's been hovering around No. 100 for about ten years.

Tate: Old Norse; "cheerful." In England, it developed into a surname, and today's it serves as both a last name and a first name. Actor Tate Donovan has a lot to be cheerful for. Although he has had steady work as a television and film actor, he's known more for his relationships with famous actresses, having been engaged to both Sandra Bullock and Jennifer Aniston. Tate is also the name of two museums in London: one filled with 18th- and 19th-century British works and the other a modern art museum.

Taylor: English; "tailor." This name is used for both boys and girls — and may be considered more of a girl's name these days. Still, it's among the top 200 boys' names. You could say that Samuel Taylor Coleridge was a master tailor when it came to the craft of poetry. The 19th-century poet's most famous poem was "The Rime of the Ancient Mariner." Another well-known Taylor (or at least known by his initials) is P(hineas) T(aylor) Barnum, the 19th-century entertainer who teamed up with competitor

☺ ☺ ☹ ☺ ☺ ☹ ☺ ☺ ☹ ☺ ☺ ☹ ☺ ☺ ☹ ☺ ☺ ☺ ☹ ☺

James A. Bailey to form Barnum and Bailey's Circus — otherwise known as "The Greatest Show on Earth."

Terence: From the Latin Terentius, a Roman family surname. The name seems to have come into use in Ireland, where it was employed on the basis of similarity of sound to replace one or two of the native Celtic names, such as MALACHI. In the United States, the name generally maintained its Irish associations through the 19th century, and to some extent, it has done so to the present on the basis of tradition. The diminutive **Terry** has become chiefly feminine, although men like Terry Bradshaw, a former pro football star and current television commentator, bear it proudly. **Terrence** and **Terrance** are alternate spellings. Film director Terrence Malick is known for *Days of Heaven, The Thin Red Line,* and other critically acclaimed movies.

Terrell: Possibly French; from a nickname meaning "one who pulls, obstinate person." Former Denver Broncos running back Terrell Davis thundered his way through many a defensive line in his seven-year career. Always humble, this Terrell helped lead the Broncos to two consecutive Super Bowl wins in 1997 and 1998; in 1998, he also became one of the very few running backs to rush for more than 2,000 yards in a single season. San Francisco 49ers wide receiver Terrell Owens is considered one of the premier receivers in the NFL. In 2002, he became infamous for the "Sharpie Incident," in which he, after scoring a touchdown, retrieved a Sharpie marker from his sock, autographed the football, and gave it to a fan in the crowd. This name is popular in the African-American community, though not particularly common generally.

Terry: See TERENCE.

Thaddeus: The origin and meaning are uncertain, but possibly Aramaic, "praise." In Matthew 10:3, Thaddeus is the surname of an apostle. In New England, the name was viable (but not used much) throughout the 18th century and until about the middle of the 19th century. It was more common in the countries of the Eastern Church than of the Western, and Jane Porter's popular novel *Thaddeus of Warsaw* (1803) may have helped the name maintain itself in English-speaking countries. Nicknames include **Tad** and **Thad.**

Theodore: Greek; "God's gift." One of a number of names that thank God for the birth of a child — for example, DOROTHY in Greek and NATHANIEL in Hebrew. In spite of that fact that a number of saints bore the name, it was scarcely used in England during the Middle Ages and was considered a name of the Eastern Church and of the countries under that domination, such as Russia. It began to appear in England during the 17th century, probably because of increased contact with eastern and central Europe. At the end of that century, Theodore was appearing in American usage. Once established, it continued steadily (although it was never common) through

☺ ☻ ☹ ☺ ☻ ☹ ☺ ☻ ☹ ☺ ☻ ☹ ☺ ☻ ☹ ☺ ☺ ☻ ☹ ☺

James A. Bailey to form Barnum and Bailey's Circus — otherwise known as "The Greatest Show on Earth."

Terence: From the Latin Terentius, a Roman family surname. The name seems to have come into use in Ireland, where it was employed on the basis of similarity of sound to replace one or two of the native Celtic names, such as MALACHI. In the United States, the name generally maintained its Irish associations through the 19th century, and to some extent, it has done so to the present on the basis of tradition. The diminutive **Terry** has become chiefly feminine, although men like Terry Bradshaw, a former pro football star and current television commentator, bear it proudly. **Terrence** and **Terrance** are alternate spellings. Film director Terrence Malick is known for *Days of Heaven, The Thin Red Line,* and other critically acclaimed movies.

Terrell: Possibly French; from a nickname meaning "one who pulls, obstinate person." Former Denver Broncos running back Terrell Davis thundered his way through many a defensive line in his seven-year career. Always humble, this Terrell helped lead the Broncos to two consecutive Super Bowl wins in 1997 and 1998; in 1998, he also became one of the very few running backs to rush for more than 2,000 yards in a single season. San Francisco 49ers wide receiver Terrell Owens is considered one of the premier receivers in the NFL. In 2002, he became infamous for the "Sharpie Incident," in which he, after scoring a touchdown, retrieved a Sharpie marker from his sock, autographed the football, and gave it to a fan in the crowd. This name is popular in the African-American community, though not particularly common generally.

Terry: See TERENCE.

Thaddeus: The origin and meaning are uncertain, but possibly Aramaic, "praise." In Matthew 10:3, Thaddeus is the surname of an apostle. In New England, the name was viable (but not used much) throughout the 18th century and until about the middle of the 19th century. It was more common in the countries of the Eastern Church than of the Western, and Jane Porter's popular novel *Thaddeus of Warsaw* (1803) may have helped the name maintain itself in English-speaking countries. Nicknames include **Tad** and **Thad.**

Theodore: Greek; "God's gift." One of a number of names that thank God for the birth of a child — for example, DOROTHY in Greek and NATHANIEL in Hebrew. In spite of that fact that a number of saints bore the name, it was scarcely used in England during the Middle Ages and was considered a name of the Eastern Church and of the countries under that domination, such as Russia. It began to appear in England during the 17th century, probably because of increased contact with eastern and central Europe. At the end of that century, Theodore was appearing in American usage. Once established, it continued steadily (although it was never common) through the 18th century. It was used more often in the 19th century, with a

Chapter 2: Bailey, Brian, or Brent? Names for Boys

☺ ☻ ☹ ☺ ☻ ☹ ☺ ☻ ☹ ☺ ☻ ☹ ☺ ☻ ☹ ☺ ☻ ☺ ☻ ☹ ☺

modest boom around 1850. Theodore Roosevelt, the highly popular president, helped to continue the interest in the name. He also helped to fix **Ted** and **Teddy** as shorter forms. Theodore Dreiser, author of *Sister Carrie* and other early 20th-century novels, is another well-known Theodore.

Thomas: Aramaic (the common language of Palestine in the time of Christ); "twin." Thomas is the name of an apostle. It may be a kind of nickname that became an independent name. After the Norman Conquest, as Christian names replaced ancient Anglo-Saxon ones, Thomas became current. The murder of Thomas Becket in 1170 transformed him into a saint and a national hero, and his name prospered accordingly. In fact, it came to stand typically in third place, exceeded only by JOHN and WILLIAM. Thomas thus became much more characteristic of English than it is of French, Spanish, or other European languages, producing such prototypes as Tom Jones, Tom Sawyer, and Uncle Tom. Being a New Testament saint's name, it survived the Reformation with little damage. It was common among the early emigrants to America, being the second most numerous name in one colony. In the 18th century, its popularity waned, possibly because of the growing popularity of Old Testament names. Although politicians Thomas Jefferson and Thomas Paine are certainly remembered, Thomas wasn't a very common name in the continental regiments. In the 19th century, however, it recovered its older popularity. In the 20th century, Thomas generally fails to make the top ten but still remains current. The name is fortunate to have highly popular nicknames — **Tom, Thom,** and **Tommy. Tomas** is an alternate spelling.

Timothy: Greek; "honoring God." Timothy was Paul's companion in the Book of Acts, and two biblical epistles are addressed to him. Although he's recognized as a saint, Timothy came to be used as an English name only in the post-Reformation period. Among the early immigrants to Massachusetts, it was a regularly used name, though not common, and it continued in use through the 17th and 18th centuries. After a small flurry of popularity around 1800, it fell off, and in the later 19th century, it was scarcely viable. It has, however, recovered. Tim Conway achieved fame as a comedian, whereas Tim McGraw is known both for his country music and for being married to fellow singer Faith Hill. **Tim** and **Timmy** are common diminutives.

Tobias: The Greek form of the Hebrew name Tobiah, which means "God is good." Tobias is a principal character in the Book of Tobit — notable if for no other reason because he has a dog. The names of characters in the Apocrypha were not used much in the American colonies, but Tobias was viable into the early 19th century. It was regularly shortened to **Toby**, and that form has become even more popular than the original, although neither is particularly common. **Tobey** is an alternate spelling of the nickname. Notable bearers of this name include writer Tobias Wolff, author of the memoir *This Boy's Life*, and actor Tobey Maguire.

☺ ☺ ☹ ☺ ☺ ☹ ☺ ☺ ☹ ☺ ☺ ☹ ☺ ☺ ☹ ☺ ☺ ☺ ☹ ☺

Todd: English; "fox." The description "wily as a fox" may be attributed to tennis player Todd Martin, who has been known to cause a lot of trouble in the tennis world's hen house. **Tod** is an alternate spelling; this version is linked to the high-fashion shoe and accessory brand Tod's. Neither spelling has achieved great prominence, though; in fact, Todd has fallen considerably in popularity in recent years.

Tony: See ANTHONY.

Travis: French; "crossroads." Also a common surname, Travis has become a popular first name for males. Country music singer Travis Tritt helped country music cross over into the mainstream in the 1990s. A Travis of a different musical ilk is Travis Meeks, songwriter, guitarist, and lead singer for the alternative rock group Days of the New.

Trevor: Welsh; from a place name meaning "large town." This name has been consistently popular for more than a decade, ranking between 50th and 80th among the most common boys' names. Trevor Howard was a well-respected character actor who had a long career. Some of his more memorable films include *The Third Man, Mutiny on the Bounty,* and *Ghandi.* Trevor Jones is one of Hollywood's elite film composers, who's credited with such films as *The Last of the Mohicans, The Dark Crystal,* and *Notting Hill.* Other Trevors of note include Trevor Griffiths, the English playwright known for his social dramas, and Trevor Nunn, the noted British stage director known for his Shakespearean productions, as well as British productions of musicals by Andrew Lloyd Webber, including *Cats* and *Starlight Express.*

Trey: Latin; "three." (The English surname Tray, another possible source of this name, means "grief, misfortune.") This name can be interpreted in a variety of ways. Christians may imagine the Holy Trinity, whereas sports fans are likely to think of basketball's three-point shot. Trey can also be a nickname for the third-generation holder of a name, as in John Smith III.

Tristan: Cornish; from a root word meaning "tumult, noise." The legend of Tristan and Isolde embodies the definition of this name. In the story, Tristan falls in love with Isolde and wants to marry her. However, Isolde becomes the wife of Tristan's uncle, King Marke. After having a brief encounter with Isolde as a result of a magic love potion that she drinks by mistake, Tristan must live out the remainder of his life full of longing and sorrow. This legend influenced the later legend of Lancelot and Guinevere; in fact, over the centuries, the Tristan and Isolde legend became part of Arthurian legend, as Tristan becomes one of the Knights of the Round Table. Most notably, however, the legend became the basis for Robert Wagner's most famous opera. As a given name, Tristan has become popular only recently. Up from over 450th place in 1994, it jumped to as high as No. 70 in recent years. Alternate spellings include **Tristen** and **Tristian.**

☺ ☺ ☹ ☺ ☺ ☹ ☺ ☺ ☹ ☺ ☺ ☹ ☺ ☺ ☹ ☺ ☺ ☺ ☹ ☺

Troy: Troy is thought to be from a family name from the city of Troyes in France, although some sources list it as deriving from an Irish name meaning "foot soldier." Given its association with the Trojan wars, it has a strong, martial feel to it. Many states have a city or town named Troy, including Michigan and New York. Troy Donahue (a pseudonym) was a 1950s teen idol and TV star, while Troy Aikman was the Dallas Cowboys' star quarterback from 1989 to 2000.

Tucker: English; "tucker of cloth." (In this meaning, "tucker" doesn't refer to tucking in your shirttails; rather, it's an archaic term that refers to the fulling of cloth.) A common surname in the United Kingdom, the name Tucker is gaining popularity as a first name for boys. One well-known Tucker is magazine and newspaper columnist Tucker Carlson, who fearlessly defends the conservative point of view as the cohost of CNN's political debate show *Crossfire*. Another Tucker of note is character actor Tucker Smallwood, known for his dependable performances in such films as *Contact* and *Traffic* and the television shows *Space: Above and Beyond* and *Malcolm in the Middle*. **Tuck** is a possible nickname, although it isn't likely to gain much prominence, at least in part because of its association with Shakespeare's Friar Tuck.

Tyler: English; "tile maker." More common as a surname, Tyler is becoming more and more popular as a first or middle name, for boys and for girls. In 2002, it was the 14th most common name given to baby boys. Notable personalities with the last name Tyler range from tenth U.S. President John Tyler (of "Tippecanoe and Tyler Too" fame) to rocker Steven Tyler of Aerosmith to actress Mary Tyler Moore. The sole nickname is **Ty** (which is also considered a name in its own right).

Tyrese: Origin and meaning unknown; possibly a made-up variant of TYRONE. The name has gained in popularity largely because of the R&B singer, actor, and model Tyrese Gibson. It's more common among African Americans than among other ethnic groups. **Ty** is a possible nickname.

Tyrone: Irish; "land of Owen." Well-known stage and screen actor Tyrone Power, Jr., came from a long line of performers, including his father, a well-respected Shakespearian actor. The latter Tyrone achieved fame in the first half of the 20th century with roles in such films as *The Mark of Zorro* and *Witness for the Prosecution*. In more recent years, this name has become increasingly popular among the African-American community, although newer names like TYRESE and TYSON are more common. A nickname is **Ty,** and **Tyron** is an alternate form.

Tyson: French; "firebrand." Historically, Tyson has been both a nickname and a surname (boxer Mike Tyson is the celebrity most likely to come to mind), but in the modern era, where last names make hip first names, it's gaining popularity as a given name. Beware the association with the chicken company. **Ty** (also associated with TYLER, TYRESE, and TYRONE) is a potential nickname.

V

Victor: Latin; "winner, conqueror." This triumphant moniker hasn't left much of an imprint on American naming, but it still hangs on among the top 500. Victor Hugo's French Revolution-era novel *Les Misérables* became a smash hit on Broadway, bringing the tragic story of Jean Valjean to life on stage. **Vic** is a common nickname.

Vincent: Latin; from *vincens*, which means "conquering." Although it's never been tremendously popular, Vincent, as the name of several notable saints, has had some use, especially among Catholics. Vincent Van Gogh's pronounced brushstrokes took the art world by storm, and his legacy as a master painter outshines his reputation as something of a wacko. Actor Vincent Price was the king of early horror films, while Vince Lombardi is known as one of the greatest football coaches of all time. **Vince** is the most common nickname, although **Vinny** and **Vinnie** are used as well. Given Vin Diesel's rise to stardom, **Vin** might appeal to today's parents, too.

W

Wade: Old English; "ford" (a place where you can wade across a river). This name is rare today. Thomas Wade Landry (or Tom Landry, as he's known to football fans worldwide) was the head coach of the Dallas Cowboys for 26 years — still the longest tenure of any NFL head coach. He took the woefully terrible Dallas Cowboys of the 1960s and turned them into a powerhouse in the 1970s, winning two Super Bowls. Another noteworthy Wade was Wade Hampton, a Confederate soldier during the Civil War. He commanded the Confederate cavalry and later served as a U.S. senator from South Carolina. Alternatives include **Wayde** and **Waydell.**

Walker: English; "fuller" (an archaic term — a fuller worked with woolen cloth). More common as a surname, Walker seems to be a preferred middle name for political notables. The 41st president of the United States, George Herbert Walker Bush, and his son, the 43rd president of the United States, George Walker Bush, need no description. Longstanding U.S. Representative from Missouri, Richard Walker Bolling, was chair of the House Select Committee on Rules for many years; and Samuel Walker Griffith, the first Chief Justice of the High Court of Australia, helped to draft the Australian Commonwealth Constitution. And don't forget about the famous Walkers from the sports world. Writer Walker Percy won the National Book Award for his first novel, *The Moviegoer*. Trained as a physician, he began writing what are deemed "philosophical novels" after contracting tuberculosis at age 26. And last but not least, Walker Smith, Jr.

Chapter 2: Bailey, Brian, or Brent? Names for Boys

(better known as Sugar Ray Robinson) is often considered the greatest boxer ever, with a record 174 victories — 109 of those victories by knockout.

Walter: German; from *vald*, which means "rule," and *-harja*, which means "folk, people." The name came to England with the Normans, who favored it. Walter was still in circulation at the time of the Reformation but had become somewhat rare. In the American colonies, the name approached extinction, but around 1800, it became popular again, possibly because Romanticism favored medieval names. This growth continued through the century until the name became common. In the later 20th century, Walter lost most of its popularity, but it remains viable, probably because it's associated with some heroic figures. For example, late Chicago Bears running back Walter Payton is considered to be one of the greatest football players in history. Walt Disney created timeless stories that transcend childhood and remain entrenched in the hearts of millions of fans. And students will likely read poems like Walt Whitman's *Leaves of Grass* for centuries to come. Writer Sir Walter Scott is another famous bearer of this name. **Walt** is a common nickname.

Wesley: English; "the west meadow." This name is among the top 200 in use today in the United States. A prominent Wesley has made headlines recently: retired general Wesley Clark. A West Point graduate, he had a distinguished career as a U.S. Army officer, rising to the rank of four-star general and supreme commander of NATO. In 2003, he announced his candidacy for president. Actor Wesley Snipes has become one of Hollywood's most bankable action heroes, having starred in such films as *Passenger 57, U.S. Marshalls,* and *Blade.* If Wesley seems too plain or old-fashioned, try an alternate spelling, such as **Wessley, Wesly, Weseley,** or **Westley.**

William: German; from *vilja*, which means "will," and *helma*, which means "helmet." As with many Germanic names, the literal meaning is of little importance — its ethnic and social history is what matters. The Normans brought the name to England in the 11th century, and it became the most popular Norman name. Because the aristocratic Norman minority favored it, the name William came to be used by the general population. During the reign of Elizabeth I, it was the most common man's name, with a staggering 22.5 percent of boys being named William; in second and third place were JOHN (15.5 percent) and THOMAS (13.5 percent). The situation was significant because it showed that William had essentially become a traditional, secular name in England, not much influenced by religion. William fell off in popularity somewhat in the 17th century but was still a common name among immigrants to the American colonies, usually standing below John and about even with Thomas in popularity. After 1800, William rose in popularity again, topping many most-popular-name lists. That popularity continues; in the most recent Social Security Administration poll, William just missed breaking into the top ten names. Present-day bearers of this name include the United States' 42nd

☺ ☺ ☹ ☺ ☺ ☹ ☺ ☺ ☹ ☺ ☺ ☹ ☺ ☺ ☹ ☺ ☺ ☺ ☺ ☹ ☺

President, William Jefferson Clinton, and the heir to the British throne, Prince William. Nicknames include **Bill, Billy, Billie, Will,** and **Willie** — think of actors Bill Murray, Billy Bob Thornton, and Will Rogers and country singer Willie Nelson.

X

Xavier: Arabic; see JAVIER. Well established as a Spanish adaptation of the Basque place name Etcheberri ("new house"). St. Francis Xavier, a Jesuit priest of the 16th century, popularized this name. He's known for bringing Christianity to India and the Far East. Canonized in 1622, he became the patron saint for all missionary work. Another famous Xavier is the Spanish bandleader and violinist Xavier Cugat, who helped introduce Latin rhythms into American culture in the 1930s. Xavier (pronounced "HA-vee-air") is a popular name in the Latino community. The name can also be pronounced "ex-AY-vee-er," like the university in Cincinnati, Ohio.

Y

York: English; a place name. Once considered a family name, York comes from the northern city and county of England. Curiously, it was one of the most common names for slaves. (It may have arisen from a similar-sounding African name.) The Duke of York (later King James II) was an important political symbol during the late 17th century. In modern times, this name conjures up images of New York, a city known for glamour, wealth, and diversity.

Z

Zachary: Hebrew; "remembrance of the Lord." Zachary makes an appearance in the New Testament as the father of John the Baptist. This biblical Zachary prayed to God to give him and his infertile wife, Elizabeth, a son; God granted their wish and said that their son John's mission would be to convert the children of Israel to the Lord. Pope St. Zachary ruled from AD 741 to 752 and was known for his benevolence to the poor. But the name Zachary isn't reserved only for religious figures; Zachary Taylor was the 12th president of the United States, taking office in 1848. His vehement opposition to Texas's threat of secession over the ownership of the territories west of the Rio Grande probably delayed the start of the Civil War. President Taylor was in office for only two years, however — he died in 1850 of cholera as a result of attending the laying of the cornerstone of the Washington Monument. Today, Zachary is quite a popular name — in 2002, it was No. 19. **Zachariah** and **Zechariah** are more traditional, biblical versions of this name; **Zackary** is an alternate, more modern spelling. **Zach** and **Zack** are common nicknames.

Chapter 3

Gennifer, Gina, or Genevieve? Names for Girls

When you see your baby daughter for the first time, the name that's likely to come to mind before any other is "Angel." And that's a perfectly lovely name — in fact, it's been among the top 100 names given to baby girls in the United States for more than ten years running. However, once the awe wears off a bit, you may find that another name suits your preferences better. This chapter gives you hundreds of options to choose from.

Don't forget to look beyond the traditional spelling(s) listed at the beginning of each entry. If you like the idea of a tried-and-true name but want to spice it up, we also include alternative forms of most names, unless there just aren't any. We also list common nicknames for those names that are often shortened — and nothing is stopping you from using a nickname as a "real" name, either!

A

Aaliyah: Arabic; "to ascend, to rise up." Aaliyah is a variation of ALIYAH, which signifies the immigration of Jews to Israel. The name was most recently made famous by **Aaliyah Haughton** (known simply by her first name), a popular R&B recording artist and actress. Aaliyah was considered to be a rising star in the music and film worlds. Two of her songs received Grammy nominations, and her third, self-titled album climbed to the No. 2 spot on the Billboard music charts. As an actress, Aaliyah distinguished herself in the films *Romeo Must Die* and *Queen of the Damned*. However, her life was tragically cut short in a plane crash in 2001. Derivatives of Aaliyah include **Aliyah, Aliya,** and **Alya.**

Abigail: Hebrew; "father rejoiced," probably as in a child's being a joy to her father. According to I Samuel 25, Abigail was a practical woman of sense and efficient action. She was, however, far from a model of high morals. After her husband died, she hastened to David's bed in a matter of days, or even hours. This action may have been necessary to preserve life and property in a world overrun by predatory gangsters; still, it sets no high ideal of human conduct, and by early Puritan standards, Abigail wasn't a heroine after whom parents wanted to name their daughters. But the name became more popular after 1675 and became common in the non-Puritan colonies. By the 18th century, Abigail was regularly among the ten most common names. Its popularity suffered, however, in the general decline of biblical names in the 19th century, and by 1900, the name was rare once again. It declined further still in the 20th century, but has made a comeback in recent years — today it stands at No. 7. The nickname **Abby** has functioned as an independent name (even more common than Abigail) since about 1800. Famous Abigails include Abigail "Dear Abby" Van Buren and First Lady Abigail Adams. **Abbigail** is an alternative spelling of the full name, and **Abbie** is a second form of the nickname.

Addison: English; "son of Adam." This name clearly began as male, given the meaning, but has since become known as feminine. A famous male Addison is James Addison Baker III, who served as Ronald Reagan's chief of staff during his first term as president and then as Secretary of the Treasury in Reagan's second term. Under George Bush, Baker served as his Secretary of State, helping in the effort to bring peace to the Middle East. Given the name's rise in popularity, famous female Addisons are sure to appear in future years.

Adrienne: Greek, Latin; "of the Adriatic (Sea)." The name Adrienne originated in the Adriatic Sea region and has become increasingly popular since the 1950s. There are many different spellings of this name, including **Adriana, Adriane, Adrianna, Adrianne, Adrina, Adrian,** and **Adrien** (the last two of which double as names for boys), but actress Adrienne Barbeau is perhaps one of the more famous women in pop culture who retains this spelling. Adrienne Rich is a well-known feminist poet.

Aileen: See EILEEN.

Ainsley: Multiple origins; one possibility is English, meaning "meadow belonging to a man named An"; another possible meaning is "hermitage meadow." Growing in popularity but still a fairly uncommon name, Ainsley first cracked the Social Security Administration's list of the 500 most popular names for girls in 2001, ranking 483rd.

Aisha: Arabic; "woman," "living prosperous." The fact that this name was borne by one of Mohammed's wives tends to account for its popularity in the African-American community via a general popularity of names with Islamic associations.

Alaina: Breton; meaning uncertain. One hypothesis relates it to the tribal name Alanni. Alaina — pronounced ah-LAY-nah — is the feminine form of the name Alain. Along with its alternate spelling, **Alayna,** it has risen steadily in popularity over the last several years.

Alana: Breton; see ALAINA. This name (based on the male form, **Alan,** with the pronunciation ah-LAH-nah) has become popular in recent years. An up-and-comer of the music world, Alana Davis, demonstrated her song-writing and singing ability with her first album, *Blame It on Me*. Variations of Alana include **Alanna.**

Alexandra: Greek; "protector of mankind," "defender." This common name has an aristocratic flair, due in part to its association with Princess Alexandra of Denmark, who married Prince Edward of Wales in 1863. Its many variations include **Alexandria,** ALEXA, and ALEXIS (all of which are popular today), with nicknames such as **Alex, Ally,** and **Allie.** The Spanish form is **Alejandra.**

Alexa: Greek; "protector of mankind," "defender." Originally a feminine form of ALEXIS and now a feminine form of ALEXANDER, Alexa is consid-ered a shorter version of ALEXANDRA. This name has remained very popu-lar with Scottish parents since the 12th century, where it's considered a royal moniker. Some people link this Alexandria with the city of the same name in Egypt (named after Alexander the Great) or the one in Virginia, just southwest of Washington, D.C. A variation is **Alexia.**

Alexis: Greek; "protector of mankind," "defender." Alexis is borrowed from the French, which in turn took it from Russian or some other lan-guage of eastern Europe. Actress Alexis Bledel has made a splash by play-ing Rory, the teenaged daughter of a young mother, on the television series *The Gilmore Girls*. Joan Collins played nasty Alexis Carrington on the long-running series *Dynasty*. **Alexus** is a secondary spelling.

Alice: Old German; from the name Adalheid, meaning "noble + sort" and therefore a variant of Adelaide. The name was filtered through the French, where it took the form Aliz/Alys/Alis, while the spelling Alice seems to have arisen in England, likely as a vernacular form of the Latin version ALICIA. It was very popular in the Middle Ages. Although it survived the first effects of the Reformation, it became rare in the colonial period. In the 19th cen-tury, its use revived, probably because of the trend toward Romanticism and a general interest in the past, especially the Middle Ages. The popular *Alice in Wonderland* (1865) also affected the situation. Around 1900, Alice was second only to MARY in popularity, and it has remained in use since, although it isn't as prominent as it once was. Most Gen X parents have a hard time thinking of this name without thinking of Mel's Diner and "Kiss my grits!" Flo from the TV series *Alice*. See also ALLISON.

Popular Scottish names

If you enjoy bagpipes, brightly colored tartans, and lilting accents, try one of these Scottish names.

* Ainsley
* Alison
* Annabel
* Cameron (or Camryn)
* Ellen
* Fiona
* Isobel (or Isabel or Isabelle if you prefer a more Americanized spelling)
* Janet
* Leslie
* Margaret

Alicia: English; "of noble birth." The name, which ranked 121st in 2002, has two different pronunciations: ah-LEE-see-ah and ah-LEE-shah. The actress Alicia Silverstone has starred in several films, including *Clueless* and *The Crush.* Soulful singer Alicia Keys took home five Grammys in 2002 for her LP *Songs in A Minor,* driven by the No. 1 hit "Fallin'." **Alisha** is an alternate spelling.

Alina: Old German; "noble." Filtered through the French, Alina is a derivative of **Adeline/Adelina**.

Allison: English; "of noble birth." Allison, a diminutive of ALICE, became popular in the Middle Ages, especially in Scotland. It came into popularity again in the 20th century. In 2002, Allison ranked 44th on the Social Security Administration's list of the most popular names for girls. Elvis Costello's song "Allison" tells the story of an admirer of Allison who let her slip away. Famous bearers of this name include actress Allison Janney, who stars on TV's *West Wing,* and bluegrass songbird Alison Krauss. Alternate spellings include **Alison, Alyson,** and **Allyson.**

Alissa: See ALYSSA.

Aliyah: See AALIYAH.

Allie, Ally: American. See ALYSSA.

Chapter 3: Gennifer, Gina, or Genevieve? Names for Girls

☺ ☺ ☹ ☺ ☺ ☹ ☺ ☺ ☹ ☺ ☺ ☹ ☺ ☺ ☹ ☺ ☺ ☺ ☹ ☹ ☺

Alyssa: Old German; "of noble birth." Alyssa is a variant of ALICE — probably a re-Latinization of the French Alis/Alys form — and not a distinct name, historically speaking. Actress Alyssa Milano is a popular Alyssa, having recently revived her *Who's the Boss?*-era stardom in the TV series *Charmed.* **Alissa** and **Allise** are variations, and nicknames include **Allie** and **Ally**.

Amanda: Latin; "worthy to be loved." In the 17th century, and even later, names were coined from Latin by poets addressing themselves to ladies they wished to remain unidentified. In addition to Amanda, there was Amata ("beloved"). Other names relating to the Latin verb *amo* ("to love") are **Amabel, Amable,** and **Amiable.** The band Boston scored a hit in the 1980s with the song "Amanda." Famous Amandas include actress Amanda Peet and Canadian singer Amanda Marshall.

Amaya: Japanese; meaning unknown. Amaya (pronounced "ah-MY-ah") has ranked among the top 300 most popular names for girls each of the last three years. One of the housemates on *Real World Hawaii* was named Amaya.

Amber: French; a fossil resin that's often used to make beads and other jewelry. Actress Tiffany Amber Thiessen starred on TV's *Saved By the Bell* and *Beverly Hills 90210* and then moved on to films, including a major role in Woody Allen's *Hollywood Ending.* The national Amber Alert system helps the authorities track down abducted children. Derivatives of this fairly popular name include **Amberlyn, Amberlynn,** and **Amberly.**

America: Italian; meaning unknown. Interestingly, this form is occasionally found in medieval Latin records representing the woman's name Amery (or Almery). However, this is extremely unlikely to have contributed to the modern use of America as a given name. In the early 16th century, Italian explorer Amerigo Vespucci followed in the footsteps of Christopher Columbus and led several voyages to what is now known as North and South America. His explorations to and findings in "the New World" are what inspired the German mapmaker Martin Waldseemuller to name the newly discovered continents after the explorer in 1507. Another famous use of the name America was by the 1970s folk-rock band America, best known for its songs "Horse with No Name," "Sister Golden Hair," and "Ventura Highway."

Amelia: Latin; "industrious, admiring." Amelia is a Latinized form of *amal,* which is a common element in early Germanic names. See EMILIO in Chapter 2. The name came to England with the Hanoverian kings and became popular there in the mid- and late 18th century — and more so in the colonies. In America, the classicism of its Latin form was becoming old-fashioned by 1800, and it was more or less replaced by the similar-sounding EMILY, although it remains among the top 150 girls' names in use today. Famous Amelias include aviation pioneer Amelia Earhart and children's book character Amelia Bedelia.

☺ ☺ ☹ ☺ ☺ ☹ ☺ ☺ ☹ ☺ ☺ ☹ ☺ ☺ ☹ ☺ ☺ ☺ ☺ ☹ ☺

Amy: Old French; "beloved." Common in the Middle Ages, the name Amy later passed out of ordinary usage but was revived as a Romantic name in the 19th century, only to become old-fashioned again in the 20th. Its early use is probably not to be attributed to the two French (male) saints of that name; it's more likely based on the meaning. By the later 20th century, however, this volatile name had again become an ordinary resident member of the top ten. Today, it just misses the top 100. Famous Amys include former first daughter Amy Carter, Christian pop singer Amy Grant, and actress Amy Irving, who's appeared in such films as *She's Having a Baby* and *Traffic.* If the classic spelling seems too plain to you, try **Aimee, Ami,** or **Amie** (the latter two meaning "friend" in French).

Ana, Anna: See ANN.

Anastasia: Greek; "resurrection." The last Russian tsar, Nicholas Romanov, and his wife, the Empress Alexandra, had a daughter named Anastasia. Nicholas and his family were arrested and killed during the Russian Revolution of 1917. Legend has it that Anastasia survived, surfacing later in Germany as woman who went by the name Anna Anderson. Anna insisted that she was Anastasia, although she was never able to prove her claim. Anastasia's story was depicted in the 1997 animated film entitled — no surprise here — *Anastasia.* Over the last decade, the name has consistently ranked among the top 500 names for girls, although it has never ranked higher than 255th.

Andrea: The Italian form of ANDREW, which in Greek means "manly." The feminine-looking form has caused it to be taken for a woman's name, and that's how it's usually used today. In 1980, at the age of 15, tennis wunderkind Andrea Yeager became the youngest semifinalist in U.S. Open history. Today she runs the Silver Lining Foundation, a nonprofit organization dedicated to improving the lives of children with cancer. CNN correspondent Andrea Koppel is the daughter of *Nightline* host Ted Koppel.

Angela: Latin, French; "angel." This name possesses many variations, including **Angel, Angeline, Angelina, Angelia, Angelica, Angelique,** and **Angie.** All are the result of attempts to derive (or adopt) a feminine name from the Latin and French words for "angel." These forms enjoyed a mild popularity in the late 19th century, and some of this popularity carried over into the 20th. Angela, for example, appeared in the top ten. Actress Angelina Jolie gives this form of the name a bit of a bad-girl image, while actresses Angelica Huston and Angela Lansbury exhibit more of its traditional angelic qualities.

Anna: Hebrew; "grace." The name Anna represents the Greek form of HANNAH, as it appears in the New Testament (Luke 2:36). This Anna became St. Anna. Much more widely known is St. **Anne,** to whom we may attribute the popularity of the name. Although this Anne isn't mentioned in the Bible, early Christian tradition identified her as the mother of the Virgin Mary. She was especially honored in the Byzantine Empire, but the name

Chapter 3: Gennifer, Gina, or Genevieve? Names for Girls

☺ ☺ ☹ ☺ ☺ ☹ ☺ ☺ ☹ ☺ ☺ ☹ ☺ ☺ ☹ ☺ ☺ ☺ ☺ ☹ ☺

failed to become popular in England until the 14th century. It survived the Reformation better than most of the nonbiblical saints' names. In their new colonies, however, the Puritans rejected it, replacing it by its alternate form, HANNAH. In the non-Puritan colonies, Anna remained about as popular as it was in England. In the 19th century, it gradually replaced Hannah and continued to be popular (usually in the top ten) until the mid-20th century. In 2002, it ranked as the 20th most common name for girls. Anna has also developed new forms. The diminutive **Annie** was popular in the 19th century as an independent name. **Ann** is popular in compounds, such as MARYANN and ANNMARIE. Anne, with its diminutive **Annette**, shows a French influence. Other forms include **Anita** and ANNABEL. Notable bearers of the name Anna or one of its variants include Tolstoy's heroine Anna Karenina, tennis diva Anna Kournikova, Swedish-born actress Ann-Margret, Holocaust-era diarist Anne Frank, and *The Vampire Chronicles* author, Anne Rice.

Annabel: Scottish; it may be a derivative of the Latin *amabilis*, which means "lovable." Although Edgar Allan Poe's poem *Annabel Lee* gave wide circulation to this name in the United States, it's never been heavily used, maybe because the funereal atmosphere of the poem was too marked. An alternate spelling is **Annabelle.**

Annika: Scandinavian; "little Ann." This name is still fairly rare, but it's risen more than 600 spots since 1995 and now ranks 344th. Golfer Annika Sorenstam, who stirred up controversy when she played against the men in a PGA tournament, seems anything but little out on the golf course. In 2001, Sorenstam finished first or second in 14 LPGA events, including a record-breaking score of 59 (13 under par) in the second round of the Standard Register PING tournament. An alternate spelling is **Anneke.**

Anya: The Russian form of ANNA, which means "grace." Anya began appearing with some regularity in the United States in the 1970s. The name made its way into popular culture most recently as a recurring character in the popular *Buffy the Vampire Slayer* series. Anya Kubrick is daughter of the late, great filmmaker Stanley Kubrick.

April: English; from the calendar month. In the 20th century, a slight use of April occurred, just as May and June are used as given names. Along with the masculine August, April seems to be the extent of personal names taken from months. (For May and August, the source is not primarily the month.) April is probably popular as a name because it conjures up images of the coming of spring and all its natural beauty. It ranked as the 258th most popular name for girls in 2002.

Ariana: The Italian form of the Greek name **Ariadne** (the daughter of King Minos in Greek mythology); "holy." A famous Ariana is Ariana Huffington, a nationally syndicated newspaper and magazine columnist and author who made headlines by running for governor of California in 2003. Derivatives of Ariana include **Arianna** and **Ariane**.

Parent's Success Guide to Baby Names

☺ ☻ ☹ ☺ ☻ ☹ ☺ ☻ ☹ ☺ ☻ ☹ ☹ ☺ ☻ ☹ ☺ ☺ ☻ ☹ ☺

Ariel: Hebrew; "lion of God," "God is a lion." A man in Ezra bears this name, and it's also used in Isaiah as a symbolic name for Jerusalem. Shakespeare used it in *The Tempest;* in the list of characters, Ariel is noted as "an airy spirit," suggesting that the playwright was attracted rather by the punning suggestion than by the linguistic meaning. In the Bible as well as in *The Tempest,* the association of the name is masculine, but in the modern American tradition, the adjective *airy* has a strong feminine suggestion, and thus Ariel is used for women. The name became extremely popular in the 1990s with the release of Disney's *The Little Mermaid,* which featured a strong-willed mermaid called Ariel. An alternate spelling is **Arielle.**

Ashanti: Swahili; a tribal name. This name recently surged in popularity, rising from 832nd most popular in 2001 to 117th in 2002. Part of the reason behind the upswing may be the success of R&B singing sensation Ashanti Douglas, whose self-titled 2002 LP debuted at No. 1 on the charts.

Ashley: English; "ash wood, ash forest." In recent years, this name has become one of the most popular names for girls; however, it was the male character of Ashley Wilkes in Margaret Mitchell's novel *Gone with the Wind* that probably initiated the name's popularity. Well-known modern-day Ashleys include Ashley Olson, half of the famous Olson twins, and Ashley Judd, who has become one of Hollywood's most successful actresses. Judd received critical acclaim for her portrayal of Marilyn Monroe in *Norma Jean and Marilyn* and has since starred in such films as *A Time to Kill, Simon Birch, Where the Heart Is,* and *Divine Secrets of the Ya-Ya Sisterhood.* Alternate spellings include **Ashlee** and **Ashleigh.**

Ashlyn: English; may be from the place-name meaning, "ash wood, ash forest." More than likely from the given name *Asceline,* another French version of an Old German name. Ashlyn is a combined form of ASHLEY and LYNN. Ashlyn has been among the 200 most popular girls' names for four years running. If you like, add an extra N to form **Ashlynn.**

Ashton: English; "ash (tree) village." Although Ashton has been more common as a male name, it can also be used as a female name. Mary Ashton Rice Livermore was a women's rights activist of the 19th century who fought for women's voting rights. She also volunteered during the Civil War, touring military hospitals and helping to collect supplies for the troops. After the war, she became well known for her writings and lectures; her most famous lecture was "What Shall We Do with Our Daughters?" in which she advocated that women should have the same opportunities for education as men. Another famous Ashton — this time male — is Ashton Kutcher, the young, comedic star of TV's *That 70's Show.* An alternate spelling is **Ashten**.

Asia: Greek; "east, where the sun rises." The name Asia has a long history; of course, everyone knows that it's the name of the world's largest continent. The name also appears in the Qu'ran as the wife of the Pharaoh who raised Moses. A notable modern-day Asia is the Italian-born actress Asia

☺ ☺ ☹ ☺ ☹ ☹ ☺ ☹ ☹ ☺ ☺ ☹ ☺ ☹ ☹ ☺ ☺ ☹ ☹ ☺

Argento. She has become known to American audiences for her portrayal of Yelena in the film *XXX*, starring Vin Diesel.

Aubrey: French, German; "elf rule." This name — another to begin as male and then transition to female — came to England with the Normans. Its later history isn't clear — it may be a Romantic revival. Today, it's among the top 200 names given to baby girls, at 199th. A couple of variations, albeit uncommon ones, are **Aubery** and **Aubury.**

Audrey: Old English; from Etheldreda, "noble strength." Etheldreda, a queen of Northumbria in the seventh century, became a highly venerated saint, and her name was passed on after the Norman Conquest. It suffered severe changes in pronunciation, and by the 16th century, the spelling was shifted to agree with the new pronunciation. The name came to have a rural and countrified association; with that suggestion, Shakespeare used it for the shepherdess in *As You Like It.* By the 17th century, the name had become rare in England, and in that period it scarcely appeared in the colonies. In the early 20th century, it revived in England and became somewhat popular. This English interest stirred up some usage in the United States. Actress Audrey Hepburn will forever be remembered for her performance as Holly Golightly in *Breakfast at Tiffany's.* The fetching Audrey Tatou starred in the popular foreign film *Amelie.*

Aurora: Greek; "dawn." In Greek mythology, Aurora was the daughter of Hyperion and Theia, sister of Helios and Selene. A steady riser, the name Aurora has gradually gained popularity over the last ten years. Astronomers know that the Aurora Borealis is more commonly called the Northern Lights. Shirley MacLaine played the character Aurora Greenway in both *Terms of Endearment* (for which she won an Academy Award) and the sequel *The Evening Star.*

Autumn: English; "the fall season." In recent years, Autumn has consistently ranked among the 100 most popular names for girls. The name would be a particularly appropriate choice for a girl born during the fall. British writer John Keats — himself a fall baby, born on Halloween — penned the poem "To Autumn" in 1819.

Ava: See EVE. Ava Gardner, perhaps the most famous Ava to date, was known for her striking beauty and screen presence. Once married to crooner Frank Sinatra, she was nominated for an Academy Award for *Mogambo* in 1953 and received high praise for her performances in *The Barefoot Contessa* and *The Sun Also Rises.* Similar names include **Avis** and **Avelyn.**

Avery: French; "nobility." This name is a form of ALFRED, although it can be given to either a girl or a boy. As with many androgynous names, it's used more often for girls than for boys today. For example, Tom Cruise's ambitious and, it turns out, unsupportive girlfriend at the beginning of the movie *Jerry Maguire* (played by John Travolta's real-life wife Kelly Preston) is named Avery. In 2002, Avery ranked as the 135th most popular name for girls.

☺ ☺ ☹ ☺ ☺ ☹ ☺ ☺ ☹ ☺ ☺ ☹ ☺ ☺ ☹ ☺ ☺ ☺ ☺ ☹ ☺

B

Bailey: English; "bailiff." A common last name, Bailey has become an increasingly popular first name for both boys and girls. Among female Baileys, Bailey White was a popular humorist and essayist. Kay Bailey Hutchison is a United States Senator from Texas. Derivatives include **Baylee** and **Bailee.**

Barbara: Greek; the feminine of *barbaros,* a term applied to any thing or person to indicate "not Greek" or, in general, "foreign, outlandish." In Christian countries, the naming tradition began with St. Barbara (Syrian, third century), one of the great virgin saints. The name wasn't popular in England before the Reformation. In the following period, with its wide-spread rejection of the idea of sainthood, Barbara almost disappeared — especially in America. In the 20th century, Barbara came into use again to some extent because of its Spanish suggestions. By 1950, it had become highly popular, a regular among the top ten. The older English familiar form was Barbary, but it has made little impression on American usage, a further indication that the recent popularity of the name isn't a development from British practice but is an independent growth, probably from a literary or Hollywood source. Notable holders of this name include singer Barbra Streisand, former First Lady Barbara Bush, and politician Barbara Mikulski, who has the honor of having been the first woman elected to the United States Senate. Nicknames include **Barb** and **Barbie.**

Bella: All three variants of this name — Bella, **Bell,** and **Belle** — are to be considered short forms of ISABEL, although the direct influence of the Latin word *bella,* which means "beautiful," is possible. *Belle,* the Southern term for an attractive girl, may have contributed to the name's popularity as well. These names are chiefly of the 19th century, although they have made something of a comeback, perhaps in part because of the Disney animated film *Beauty and the Beast,* whose heroine is named Belle.

Bernadette: French; "brave as a bear." In the mid-19th century, a woman claimed to have seen the Virgin Mary on 18 separate occasions at Massabielle Rock, a place that has since become a popular destination for Christian pilgrims. In 1933, she was canonized and forever became known as St. Bernadette of Lourdes. Another famous Bernadette is Bernadette Peters, the Tony Award-winning Broadway and film actress known for her daring choices of roles, as well as her fearless performances. She has starred in such Broadway musicals as *Sunday in the Park with George, In the Woods, Song and Dance,* and the revival of *Gypsy,* in which she earned critical acclaim for her portrayal of stripper Gypsy Rose Lee. Derivatives include **Bernadina, Bernadine, Bernette,** and **Bernita**.

Bethany: Hebrew; a place name. Bethany, a village just east of Jerusalem, was the site of one of Jesus's most famous miracles. According to the Bible, Lazarus lived in Bethany with his two sisters, Martha and Mary, and

Chapter 3: Gennifer, Gina, or Genevieve? Names for Girls

☺ ☺ ☹ ☺ ☺ ☹ ☺ ☺ ☹ ☺ ☺ ☹ ☺ ☺ ☹ ☺ ☺ ☺ ☹ ☹ ☺

here Jesus raised Lazarus from the dead. And it was near Bethany that the Bible says Jesus ascended to heaven after His crucifixion. The biblical significance of the name has led to its becoming a fairly common female name — today, it's among the top 200. Variations include **Bethanie.**

Bianca: Italian; "fair-skinned." Bianca, the sister of Katherine in Shakespeare's *The Taming of the Shrew,* is soft-spoken, sweet, and unassuming. Another beautiful Bianca is Bianca Jagger, who left behind a rock-and-roll lifestyle to become a respected advocate for human rights and victims of violence against women. Bianca Montgomery is the fictional daughter of one of the soap opera industry's most famous divas, *All My Children's* Erica Kane. The French version of this name is **Blanche.**

Brenda: Old Norse; "sword." Brenda is a literary name, used by Sir Walter Scott. It came into fashion in the mid-20th century — rising in sync with comic-strip character Brenda Starr — and has continued to be moderately popular. Actress Brenda Blethyn earned Academy Award nominations for her performances in *Secrets and Lies* and *Little Voice.* **Brenna** is a variant of Brenda.

Brianna: American; Brianna is a feminine variant of the name BRIAN. It ranked as the 17th most popular name for girls in 2002, and since 1994, it has never ranked lower than 28th. A multitude of alternate spellings and forms exist: **Briana, Brianne, Breanna, Breanne, Briannah, Briannon, Brienna, Bryana,** and **Bryanna.**

Bridget: Gaelic; "high one, noble one." Bridget is the English adaptation of the Irish form Brighid, a pagan fire goddess. It has traditionally been the most common woman's name in Ireland after MARY. Because of the tremendous transatlantic immigration of the Irish in the mid-19th century, the name became common, but it failed to establish itself in general usage in the United States. It thus became a mark of the Irish (especially of domestic servants), and the Irish themselves tended to abandon it as a handicap to their integration into American life. Although a revival seems possible, the name is only moderately popular today. Actress Bridget Fonda, daughter of Peter Fonda and granddaughter of Henry Fonda, has starred in numerous films, including *Singles* and *A Simple Plan.* In the literary world, Helen Fielding's comedic novel *Bridget Jones's Diary* was a hugely popular bestseller. An alternate spelling of the name is **Bridgette.**

Brittany: American; "from Britain," "from the region called Brittany." The name Brittany originally referred to the Briton settlers from England who fled to France after the Anglo-Saxon invasion. Today, it's a moderately popular name in the United States, ranking 175th in 2002. Up-and-coming actress Brittany Murphy wins hearts by taking roles like loveable Tai in *Clueless* and the voice of Luanne on TV's animated comedy *King of the Hill.* And from Mousketeer to pop sensation, daring yet adorable **Britney** Spears continues her ascension to divadom. Other variants include **Brettany, Brettani, Brite, Britani, Brittney, Brittanie, Brittnee,** and **Brittni.**

☺ ☹ ☺ ☺ ☹ ☹ ☺ ☹ ☹ ☺ ☹ ☹ ☺ ☹ ☹ ☺ ☺ ☹ ☹ ☺

Brooke: English; "lives near water," "stream," "brook." Model-turned-actress Brooke Shields graced more than 250 magazine covers from 1980 to 1985 and went on to graduate from Princeton and become an advocate for children's rights and literacy. Her legacy lives on in this popular name, which consistently hovers around No. 50 on the list of the most common girls' names in the United States. Variations include **Brook, Brooklyn, Brooklynn,** and **Brooklynne**.

Bryanna: See BRIANNA.

C

Caila: See KAYLA.

Caileigh, Cailey: See KAYLEIGH.

Caitlin: Irish; "pure (beauty)." This name comes from an Irish borrowing of the Middle English CATELINE, a variant of KATHERINE. Caitlin — poet Dylan Thomas's wife and an author in her own right — appears in one of his famous love poems. Actress Caitlin Clarke *(Dragonslayer)* is another notable Caitlin. The perky actress Heather Locklear played Caitlyn Moore on the television series *Spin City* for several years. A very popular girl's name in the 1990s, Caitlin and its various permutations reached the No. 1 spot in 1998. Alternative spellings include **Caitlyn, Kaitlin, Kaitlyn, Kaitlynn, Katelin,** and **Katelyn**. Nicknames and short forms include **Cate, Caty, Kait, Kate,** and **Katy.**

Callie: English; a nickname from the Greek **Callista,** which means "beautiful." The name Callie has, in recent years, consistently ranked among the 500 most popular names for girls, although it's never reached higher than 265th. Callie Khouri wrote the screenplay for the film *Thelma & Louise* and directed *Divine Secrets of the Ya-Ya Sisterhood,* adapted from the bestselling novel.

Cameron: Gaelic; "crooked nose." Like many Scottish names, Cameron attained popularity along with the Romantic movement. The name is appropriate for girls and boys, although it's more commonly given to the latter. Spunky actress Cameron Diaz has appeared in a wide variety of films, from the slapstick comedy *There's Something About Mary* to Martin Scorsese's dark period piece *Gangs of New York.* Alternate spellings include **Camron** and **Camryn.** Emmy-winning actress Camryn Manheim uses this form of the name.

Camilla: Italian; meaning unknown. This name comes from the Roman family surname Camillus, which some historians speculate may be of Etruscan origin. It probably didn't occur in the United States before the 19th century, and it has always been rare. Prince Charles's paramour, Camilla Parker Bowles, is likely the most famous bearer of this name. **Camila** and **Camille** are variations.

Chapter 3: Gennifer, Gina, or Genevieve? Names for Girls

☺ ☺ ☹ ☺ ☺ ☹ ☺ ☺ ☹ ☺ ☺ ☹ ☺ ☺ ☹ ☺ ☺ ☺ ☹ ☺

Candace: Origin and meaning uncertain. In ancient times, Candace was the hereditary name or title of the queens of Ethiopia or Nubia. One of these queens figured in a story that represented her as involved in incest with her brother. Chaucer, though attributing the story to Canace, contributes the line "Who loved her owne brother synfully." The name was also attributed to the queen of Sheba who visited Solomon. In addition, "Candace queen of the Ethiopians" has a passing mention in Acts 8:27. For some reason, American parents began using the name in spite of the suggestion of incest that clung to it. In fact, that taboo topic might even have an attraction, as it has in Faulkner's *The Sound and the Fury.* An alternate spelling is **Candice.** Candice Bergen, widow of the late filmmaker Louis Malle, starred with Jack Nicholson in the movie *Carnal Knowledge,* but she may be best known for playing the title role on the TV series *Murphy Brown.*

Cara: Latin; "dearest, beloved." Moderately common, Cara consistently manages to rank among the top 500 most popular names. While famous people with the first name Cara are few and far between, singer Irene Cara got her moment in the sun when she topped the charts with the title song to the movie *Flashdance.*

Carissa: Greek; "grace." Carissa, which peaked in popularity in the early 1990s, is also the name of a thorn-bearing plant that's native to South Africa, although it's now commonly found in Florida. A variant spelling is **Charissa.**

Carla: A feminine form of CARL, a German name than means "man." Until the 1950s, it was far more common in the United States than in Britain, but the name has since gained popularity across the Atlantic as well. Actress Carla Gugino *(Spy Kids),* model Carla Bruni, and Carla Tortelli, the irascible barkeep from the television show *Cheers,* are a few famous Carlas. A variant spelling is **Karla,** and nicknames include **Carly, Karly, Carley,** and **Karley.** Today, Carly is even more popular than Carla.

Carmen: Spanish; based on the place name Carmel (which itself has a Hebrew origin meaning "garden"). The Spanish adopted Carmen as one of a group of names — including Mercedes, Dolores, and others — referring to attributes of the Virgin Mary. The name Carmen was immortalized in Bizet's opera of the same name. Modern-day Carmens include Dennis Rodman's ex-wife Carmen Electra. It's not especially common these days, although it ranks among the top 300 girls' names.

Carol: A feminine form of CARL, a German name than means "man." In Great Britain, the name Carol, beginning to appear near the end of the 18th century, applied to men. In America, however, it soon was used for women — perhaps being influenced by parents' attraction to the obvious Caroline. As a result, Carol (applied to a man) is so rare in the United States as scarcely to exist. Instead, the spelling **Carroll** has been used, as if it were a family name. Carol continues to be used for women; two later coined forms are **Carole** and **Carola.** The comedian Carol Burnett drew millions of television viewers to her self-titled variety show in the 1970s.

109

☺ ☹ ☺ ☺ ☹ ☺ ☺ ☹ ☺ ☺ ☹ ☺ ☺ ☹ ☺ ☺ ☺ ☹ ☺ ☺

Other famous Carols include entertainer Carol Channing and prolific author Joyce Carol Oates.

Caroline: A feminine form of CARL, a German name than means "man." The popularity of this name came to England from Germany in the mid-18th century with the marriage of George II to Princess Caroline of Ansbach. The name Caroline was moderately popular in the United States throughout the 19th century, before disappearing for several decades. In the mid-20th century, it again became popular. John F. Kennedy and his wife, Jackie, liked the name so much that they gave it to their daughter, Caroline Bouvier Kennedy, when she was born in 1957. Variations and nicknames include **Carolyn** and **Carolina,** and **Carrie** is a possible nickname. The latter was considered an independent name even before Carrie Bradshaw, played by actress Sarah Jessica Parker, became a phenomenon — and an embodiment of female independence — on the hit HBO series *Sex and the City.*

Carson: English; more than likely from some unidentified nickname with "son" added. What began as a surname is now gaining in popularity as a first name for either a girl or boy. Frontiersman Kit Carson is one of the first notable Carsons in the United States, after whom Carson City, Nevada, is named. Popular talk show host Johnny Carson may be the best-known Carson ever. Among female Carsons are the author Carson McCullers, best known for her novel *The Heart Is a Lonely Hunter.*

Casey: Irish; more than likely derived from a reduced form of the Irish surname O'Cathasaigh (O'Casey), from the given name Cathasach, meaning "war vigilant." In modern times, the nickname based on the initials *K. C.* may also have contributed to the development of this name (similar to the conversion of Olympic athlete J. C. Owens' name to "Jesse"). Casey is derived from the word *acacia*, which is a biblical reference to the wood that was used to build the arc of the covenant and the tabernacle. This name is suitable for a boy or a girl. In fact, Casey and the alternate spelling **Kasey** both ranked among the 500 most popular names for girls in 2002. The best-known poem about baseball is *Casey at the Bat,* and the most famous locomotive engineer hero is Casey Jones, who died in the line of duty. Variations and derivatives include **Kaycee, Kayce, Caycee, Kaysee, Kayse,** and **Kacey.**

Cassandra: The name of a character in *The Iliad.* The second half of the name is probably the same as that in ALEXANDER, meaning "man." Cassandra is one of Priam's daughters, notable as being the prophetess who was never believed. Like Hector, her brother, Cassandra became well known to the English. Her name was common in the Middle Ages, and a faint tradition of it hung on, usually in the diminutive **Cassie.** Local-color writers of the 19th century, like Bret Harte, used the name as a characteristic one for a primitive American of the period. The name's popularity has diminished somewhat in recent years, although it managed to rank as the 125th most popular name for girls in 2002.

☺ ☺ ☹ ☺ ☺ ☹ ☺ ☺ ☹ ☺ ☺ ☹ ☺ ☺ ☹ ☺ ☺ ☺ ☹ ☺

Cassidy: Gaelic; it derives from a shortening of the Irish surname O'Caiside, meaning "curly (haired)." In modern usage, it can be given to a boy or a girl, and as a girls' name, it recently slipped out of the top 100. Twenty-eight western novels chronicle the tales of the heroic Hopalong Cassidy, written by Clarence E. Mulford in the early to mid-20th century. The late pop-blues singer Eva Cassidy remains a soulful favorite among folk music fans. Singer and actor David Cassidy was considered a dreamboat by many a teenage girl in the 1970s.

Catharine, Catherine: See KATHERINE.

Cayla: See KAYLA.

Caylee, Cayley: See KAYLEIGH.

Cecilia: Latin; from the family name meaning "blind." The feminine of Cecil, its use is based more particularly on the cult of St. Cecilia, the patroness of music. As a nonbiblical saint, Cecilia was not much regarded in the Protestant tradition, and the name has been rare in the United States. In the 20th century, its use increased somewhat, and these days it's around 250th in popularity. Folk rockers Simon & Garfunkel immortalized the name with the catchy 1969 hit "Cecilia."

Celeste: French; "heavenly." In terms of popularity, Celeste has been a consistent, if not stellar, performer: Between 1994 and 2002, it ranked no higher than 244th and no lower than 309th. Celeste is the name of Babar the elephant's wife in the beloved series of children's books. Actress Celeste Holm has been acting for the last seven decades, with appearances on TV shows such as *Falcon Crest* and *Columbo* and in films such as *All About Eve* and *Three Men and a Baby.*

Charlotte: French, German; the feminine form of CHARLES. Charlotte has evolved through the use of the French diminutive-feminizing suffix *-otte*. In British-American usage, however, the connection of Charlotte with Charles has been forgotten, or the idea of the association with Charles failed to make the transition from French to English. Before the later 18th century, Charlotte was essentially a French name, rare in England and scarcely existing in America. The shift came with the marriage of George II to the German princess who bore the half-French name Charlotte Sophia. As queen, she was a popular figure, and the name crossed the Atlantic. The establishment of Charlotte drew support from its uses for fictional characters, because it seems to have appealed to writers. In Goethe's widely read *Sorrows of Young Werther,* it's the name of the heroine, and it serves both as heroine and title for Rowson's immensely popular *Charlotte Temple* (1791). However, the name failed to equal the success of Charles and enjoyed only a moderate popularity throughout the 19th and 20th centuries. Charlotte Brontë wrote the literary classic *Jane Eyre,* which was first published in 1846.

Chelsea: English; "chalk landing." Ranked No. 15 in 1992, this name has since slipped to 181st, with its popularity waning. Having attended both Stanford and Oxford universities, Chelsea Clinton, daughter of former president Bill Clinton and Senator Hillary Rodham Clinton, always exhibits poise in spite of her sometimes controversial parents. On the geographical front, Chelsea is the name of an upscale neighborhood in London.

Cheyenne: The name of a Native American tribe. Between 1995 and 2000, Cheyenne consistently ranked among the 100 most popular names for girls. Since then, it's become slightly less common. The name may be a good choice for natives of the U.S.'s 44th state, as Cheyenne is the capital of Wyoming. An alternate spelling is **Cheyanne.**

Chloe: Greek, "a burgeoning shoot, verdant and blooming." A name used once in the New Testament, Chloe has been a steady riser, reaching the 24th slot on the Social Security Administration's list of the most popular names for girls in 2002. Actress Chloe Sevigny was nominated for an Academy Award in the Best Supporting Actress category for her performance in the 1999 film *Boys Don't Cry.*

Christina: Greek; "a Christian." Christina and its slightly less common French variation, **Christine,** have been favored names since the 19th century. Famous holders of this name include pop diva Christina Aguilera, *Married with Children* star Christina Applegate, and actress Christina Ricci, who has appeared in such films as *The Addams Family, The Ice Storm,* and *Fear and Loathing in Las Vegas.* Alternate spellings include **Kristina** and **Kristine.**

Ciara, Cierra: See SIERRA.

Cindy, Cyndy: See CYNTHIA.

Claire: French; "clear, bright." In the 19th century, this name was commonly used for men. Gradually, however, the name came to be used ordinarily for women. Actress Claire Danes got her start in show business on TV's *My So-Called Life* before moving on to the silver screen, with roles in films like *How to Make an American Quilt, The Rainmaker,* and *The Hours.* Spelling variations include **Clair** and **Clare.**

Clara: Latin; the feminine of *clarus,* "bright," but more directly from one of the several saints so named. Used in the Middle Ages, Clara was revived in the Romantic period, maintaining its popularity in the United States throughout the 19th century. The name is moderately common today. Humanitarian Clara Barton founded the American Red Cross, while actress Clara Bow starred in numerous silent films of the 1920s, including *Wings.*

Clarice: English, French; "bright." Clarice is a variant of CLAIRE. Antiquers are always on the lookout for the highly collectible work of Clarice Cliff, a top potter from the 1930s. Clarice Starling proved herself to be the only person gentle yet brave enough to go head to head with Dr. Hannibal Lecter in Thomas Harris's contemporary crime books, including *The Silence of the Lambs.*

Clarissa: Latin; "brilliant." Various forms evolved in France from CLARA, such as CLARICE and **Clarisse.** The novelist Samuel Richardson apparently Latinized (or Hellenized) the name to produce the heroine of his novel *Clarissa Harlowe* (circa 1747). We have here the rare case of a name that evolved from Latin to French and then back to Latin. It appears occasionally in American usage.

Claudia: Latin; the feminine of Claudius, a tribal name that derives from *claudus,* "lame." It was a common name under the Roman Empire, and some half-dozen saints are named Claudius. In the United States, it's been somewhat common — today, it ranks 221st. Among famous Claudias is German-born supermodel Claudia Schiffer.

Colleen: Gaelic; "girl." Colleen has fallen in popularity of late, sinking to 546th on the Social Security Administration's 2002 list of the most popular names for girls, but if you're looking for an Irish name, it's a classic choice. Emmy Award-winning actress Colleen Dewhurst will be remembered for her performance in *Anne of Green Gables* and as Candice Bergen's mother on the hit TV show *Murphy Brown.* Variations include **Collena, Collene**, and **Colene.**

Cora: Greek; "maiden, daughter." Cora first appeared in the United States around the end of the 19th century. In recent years, the name has become more common, rising from the 859th most popular name for girls in 1992 to the 467th most popular in 2002. Corazon Aquino, sometimes known as Cory, served as the president of the Philippines from 1986 to 1992.

Corinna: Greek; "maiden." In England, the writer Robert Herrick used this name for his famous poem "Corinna's Going A-Maying" (1648), and from there, it's been taken over as an actual name, although its appearances in America did not occur until the 19th century. **Corinne** is the French form, which was somewhat popularized by Madame de Staël's novel *Corinne* (1807). Whoopi Goldberg starred in *Corinna, Corinna,* a 1994 film about a housekeeper who develops a romantic relationship with her boss, a widower played by actor Ray Liotta.

Courtney: French; originally derived from a man's name **Courtenay,** meaning "short." Smart and sexy Courtney Thorne Smith is usually the epitome of poise in a cast full of weirdoes *(Melrose Place, Ally McBeal).* Courteney Cox Arquette remains one of America's favorite *Friends,* and who could forget one of the most recognized females in the music industry, Courtney Love? The name has consistently ranked among the 100 most popular names for girls, reaching as high as 19th in 1995. Alternative spellings include **Courtny.**

☺ ☺ ☹ ☺ ☺ ☹ ☺ ☺ ☹ ☺ ☺ ☹ ☺ ☺ ☹ ☺ ☺ ☺ ☺ ☹ ☺

Cristina: See CHRISTINA.

Crystal: English; used as a pet name for CHRISTOPHER, especially in Scotland. Today, this name is falling in popularity from a peak in 1991 at No. 42, but it remains near the top 150 girls' names in use. In 1976, Crystal Gayle broke records by taking country music over to the pop charts as her album containing the song "Don't It Make My Brown Eyes Blue?" became the first by a female country artist to sell over a million copies. Alternate spellings include **Christal**, **Christel**, **Christelle**, **Kristal**, **Krystal**, and **Krystle**, the latter made popular in the 1980s by Linda Evans, who portrayed *Dynasty's* Krystle Carrington.

Cynthia: Greek; "from Mount Cynthos." An epithet of the ancient Greek moon goddess Artemis. Artemis was a virgin goddess, and in the later 16th century, the poets often celebrated Elizabeth, "the Virgin Queen," by comparing her with Artemis, often using the name Cynthia. Thus inspired, a few uses of the name are cited in England from the 17th century. Cynthia was very rare in America in the 19th century. For some unknown reason, however, it became popular in England at the end of that century and also began to be used freely in America. In the 1970s, it rose to fifth place. Noteworthy bearers of this name include *Sex and the City* actress Cynthia Nixon and children's book author Cynthia Leitich Smith. The shortened forms are **Cindy** and **Cyndy.**

D

Dakota: The name of a Native American tribe. A name that evokes images of expansive Western vistas, Dakota is suitable for a boy or girl, although it's considerably more common among the former. Young actress Dakota Fanning has appeared in such films as *Uptown Girls* and *The Cat in the Hat.* An alternate spelling is **Dakotah.**

Dana: English; "Danish, from Denmark." Dana was used occasionally as a given name for men in the 19th century. Since the 20th century, however, the name has been used for women. The shift to femininity probably results from the fact that Dana looks like what the average American considers to be a name for a woman — particularly its ending in *a*. Dana Delany gained fame as the military nurse Colleen McMurphy on TV's *China Beach*, while child star Dana Plato, who died of a drug overdose in 1999, costarred on the hit show *Diff'rent Strokes.*

Danielle: Hebrew; "God is my judge." The feminine version of DANIEL. Having peaked at No. 18 a decade ago, Danielle is less common today, but it's still quite a popular name. Danielle Steel remains one of the most prolific and well-accepted writers in U.S. history, having sold more than 500 million copies of her books. Derivatives and similar-sounding names include **Daniele, Dannell, Daniela, Daniella, Dannia, Danila, Danise, Danice, Danna, Dannon, Dannah, Dannalee, Dania, Danya. Dani** is a common nickname.

☺ ☹ ☻ ☺ ☹ ☻ ☺ ☹ ☻ ☺ ☹ ☻ ☺ ☺ ☹ ☻ ☺

Darian: Latin; meaning unknown. Darian perhaps comes from **Daria** ("queenly"), a third-century Greek woman martyred under the Roman Empire. The name is used far more extensively in Britain than in the United States and combines a number of popular naming elements in a unique way. The name has many variations, including **Darion, Darien, Daryn,** and **Darria**.

Dawn: English; "the beginning of a new day." Described by one source as "a 20th-Century invention of novelette writers," Dawn has failed to gain widespread popularity, even though it offers advantages like brevity and euphony. The name has become even less common of late, failing to rank among the Social Security Administration's 2002 list of the 1,000 most popular names for girls. This lackluster history probably explains why there are few notable Dawns to speak of. One exception is Australian swimmer Dawn Fraser, who in the 1950s and '60s won the same race in three consecutive Olympic Games — to date, she's still the only swimmer to have accomplished this feat. An alternate spelling is **Daunn.**

Deborah: Hebrew; "bee." Deborah's meaning is unusual for a personal name, and it may (like other early biblical names) represent a name borrowed from one of the many languages with which early Hebrews were in contact. As prophetess, poet, and ruler of the people, the great Deborah (Judges 5) was encroaching upon fields of endeavor that the Puritans reserved for males. Like ABIGAIL, Deborah scarcely appears until after 1675. It then enjoyed some popularity, only to decline sharply in the early 19th century. In 1863, Victorian writer Charlotte Mary Yonge stated that the name was no longer used in England "except by the peasantry." Revived once more in the 20th century, it prospered, and for children born near the mid-1900s, it stood close to the top. Today, however, this name seems dated, and it's not longer among the top 500. Famous bearers of this name include actresses Deborah Kerry, Debra Winger, and Debbie Reynolds, as well as pop singer Debbie Gibson. Variations and nicknames include **Debora, Debra, Debbie,** and **Deb.**

Delaney: An English adaptation of a French locative surname, probably something like del Aunay. Appropriate for a boy or a girl, Delaney gained footing as a first name over the course of the 1990s. It ranked as the 183rd most popular name for baby girls in 2002, rising from 934th in 1991. As a surname, notable Delaneys include the actresses Dana and Kim Delaney.

Denise: French; the feminine form of DENNIS. Like its masculine counterpart, but to a lesser degree, it saw an increase in use in the later 20th century. Actress Denise Richards starred alongside Matt Dillon in *Wild Things* and as a Bond girl in *The World Is Not Enough*.

Desiree: French; "the desired one." Victorian-feminist author Kate Chopin popularized the name in the 1920s with her short story "Desiree's Baby," in which the main character transforms from a symbol of weakness into a stronger, more independent woman. Variations and nicknames include

Desire, Desirae, Desideria, Desaree, Desarae, Dezirae, Deziree, and **Des.**

Destiny: English; "certain fortune" and "fate." Destiny was also the name of the God of fate who was worshiped by the Babylonians. The name ranked among the 50 most popular names for baby girls from 1997 to 2002. Variants and nicknames of Destiny include **Destinie, Destinee, Destin,** and **Des.**

Diana: Latin; "little goddess." The name of the virgin goddess whose Greek counterpart was Artemis. Her name was well known among the European aristocracy of the Renaissance, a period in which the authority of the church was slack. One of the first modern uses of the name was that by Diane de Poitiers, mistress of King Henry II of France. Diana made little impression on the United States until the mid-20th century, when the French form **Diane** became popular enough to make the top ten on occasion. In that period, the name was plagued by the development of many spelling variants, such as **Deanna, Deanne,** and **Dyanne.** Today, Diana is considerably more popular than Diane. Famous bearers of this name include singer Diana Ross, talk-show host Diane Rehm, and actresses Diane Keaton and Diane Lane.

Dina: Hebrew; "judged, vindicated, avenged." Dina was first used with some regularity in the 16th century, when it was popular among the Puritans. Interestingly, when Dina made her way to the United States, the name was preferred by African Americans in the southern states. Dina is also a Biblical name; she was the daughter of Leah and Jacob. Dina is sometimes a shorter form of names like Bernardina (where it sometimes becomes Deena). A common variation of Dina is **Dinah,** the feminine version of DEAN. Dinah Shore was a popular talk show host in the early years, way before anyone had ever heard of a certain woman named Oprah.

Dominique: French; "belonging to God," "of God." Dominique is the feminine version of DOMINIC; its visibility has increased since the 1960s. Interestingly, *two* popular women named Dominique are champion gymnasts: Dominique Dawes and Dominique Moceanu. Basketball star Dominique Wilkins is one of the better-known male Dominiques.

Dora: Greek; "gift." Although the ending in *a* is unusual, Dora probably should be considered merely a short form of **Dorothy.** The name is rare, but it was found occasionally in the 19th century. Today, it's still uncommon, but the cartoon heroine Dora the Explorer just might change that in the coming years.

Drew: Old French; from the given name Drogo, meaning "to carry, to bear" (more rarely as a short form of ANDREW or from a French nickname meaning "sturdy" — all unrelated). Although its meaning suggests masculinity, Drew is a girl's name as well; actress Drew Barrymore is one popular example. Actor and comedian Drew Carey and NFL quarterback Drew Bledsoe are other well-known male Drews. It's occasionally spelled **Dru** or **Drue.**

☺ ☻ ☹ ☺ ☻ ☹ ☺ ☻ ☹ ☺ ☻ ☹ ☺ ☻ ☹ ☺ ☺ ☻ ☹ ☺

Dylan: Welsh; "ocean," "wave." In Welsh mythology, Dylan was a god of the sea who died when his uncle accidentally killed him. The name was in the top 50 most popular names for boys in the late 1990s and, in the United States, is making headway as a name for girls as well. Welsh-born poet Dylan Thomas is known for his fluid and powerful poetry. American singer/songwriter Bob Dylan was born Robert Zimmerman but took the poet's name as his own as a tribute. He writes and sings folksy songs that have an elemental attraction as strong as the tide. **Dillon** is an alternate spelling.

E

Eden: Hebrew; "place of pleasure, paradise, and delight." In the Bible, the home of the first man and woman — Adam and Eve — was called Eden. Perhaps in an effort to regain that wondrous atmosphere, Eden is a popular name for fictional characters — especially soap opera characters. *The Guiding Light* and *Santa Barbara* both followed the attempts of Edens to find daytime delight. In Woody Allen's movie *Bullets Over Broadway*, Tracey Ullman's Eden Brent is a slightly skewed namesake. Michelle Rodriguez as a surfer-babe named Eden gave young men a glimpse of paradise in the movie *Blue Crush*. Actress Barbara Eden brought viewers of television's *I Dream of Jeannie* to a fantastical version of one man's imagined paradise. An alternate spelling is **Edan,** although that spelling has a Gaelic derivation.

Eileen: Gaelic; "light." Though actually from an Irish name, Eibhilin, Eileen is an Irish borrowing and adaptation of the English EVELYN. It shared in the general revival of Irish names in the 20th century, although it was scarcely used before then. One-hit wonder Dexy's Midnight Runners gave us the ditty "Come on Eileen" in the early 1980s. **Aileen** is a second spelling option.

Elaine: French; an adaptation of a Greek name that means "light." Elaine is the medieval French form of HELEN, occurring in Malory's *Morte D'Arthur*. From that work, Tennyson took it for his *Idylls of the King* in the mid-19th century, and it has remained in occasional use. Julia Louis-Dreyfus played the irrepressible Elaine Benes on the wildly popular sitcom *Seinfeld.*

Elena: Latin; a form of a Greek word meaning "light." A form of HELEN, Elena is a popular girl's name in a wide range of cultures. Russian playwright Anton Chekhov used the name in his famous play, *Uncle Vanya* (although the spelling is usually **Ilenya**). American actress Joan Allen played a somewhat dark Elena Hood in *The Ice Storm*. In *The Mask of Zorro*, Welsh actress Catherine Zeta-Jones lit up the silver screen and ignited her career with her illuminating turn as Elena Montero/Elena Murrleta — the daughter stolen from Anthony Hopkins's Zorro and raised as the daughter of his enemy. A few of the numerous spelling variations include **Alena, Elaina** and **Ilyena.**

☺ ☹ ☹ ☺ ☹ ☹ ☺ ☺ ☹ ☹ ☺ ☺ ☹ ☺ ☹ ☹ ☺ ☺ ☹ ☹ ☺

Elizabeth: Hebrew; "God has sworn," with reference to the oath or covenant that God swore to Abraham (Genesis 17). The spelling with z has been the regular English usage, s (**Elisabeth**) indicating French influence. The name was borne by the mother of John the Baptist (Luke 1). The name entered the royal family in the 15th century, from Elizabeth Woodville, the queen of King Edward IV. The still rare name eventually passed on to the younger daughter of King Henry VIII. In her early years, that Elizabeth was little known, but circumstances put her into the position of being the symbol of Protestantism as opposed to her Catholic sister Mary. One curious result of this rivalry was the sudden popularizing of the name Elizabeth. Elizabeth Tudor eventually became queen and ruled gloriously for almost half a century, usually with great personal popularity. The glamour of the queen, who was a symbol of the nation itself, shed glamour also on her name. Elizabeth was the leading woman's name in that reign, and so continued into the 17th century, after the queen's death. Also much favored during her actual reign was the Latinate form **Eliza.** The classical tastes of the times kept Eliza in a strong position until the 19th century, when **Lizzie** and **Liz** began to take over. In the 20th century, **Beth** showed some strength, as did **Betty.** For the past decade, it's consistently been between 9th and 11th. Notable bearers of the name Elizabeth are many: Queen Elizabeth I and II, actress Elizabeth Taylor, suffragist Elizabeth Cady Stanton, politician Elizabeth Dole, and actress/model Elizabeth Hurley.

Ella: An English borrowing of a French form of an Old German name, occurring in the post-Conquest period but of uncertain meaning. It's easily confused with HELEN and ELLEN, and its history is comparable. It passed through a period of popularity in the mid-19th century but didn't attain the status of Helen until recently — since 1991, it's jumped more than 900 spots to break into the top 100. Its brevity and easy phonetic quality led to its use in compounds, such as **Ellamay.** Ella on its own draws references to legendary blues singer Ella Fitzgerald, which many people find to be a favorable comparison. BELLA and STELLA are similar-sounding options.

Ellen: Having begun as a form of HELEN (Greek; "bright"), Ellen is now an independent name, particularly common in Scotland. Like Helen, it rose in popularity in the 19th century under the influence of Romanticism, reaching its height at about 1850. Famous Ellens include comedian Ellen DeGeneres, journalist Ellen Goodman, and actresses Ellen Barkin and Ellen Burstyn.

Emily: Latin; from the Roman family name Aemilius, "eager to please," "industrious." The curious circumstance of this name's being current only in the feminine reinforces the likelihood that its use sprang primarily from literary sources, such as Chaucer. It didn't come into common use until after 1800, and its continuing popularity in the 19th century can be attributed partly to its taking over of the name Amelia and partly to Romanticism. It's also pleasant sounding and thus is suitable for poetry. Today, Emily is the top name for baby girls, so if you want your daughter to have the name of the moment, this is it. With EMMA and Emmeline, it shares the nickname **Emmy.** Alternate spellings that also reside among

Chapter 3: Gennifer, Gina, or Genevieve? Names for Girls

☺ ☺ ☹ ☺ ☺ ☹ ☺ ☺ ☹ ☺ ☺ ☹ ☺ ☺ ☹ ☺ ☺ ☺ ☹ ☺

the top 500 names in use include **Emely, Emilie,** and **Emilee.** Emily Dickinson penned such poems as "I Felt a Funeral in My Brain" and "She Sweeps with Many-Colored Brooms." Emily Watson was nominated for Best Actress Academy Awards for her performances in *Hilary & Jackie* and *Breaking the Waves.*

Emma: Old German; "whole, universal." It was a much-favored name among the Normans, and it persisted strongly throughout the Middle Ages. The name fell into disuse in the 16th century, and it hardly existed in the American colonies. With the Romantic interest in the Middle Ages came a revival of Emma, and by the middle of the 19th century, the name was sometimes making the top ten. By the middle of the century, that popularity had fallen off sharply, and for much of the 20th century, the name was only moderately common. At the close of the century, though, Emma's fortunes turned dramatically, with the name rising from the 125th most popular name for baby girls in 1991 to the 4th most popular in 2002. Nicknames include **Em** and **Emmy.** Emma Thompson has won two Academy Awards: in the Best Actress category for her performance in *Howards End* and in the Best Adapted Screenplay category for *Sense and Sensibility.*

Erica: Scandinavian, Latin; "honorable leader," "heather." In the United States, the male form ERIC is closely connected with Scandinavian immigration, showing up in lists of names toward the middle of the 19th century. Erica is also the Latin name of the plant known in English as heather, and so may be the occasional source of the name from the late 19th century on among namers who had taken up the fad of drawing girls' names from flowers and bushes. Fans of daytime drama surely are familiar with the legendary Erica Kane, from *All My Children.* Writer Erica Jong is best known for her sexually frank novel *Fear of Flying.* For a more exotic feel, try the alternate spellings **Erika** or **Eryka,** used by singer Eryka Badu.

Erin: Gaelic; "belonging to Ireland," "of Ireland." The anglicized spelling of the original Irish is **Eirinn,** from which both male and female versions of the name are derived. *Happy Days* fans will remember Erin Moran, the actress who played Ritchie Cunningham's little sister Joanie. Another popular television family boasted an Erin also — Mary Beth McDonough made Erin Walton her own ("Goodnight, John-Boy"). Probably the most notable Erin of recent memory is Erin Brockovich, the environmental crusader and the subject of the movie that garnered actress Julia Roberts an Academy Award. Today, Erin is among the top 75 names for girls.

Esmeralda: Spanish; "emerald." Esmeralda is fairly common, ranking as the 207th most popular name for baby girls in 2002 — maybe due in part to the fact that the name appears in the Disney animated films *Cinderella* and *The Hunchback of Notre Dame.* **Esme** is a potential nickname, although it's also a given name in its own right.

Etta: American; "ruler of the home." This Italian diminutive suffix, as in **Henrietta,** developed the ability to stand on its own in the late 19th century. It's never been a wildly popular name, but its use has remained steady. Soulful singer Etta James is the best-known holder of this moniker.

Eve: Hebrew; "life-giving." As Eve was believed to have brought sin into the world, and because her friendship with the serpent was not to her credit, her name was not a popular one. During the Middle Ages, Eve was a reasonably common name. However, the Puritan colonists didn't seem to use it at all, and in other colonies, it was rare. The appearance of little **Eva** in Harriet Beecher Stowe's 1852 novel *Uncle Tom's Cabin* lent some popularity to the name in the Latinized form, while the 1950 film *All About Eve*, starring Bette Davis, kept it in the minds of mid-20th-century namers. Eva Gabor of *Green Acres* fame was known for her many marriages. Rapper Eve proves that this very old name hasn't gone out of use.

Evelyn: An English adaptation of a French diminutive of the Old German root *Avi*, meaning "eager." In Great Britain, this name is pronounced with a long *e* and is used for either a man or a woman; in the United States, it has a short *e* and is used almost exclusively for women. Dating from the Normans, the feminine usage is older. It's a viable name in the United States, but Evelyn has never been common. The feminine **Evelina,** which flourished in the Middle Ages, may be the original form. With its three quickly pronounced syllables, Evelyn has a musical quality to it. Consider it if you're looking for a traditional, more formal-sounding name. Sprinter Evelyn Ashford participated in three different Olympiads (1984, 1988, 1992), winning four gold medals in her career. The name Evelyn is commonly shortened to **Eve** or **Lynn.**

F

Faith: Latin; "trust, belief." Faith is a common word in the New Testament. As a name, it derives from the famous 13th chapter of I Corinthians — "And now abideth faith, hope, charity . . . ." The meager use of this name, as well as HOPE and Charity, in New England may be a result of their common use in Elizabethan England — the colonists didn't want to associate themselves with those they had left behind. Beautiful singer Faith Hill gives country music fans someone to be faithful to, while actress Faith Ford played a perky counterpoint to Murphy Brown (portrayed by Candice Bergen) in the popular 1980s TV series of the same name.

Fatima: Arabic. Fatima was the daughter of the prophet Mohammed and the wife of the fourth Muslim caliph, Ali. This name is popular in the Spanish-speaking community, as well as among the Arabic population, perhaps because it's the name of a town in Portugal where, legend has it, the Virgin Mary revealed herself six times to three shepherd children. Alternative music fans may be familiar with the 1990s Camper Van Beethoven song "Eye of Fatima."

Felicia: Latin; "great happiness." One of several feminine forms of the name FELIX, Felicia is one of the more graceful variations. Fictional

Felicias include Felicia the tattoo artist in Ray Bradbury's book *The Illustrated Man.* In the movie *Priscilla, Queen of the Desert,* Guy Pearce plays a man pursuing happiness as drag queen Felicia Jollygoodfellow. For real-life Felicias, turn to early 19th-century poet Felicia Hemans, a contemporary of Shelley (with whom she corresponded for a time) and Byron. A more modern Felicia is Felicia Bond, who illustrates the popular children's books *If You Give a Mouse a Cookie, If You Give a Moose a Muffin,* and so on. **Felice, Felicidad,** and **Felicity** are all variations of Felicia.

Finn: Gaelic; "white," "fair." Used for both boys and girls, although mostly for boys, Finn is a form of the anglicized Irish name **Fionn.** An early Irishman with the name was Fionn Mac Cumhail, a third-century hero along the lines of Robin Hood, who reportedly gained wisdom when he ate an enchanted fish. Another fair fighter from the American Old West was Finn Clanton, one of the Clanton Boys, who, legend has it, fought it out with the Earp brothers and Doc Holliday at the O.K. Corral. The most famous fictional Finn is found in tales by Mark Twain — Huckleberry Finn. Like Huck, a girl with this name is likely to be independent and headstrong. Variations of Finn include **Fin, Findlay, Finlay, Findley,** and **Finley.**

Fiona: Gaelic; "white." This name was apparently coined by the Scottish author William Sharp (1855 to 1905); he used it as a pseudonym. (Actually, the term "literary *persona*" may be more accurate, since he didn't admit to the identification.) The name is a feminization of the Gaelic masculine name **Fionn.** It's been used occasionally in America, chiefly in the late 19th century. Singer Fiona Apple released her debut album, *Tidal,* in 1996 at the age of 18; the LP earned a spot on the Top 40 charts, driven by the single "Shadowboxer." This name certainly isn't topping the charts these days, but it is among the top 350 girls' names.

Francesca: The Italian version of FRANCES. If you have a romantic spirit, this melodious, though rare, name may be an excellent choice for your daughter. It conjures up images of lush Tuscan fields and tranquil Venetian canals. Piero della Francesca was a prominent artist in the 1400s. **Fran** is a nickname, as is FRANNIE.

G

Gabriela: Spanish; the feminine form of the Hebrew name GABRIEL, which is often translated as "God gives strength." Gabriel was the archangel who told Mary that she would give birth to God's son. One hero to her fellow Argentines — and tennis fans everywhere — is tennis player Gabriela Sabatini, a strong presence on the professional women's tennis circuit in the 1980s and '90s. She won the U.S. Tennis Open in 1990 and was an even more successful doubles player, winning the French Open and Wimbledon women's doubles finals. In *Gabriela, Clove and Cinnamon,* Brazilian author Jorge Amado wrote a book about a heroic Gabriela — a woman who emerges triumphant through changing cultural

Parent's Success Guide to Baby Names

☺ ☺ ☹ ☺ ☺ ☹ ☺ ☺ ☹ ☺ ☺ ☹ ☺ ☺ ☹ ☺ ☺ ☺ ☹ ☺

mores. **Gabriella** is an alternate spelling from the French and Italian; nicknames include **Gaby, Gabby, Gabbee, Gabbie,** and **Brie.** Both Gabriela and Gabriella are among the top 100 names given to baby girls in the United States today.

Gabrielle: French; from the Hebrew name GABRIEL, which means "God gives strength," "God's able-bodied one." This 67th most popular name appears in Anne Rice's series of books, *The Vampire Chronicles*, in which Lestat "saves" his beautiful mother, Gabrielle de Lioncourt, from death. Another fictional Gabrielle is the spunky, comedic sidekick on television's *Xena: Warrior Princess*. A real-life Gabrielle is Gabby Reece, a professional volleyball player and sometime model. This name shares nicknames with the Spanish form GABRIELA.

Genesis: Hebrew; "birth." The first book of the Bible is Genesis, and it is here that the creation of the world and of the first humans is recounted. It's a strong name, suitable for either a boy or a girl, and naming a daughter Genesis ensures that the child comes into the world with history and tradition on her side.

Genevieve: Gaulish, through the French; meaning uncertain. It's a popular name in France, promoted by the adoption of St. Genevieve as the patron saint of Paris. In the United States, it's fairly rare. It's probably a literary name or else borrowed directly from the French. Bearers of this name are often nicknamed **Genny.** Designer Genevieve Gorder brings a sassy touch to the home-improvement series *Trading Spaces.*

Gillian: See JILLIAN.

Ginger: English; "flower," "the spice." As a flower or as a spice, ginger is both subtle and spicy — traits that carry over to the most famous Ginger. Actress/dancer Ginger Rogers was a renowned dancer in her own right before hooking up on-screen with Fred Astaire, where, as the modern axiom goes, she did everything he did backwards and wearing high heels. Despite the positive association, this name is rare today. Variations include **Ginjer** and **Ginny.**

Giselle: The French form of an Old German name that means "pledge." *Giselle* is also the name of a ballet by Adolphe Adam, which is perhaps the most famous ballet of the Romantic era. It tells the story of a gentle and forgiving peasant girl, appropriately named Giselle. Probably because it sounds a lot like *gazelle,* the name seems graceful, like a ballerina. It's a rare name, but if you like names that sound foreign and romantic, it's an interesting option. Another Giselle affiliated with the arts is children's illustrator and author Giselle Potter, who gained critical acclaim with the release of her story, *The Year I Didn't Go to School.* An alternate spelling is **Gisselle**.

Glenda: Gaelic; "valley." A feminine form of Glen, Glenda evokes quiet and peace. Glenda came about as an American coinage that only later made its way to Britain. British actress Glenda Jackson could portray a

☺ ☻ ☹ ☺ ☻ ☹ ☺ ☻ ☹ ☺ ☻ ☹ ☺ ☻ ☹ ☺ ☺ ☻ ☹ ☺

quiet, peaceful country girl or a raging shrew. The Americanized version **Glennesha** is a possible derivation. And **Glinda,** the good witch from *The Wizard of Oz,* bears a variation of the name. Another form of Glenda is **Glenna; Glynnis** is similar.

Gloria: Latin; "glory." In the United States, its use seems to fall entirely within the 20th century. Although it may be called overemphatic and requiring rather too much of its bearer, it has maintained itself as a viable name. Feminist leader Gloria Steinem certainly lived up to the moniker through her work to earn equal rights for women.

Grace: English; "grace of God." As a name — at least in its earlier usage — it's to be taken in the theological sense, indicating a person who has attained, or hopes to attain, a state of grace — that is, one who is a recipient of God's favor or mercy. In some instances, Grace may be a translation of HANNAH or ANNA. In the 19th century and later, Grace became physical in its suggestion — that is, "a graceful person." The name was current in the Puritan colonies and, to a lesser degree, in the non-Puritan colonies. Shifted to its later meaning, it enjoyed a brief period of mild prosperity in the late 19th century. It's still current — in fact, it's among the most popular girls' names in use today. **Gracie** is a common term of endearment for bearers of this name. The actress Grace Kelly starred in several Hitchcock films, including the classic *Rear Window,* before exiting show business to become a princess — literally — by marrying Prince Rainier III of Monaco. And the TV series *Will and Grace* has legions of fans.

Gretchen: German; originally a nickname for MARGARET, which means "little pearl." This classic name is not particularly popular today. Actress Gretchen Mol gained attention for her work in movies such as *Cradle Will Rock* and *Sweet and Lowdown.* Country music fans are certainly familiar with singer-songwriter Gretchen Peters, winner of 1995's Country Music Association's Song of the Year, "Independence Day," recorded by Martina McBride.

Guadalupe: Spanish; similar to CARMEN, this is one of the Spanish names inspired by the attributes of the Virgin Mary — in this case, by a miraculous vision of the Virgin at Guadalupe in Spain. It's suitable for a boy or girl, although it's more common as a feminine name. Today, it sits at No. 250 on the list of the most common baby names in use in the United States. **Lupe** (pronounced "LOO-pay," not "LOOP") is a common nickname.

Gwen: Welsh; based on *fionn,* meaning "white" and "fair, blessed." Often considered a diminutive of GWENDOLYN, Gwen also stands alone as a distinctive girl's name. Gwen Ifill is the moderator and managing editor of *Washington Week,* a public affairs program, and a senior reporter for *The NewsHour with Jim Lehrer,* a nightly news show on the PBS. Gwen Stefani is the navel-baring lead singer for the band No Doubt. A variant of the name is **Gwynn** (in Welsh usage, it's a boys' name, with either one or two *n*s).

Ten popular Spanish names

Here are ten common Spanish names for girls.

- Gabriela
- Ana
- Alejandra
- Paola
- Esmeralda
- Selena
- Guadalupe
- Yesenia
- Mercedes
- Carmen

Gwendolyn: A name coined by Geoffrey of Monmouth, the man responsible for much of early Arthurian legend. He probably created it from a misreading of the Welsh masculine name Guendoleu as Guendolen. American poet Gwendolyn Brooks was the first African-American poet to win the Pulitzer Prize. An uncommon spelling variation of this rare name is **Gwyndolyn,** and **Gwen** is the usual nickname.

H

Hailey: English, Gaelic; "hay meadow." An uncommon yet distinctive name for either a boy or a girl, Haley is adaptable to many different spellings, including **Haley, Haleigh, Hailee,** and **Hayley.** The twin sisters whom actress Haley Mills played in the movie *The Parent Trap* exhibited ingeniousness in getting their divorced parents back together.

Hallie: English; as a surname, from a place name meaning "meadow at the hall" ("hall" in this case means "great hall, mansion"). **Halle** and **Hally** are alternate spellings. All three forms are considerably less popular than Haley and Hailey, although Hallie does appear at No. 356. Actress Halle Berry won an Academy Award for her performance as a damaged widow trying to rebuild her life in the film *Monster's Ball*. She also received acclaim — and an Emmy — for her portrayal of Dorothy Dandridge in a made-for-television movie.

Chapter 3: Gennifer, Gina, or Genevieve? Names for Girls

☺ ☺ ☹ ☺ ☺ ☹ ☺ ☺ ☹ ☺ ☺ ☹ ☺ ☺ ☹ ☺ ☺ ☹ ☺

Hannah: Hebrew, "grace." Hannah appears in I Samuel as Samuel's mother, herself a prophet. The name is the same as ANNA, being so spelled in the Greek of the New Testament. As pronounced, the two names differ little, and in an *h*-dropping environment, they would be indistinguishable. A tradition for the use of both Hannah and Anna existed in England at the time of heavy migration to New England, the latter being common, the former rare. In the Puritan colonies, the situation rapidly reversed. In a Boston list of births in the 1640s, Hannah appears 45 times, topping ELIZABETH and SARAH and barely being exceeded by MARY. As late as the first quarter of the 19th century, Hannah still occurred among the top ten most popular names for girls. Shortly after, however, Hannah rapidly disappeared, with Anna becoming correspondingly common. By the middle of the 19th century, the palindromic Hannah (it spells the same word forwards and backwards) was all but obsolete. Over the course of the 20th century, though, the name regained its footing. Today, it stands as a perennial top-five favorite, ranking as the third most popular name for baby girls in 2002. During the Holocaust, the Jewish political theorist Hannah Arendt fled from Germany to France and then from France to the United States, where she established herself as one of the most compelling intellectuals of the 20th century. Hannah Storm has served as a co-anchor of CBS's *The Early Show* as well as a reporter for NBC Sports.

Harper: English; "harp player." Harper is suitable for a boy or girl, although it has become uncommon for both. Harper Lee authored the classic novel *To Kill a Mockingbird*, which was later adapted into a film starring Gregory Peck as the virtuous father and small-town lawyer Atticus Finch. (Bruce Willis and Demi Moore took the name Scout, another central character in this book, for one of their daughters.)

Hart: English; "deer." Although it's more common as a last name, Hart can be a distinguished first or middle name for a boy or girl. Actor Hart Bocher carries the name with distinction. Playwright Moss Hart teamed with George Kaufman to write plays in the 1930s and '40s that took Broadway by storm, such as *You Can't Take It with You* and *The Man Who Came to Dinner*. On his own, he continued to write outstanding dramas, including *Winged Victory*.

Haylee, Hayley: See HAILEY.

Heather: One of several names that comes from a plant or flower. See ERICA and LILY.

Heidi: German; a pet form of Adelheide, meaning "noble + sort." The name may be from two sources. First, it may be (shown in such forms as **Hedy** and **Heidy**) from the Germanic Hedwig, "refuge war." Second, it appears as **Haidee,** for a Greek girl, in Byron's *Don Juan*, with no clear source, and perhaps to be considered primarily a Romantic coinage for poetry. It was rare in the United States until the mid-20th century, when it appeared occasionally. Today, it maintains modest popularity. Famous

carriers of this name include the model Heidi Klum and the "Hollywood Madam" Heidi Fleiss.

Helen: Greek; "bright light." Beginning with Helen of Troy, this name assumed a post-classical Latin form, HELENA. This was the name of the mother of the Emperor Constantine. Sainted, and closely associated with the story of the discovery of the True Cross, she passed her name on to the nations of western Europe. In medieval England (as Helen, Helena, or ELLEN), the name had some currency, but with the Reformation, being that of a nonbiblical saint, it nearly disappeared in English. It survived, chiefly as Ellen, in the non-Puritan colonies. Under the influence of Romanticism, Helen became suddenly popular toward the middle of the 19th century. Phonetically attractive, it became a poet's word, as in Poe's "To Helen." Around 1900, it was one of the most popular names. By the middle of the 20th century, however, the popularity had receded, and little has changed since then. In contemporary times, the name holds scant popularity, perhaps being perceived as old-fashioned.

Helena: Greek; "bright light." British actress Helena Bonham Carter bears this rare name with elegance and strength. William Shakespeare used the name in two of his lighter plays — *A Midsummer Night's Dream* and *All's Well That Ends Well.*

Hillary: Latin; "cheerful." As a first name, Hillary is distinctly feminine, although Sir Edmund Hilary, climber of Mount Everest, bears it as a last name. The name has experienced a dramatic drop in popularity in recent years, falling from 136th in 1992 to the high 800s in 2002. Distinguished female Hillarys include former First Lady and U.S. Senator Hillary Rodham Clinton (who, given the timing of the drop in status of the name, may be largely responsible). **Hilary** is an alternate spelling. Young star Hilary Duff was the focus of not one but two television series — *Cadet Kelly* and *Lizzie McGuire* — while still in her teens. Given these two examples, they may have to add "accomplished" to the meaning of the name.

Holden: English; "hollow, valley." Traditionally a boy's name, Holden is also a distinctive name for a girl. The name immediately brings to mind the main character in author J. D. Salinger's novel *The Catcher in the Rye.* Although the protagonist, Holden Caulfield, is a troubled and ultimately tragic figure, his engrossing account of himself has become shorthand to express teenage angst. Alternate spellings include **Holdan** and **Holdun.**

Holly: One of several names that comes from a plant or flower. See LILY.

Hope: English; "hope." The common English word furnished an occasional name in early New England — ordinarily for women, but occasionally for men. Curiously, the members of the famous trio "faith, hope, and charity" are so rare as names in the 17th century that historians search for some special reason for their disbarment. Hope, like GRACE, survived, however. It's found down to the present, and it regularly ranks among the 200 most popular names for baby girls. Hope Sandoval emerged on the music scene

Chapter 3: Gennifer, Gina, or Genevieve? Names for Girls

☺ ☺ ☹ ☺ ☺ ☹ ☺ ☺ ☹ ☺ ☺ ☹ ☺ ☺ ☹ ☺ ☺ ☺ ☹ ☺

as the vocalist in the alternative-rock duo Mazzy Star before embarking on a solo career, while actress Hope Davis has appeared in such acclaimed films as *About Schmidt.*

I

India: The name of a densely populated country in Asia. As a first name, India has an exotic quality. Singer india arie, with her unusual lack of capitalization, has brought prominence to this name in recent years. **Indie** is a possible nickname.

Ingrid: Old Norse; from Ingir, the name of an ancient hero, and *rida,* a word that means "ride." In the United States, this name was originally limited to Scandinavian immigrants, but since the mid-20th century, it's been used more generally, borrowed from stage and screen. Iconic actress Ingrid Bergman, born in Sweden, surely helped bring popularity to the name. Bergman radiated sophistication in Hollywood films like *Casablanca, Murder on the Orient Express,* and Alfred Hitchcock's *Spellbound* and *Notorious.* Any girl with this name is bound to be compared to her.

Irene: Greek; "peace(ful)." This name appeared in the late 19th century on both sides of the Atlantic. The three-syllable pronunciation "eye-REE-nee" that the British use is close to the classical Greek, suggesting that the name was brought into English self-consciously and at a sophisticated or learned level — that is, by someone who had studied Greek. The name may have entered American usage in writing rather than orally, so the pronunciation became that which the spelling suggested: "eye-REEN." Irene enjoyed mild popularity in the earlier 20th century, and a highly popular song of the 1950s gave the name much publicity. Today, it's less common but still in use. Jim Carrey and Renee Zellweger starred in the 2000 movie *Me, Myself, and Irene.*

Iris: One of many flower- and plant-related names, like LILY. The 2000 film *Iris* tells the story of writer Iris Murdoch and her struggle with Alzheimer's disease.

Isabella: Hebrew; "God has sworn" — a reference to the oath or covenant that God swore to Abraham (Genesis 17). Isabella is a girlish name whose second syllable, *-bella,* means "beautiful." That may be why it's so popular today, at No. 14 on the girls' list. Actress Isabella Rossellini (the daughter of Ingrid Bergman) has played a nun, as well as a wide variety of other roles, in her distinguished acting career. And Queen Isabela of Spain was at least partly responsible for the discovery of the Americas because she and her king, Ferdinand, funded Christopher Columbus's voyages of discovery in the late 15th century. **Isabela, Izabela,** and **Izabella** are alternate spellings, and **Isabel** and **Isabelle** are variations that are also quite popular among parents.

Ivana: Russian (among others); a feminine form of IVAN, and thus related to JOHN, originally from Hebrew, meaning "God is gracious." Probably the best-known Ivana is Ivana Trump, former spouse of wealthy power broker Donald Trump. After their divorce, Ivana made a name for herself in the beauty and fashion industry. Today, the name is rare in the United States.

Ivy: This fairly rare name may be from a family name or may refer to the plant (see also LILY). Dame Ivy Compton-Burnett was a prolific novelist in England whose novels focused on wealthy Victorian and Edwardian society. Ivy is also the name of an alternative pop band.

J

Jacqueline: French; a diminutive-feminine of JACQUES, the French equivalent of — you guessed it — JAMES. In English, though, it's equated with JACK, with **Jackie** as the most common nickname. Historically, Jacqueline has never been a common name, but in the past decade, it has consistently cracked the top 100, sometimes with the spelling **Jacquelyn.** (**Jaqueline** is another option.) Former first lady Jacqueline Kennedy Onassis brought style and grace to the White House. After her second husband, Greek oil tycoon Ari Onassis, died, she returned to New York and became a book editor. Jackie Joyner-Kersee is known as one of the greatest female athletes of all time and holds the world record in the heptathlon, despite having asthma. Author Jackie Susanne is best known for her bestselling first novel, *Valley of the Dolls*, about drug use in Hollywood.

Jada: Arabic; meaning unknown. The most famous bearer of this fairly popular name is Jada Pinkett Smith, who is adored for her roles in such films as *The Matrix Reloaded* and *The Nutty Professor*, with Eddie Murphy. To avoid the possible mispronunciation "JAD-ah," try the alternate spelling **Jayda.**

Jade: English; a precious stone. The green jewel jade is common in the Orient, thus the name may conjure up images of the Far East. This exotic association may be why the name has risen to 87th on the list of the most popular girls' names. **Jadine** is a related option.

Jaden: Hebrew; "God has heard." This name's popularity has skyrocketed in recent years: It's still more popular for boys, but for girls, it has broken into the top 250, and it's likely that it will continue to rise up the charts. Other possible spellings include **Jaiden** and **Jadyn.**

Jamie: From JAMES, a Hebrew name that means "following after," "supplanter." Since its modern-day peak at number 60 in 1990, the popularity of this name has fallen a little bit each year, but it remains in the top 200 names for girls. Jamie Lee Curtis, the daughter of Tony Curtis and Janet Leigh, made her acting debut in the horror film *Halloween* and also played major roles in *Trading Places*, with Eddie Murphy and Dan Aykroyd, and

True Lies, with Arnold Schwarzenegger. Today she's gaining prominence as a children's book writer.

Jane: The most common feminization of JOHN, which in Hebrew means "God is gracious." It apparently developed from the French. (After the Norman Conquest, the upper classes in England spoke French for several generations.) Although other forms of John, like Joan, JOANNA, and Jean, have kept Jane from reaching first place, Jane has often stood in third place behind MARY and ELIZABETH. In the early New England colonies, Jane was not much favored because it wasn't biblical. Elsewhere, it flourished in the 18th century and declined in the 19th. But it was often used as an auxiliary in names like Mary Jane. Around 1900, Jane became popular again — so much so that *jane* became slang for "girl." The Dick and Jane Readers that developed in the 1950s are further evidence that this name was considered very ordinary. When a name becomes so commonplace, its popularity naturally falls. But there are many, many past and present famous Janes, including writer Jane Austen; frontierswoman Martha "Calamity Jane" Burke; actress, political activist, and 1980s fitness guru Jane Fonda; filmmaker Jane Campion; and Jane Goodall, known for her groundbreaking work with primates in Africa despite the fact that she had no formal education in the field. If you don't want your daughter to be a plain Jane but you like the sound of this name, try **Jayne. Janie** is a common pet name.

Janelle: An American variation of JANE (from JOHN, Hebrew, "God is gracious"), with the suffix *-elle* added on. If Jane seems too dull, Janelle is a more upscale, French-sounding version. The fact that it sounds a lot like upscale designer Chanel certainly doesn't hurt in this regard. **Janel, Janell,** and **Jeanelle** are alternate spellings.

Janet: A diminutive of JANE, of French origin. It developed a strong Scottish usage and was highly popular in the 20th century. Its use has fallen off, but it's still among the top 500 names for girls. Singer Janet Jackson brought girl power — and great abs — to the pop music scene in the late 1980s. Janet Reno wielded a different form of power, serving as attorney general under President Bill Clinton. **Janette** and **Jeanette** are derivatives.

Janine: English; "gracious, merciful." A name more popular in the early part of the 20th century than in the latter, Janine is making a bit of a comeback in the 21st century as a feminine, but not *too* feminine, girl's name. The name is open to a variety of spellings — **Janeane, Janene, Jannine,** and **Janinne,** for example. Actress/comedian Janeane Garofalo uses a unique spelling, while actress Janine Turner, star of television's quirky *Northern Exposure* series, adopts a more traditional spelling. See also JANE.

Jasmine: Persian; "jasmine flower." The jasmine flower is associated with the Zodiac sign Gemini, so naming a girl born in late May through mid- to late June Jasmine is especially appropriate. Variations in spelling include

☺ ☺ ☹ ☺ ☺ ☹ ☺ ☺ ☹ ☺ ☺ ☹ ☺ ☺ ☹ ☺ ☺ ☺ ☺ ☹ ☺

Jasmin, Jazmin, Jazmine, Jasman, Jasmyn, and **Jazzmyn** — the name invites a great deal of creativity and is often used by creative types. Highly popular throughout the 1990s — Michael Jordan gave the name to his daughter — the name shows no signs of waning. Jasmine is the name of the princess in the animated movie *Aladdin*, released in 1992, which may explain part of the name's popularity.

Jayda: See JADA.

Jayden: See JADEN.

Jayla: English; "daughter of Jay." This name was created by combining the male name JAY and the traditionally feminine suffix *–la*. It currently sits at No. 211 among the most popular names in use. Traditionally, Jay is used in reference to the blue jay, or jaybird.

Jenna: See JANE. Jenna, along with alternate spellings **Jena** and **Jennah,** was a very popular girl's name in the 1990s and remains a feminine standby. American actress Jena Malone started garnering awards and nominations as soon as she started acting. She plays the young Jodie Foster in *Contact* and stars in the movie adaptation of the bestselling novel *Cold Mountain*. Jenna Elfman was the star of the television series *Dharma & Greg* popular in the late 1990s and early 2000s and is active on the silver screen as well.

Jennifer: An English adaptation of the Welsh name Gwenhwyfar (Guinevere), often associated specifically with Cornwall; "white wave." The resemblance to JENNIE is coincidental. It became suddenly popular in England around 1950, probably because of its use by actresses. In the United States, a similar but not-so-striking popularity occurred in the same period, and the name has remained popular ever since. In the 1970s, '80s, and '90s, it was among the top ten most common names in the United States. This trend is beginning to fade, but celebrities like singer and actress Jennifer Lopez, actress Jennifer Aniston, and actress Jennifer Garner are likely to keep it in parents' minds as they choose girls' names in the future.

Jenny, Jennie: Although you probably think of the two spellings of this name as nicknames for JENNIFER, Jenny and Jennie are actually diminutives of JANE (which comes from JOHN, a Hebrew name meaning "God is gracious." Earlier, they were usually pronounced and even spelled **Jinny.** The height of Jenny's popularity was around 1870, when it sometimes approached or even reached the top ten. There are still plenty of Jennys and Jennies around today, but it's likely that they have the given name Jennifer rather than Jenny or Jennie. Well-known Jennys include diet guru Jenny Craig, talk show host Jenny Jones, and Playboy bunny turned MTV VJ and actress Jenny McCarthy. Tommy Tutone immortalized this name, along with a certain phone number, with the 1981 hit song "867-5309 (Jenny)."

Jessica: Hebrew; "He beholds." This name appears in various editions of the Bible as Iscah or Jesca, and Shakespeare used it in *The Merchant of*

Venice. Historically, it has carried Jewish connotations with the non-Jewish community, although that association has pretty much fallen by the wayside in modern times. Jessica became quite popular in the 1980s, and from 1991 to 1995, it was the No. 1 name in the United States. It has since slipped a bit, but it remains very common. Famous Jessicas range from actresses Jessica Lange and Jessica Tandy to singer Jessica Simpson to rescued prisoner of war Jessica Lynch. *Sex and the City*'s Sarah Jessica Parker makes use of it as a middle name. Nicknames include **Jessie, Jessy,** and **Jess.**

Jessie: Hebrew; "God is." A feminized version of JESSE. Being the father of David, Jesse was a well-known biblical character, and his name was used steadily after 1750, although it never attained great popularity. It remained in use later than most biblical names, still current as a boy's name as late as 1875. Today, Jessie isn't a particularly common given name for girls; parents tend to use JESSICA as a given name and Jessie as a nickname. Prominent Jessies from history include suffragist and civil rights activist Jessie Daniel Ames. **Jessy** is an alternate spelling.

Jewel: French; a precious gem. A jewel by any other spelling might be **Jewell** or **Juill.** An unusual name, Jewel is in good company with other names based on precious gems, such as Pearl and Ruby. Singer, songwriter, and poet Jewel was christened Jewel Kilcher but uses only her first name in public life. Jewel Jackson McCabe founded the National Coalition of 100 Black Women to advocate meaningful change and advancement in the lives of African Americans.

Jillian: Old English; from the Latin JULIANA. Jillian and its alternate form, **Gillian,** have become increasingly popular in recent years. Jillian is near the top 100 names, and Gillian climbed 600 spots from 1992 to 2002. The name is often shortened to **Jill.** In her role as FBI detective Dana Scully, actress Gillian Anderson became a cult heroine on the TV series *The X-Files.*

Jill: English. Although it developed as a short form of Gillian, which means "youthful" or "young," Jill became much more popular than Gillian ever was. Along with her brother JACK, she even became the subject of a favorite nursery rhyme. Today, Jill's popularity has waned considerably; it has fallen out of the top 1,000 names in use. To be more current, opt for JILLIAN, which has overtaken the G spelling.

Joanna: From **Joan,** a feminization of JOHN. The name Joan was popular in the Middle Ages and remained popular throughout the 16th century, but by 1600 had apparently become common in the not-so-positive sense, as Shakespeare's derogatory "greasy Joan" suggests. Although it remained current in the American colonies and later, it hasn't been a wildly popular name in the United States. The forms **Joanna** and **Johanna** have surpassed it of late, Joanna being among the top 250 girls' names in 2002. Famous Joans include French resistance leader Joan of Arc, talk show host Joan Rivers, and writer Joan Didion. **Joann** and **Joanne** are similar, and **Joanie** and **Joni** are common nicknames.

☺ ☹ ☹ ☺ ☹ ☹ ☺ ☹ ☹ ☺ ☹ ☹ ☺ ☹ ☹ ☺ ☺ ☹ ☹ ☺

Jocelyn: Old German; based on the root *Gauta*, equivalent to the tribal name "Goth." This name was common among the Normans but fell out of use in the 14th century. It began as a man's name and remains masculine in Great Britain. In the United States, it's more commonly feminine, perhaps because of the similarity of JACQUELINE. Dr. Jocelyn Elders served as U.S. Surgeon General under President Bill Clinton. Controversy surrounding her position on sex education forced her to resign just over a year after she was appointed. She remains an outstanding role model for girls and for African Americans. **Jocelin, Joselyn,** and **Josslyn** are variations.

Jordan: Hebrew; "something that descends, flows down." The River Jordan figures significantly in the Bible and in the history of the Middle East. As far as names go, there's an interesting split in whether Jordan is given to a boy or to a girl. African-American parents are more likely to name their sons Jordan, perhaps in honor of basketball great Michael Jordan, while Caucasians name their daughters Jordan more often than their sons. Whether given to a boy or a girl, Jordan — and it variations **Jordyn, Jordann,** and **Jourdan** — became quite popular in the 1990s and continues to be the choice of many parents. Actress Jill Hennessy plays a medical examiner named Jordan in the television series *Crossing Jordan.* **Jory** is a possible nickname.

Josephine: A French feminine-diminutive of JOSEPH, popularized in the 19th century by Empress Josephine, Napoleon's wife. As with most feminine forms, it gained only enough vitality to keep it alive. Women so named are usually called **Jo,** leaving Joe as the masculine. **Josie** is a common nickname that's become even more popular than the long form. It climbed into the top 300 in the 2000s.

Joy: English; "great happiness." There isn't much to say about this name that means what it says: What could be simpler than pure joy? As a name, Joy has been around since the Middle Ages; these days, it's fairly uncommon, ranking 477th among girls' names. One well-known Joy is Joy Philbin, the wife of talk-show host Regis Philbin. Variations include **Joi** and the French **Joie.**

Joyce: A French adaptation of the Breton saint's name Jodoc; the root is an element meaning "lord, prince." Joyce was used often in the Middle Ages — for either a man or a woman. By 1400, however, it had become strictly feminine. It then went almost out of use until a revival in the early 20th century. The word *joy* in the name has probably helped establish Joyce. It remains current, although it's not especially popular today. Well-known Joyces include psychologist and radio personality Dr. Joyce Brothers and contemporary novelist Joyce Carol Oates.

Julia, Juliana: Latin. Julia is the feminine form of Julius, the name of a Roman clan that was especially well known because of the historical prominence of Julius Caesar. Along with the masculine JULIAN, Juliana is from Julianus, a form that was current in the later Roman period. As the

☺ ☺ ☹ ☺ ☺ ☹ ☺ ☺ ☹ ☺ ☺ ☹ ☺ ☺ ☹ ☺ ☺ ☺ ☹ ☹ ☺

name of a number of saints, Julian was frequently used in English during the Middle Ages, and Juliana became viable as well. The more classical Julius and Julia appeared in the Elizabethan period — for example, Julia was the name of a character in Shakespeare's *Two Gentlemen of Verona*. In the United States, these names made little showing before the later 18th century, when the classical influence worked in their favor and they became current. Many women with the names Julia and Juliana have achieved fame: former First Lady Julia Grant (wife of Ulysses); Julia Ward Howe, who wrote "The Battle Hymn of the Republic"; and chef Julia Child; as well as comedic actresses Julia Roberts and Julia Louis-Dreyfus and alternative pop singer Juliana Hatfield. **Juliet,** based on Shakespeare's heroine, and **Juliette** also appear, but rarely. **Julianne** is another option to consider.

Julie: The French version of JULIA. Personalities known by this name include film actress and beauty Julie Christie and *Sound of Music* songstress Julie Andrews. In recent years, the rather plain-and-simple Julie has been surpassed by the more flowery Julia, JULIANA, and JULIANNA; it sat at No. 220 in 2002.

K

Kaitlyn: See CAITLIN.

Kamryn: See CAMERON.

Kara: A variation of CARA, a Latin name that means "dearest, beloved."

Karen: The Danish form of KATHERINE, which means "pure." In the 20th century, this name showed spectacular growth in the United States. At the opening of the century, it was very rare, but among children born around 1950, the name stood high, often in the top ten. No particular reason accounts for such growth. It was probably somewhat influenced by the usage of the numerous Scandinavian immigrants. It's also a short and euphonic name. Famous carriers of this name include "Close to You" singer Karen Carpenter, union activist Karen Silkwood, and actress Karen Allen, who had leading roles in *Animal House* and *Raiders of the Lost Ark.* A moderately popular derivative of Karen is **Karina.**

Karissa: See CARISSA.

Karla: See CARLA.

Kasey: See CASEY.

Kassandra: See CASSANDRA.

Kassidy: See CASSIDY.

Names that recall beautiful places

If a certain locale has a special significance to you, consider naming your daughter after it. The following are some of the more common place names given to girls:

- ❀ America
- ❀ Asia
- ❀ Carolina
- ❀ Charlotte
- ❀ Dakota
- ❀ Eden
- ❀ Georgia
- ❀ Heaven
- ❀ India
- ❀ Madison
- ❀ Paris
- ❀ Savannah

Kate, Katie: See KATHERINE.

Katelyn, Katelynn: See CAITLIN.

Katherine: Greek; "pure." This name goes back to the Greek form Aikaterine. Latin rendered the name as **Katerina** or **Katharina,** making it a derivative of the Greek adjective *katharos,* meaning "clean, pure," an apt and meaningful name for a virgin martyr. Although six saints bear the name, its popularity in western Europe rests on the story of St. Catherine of Alexandria and her martyrdom around 310. The western nations inherited the Latin form, but early spellings differ greatly, the most common probably being **Katerine.** St. Catherine's cult can be traced in England from 1100. The name itself rapidly took root, and its shortened form **Kate** became one of the stalwart English names. Baptismal lists soon reflected that popularity by showing the name to be one of the most used. Katherine survived the Reformation better than did the names of most of the nonbiblical saints. Among the more vehement Protestants, her name naturally could find no favor. Less fanatical English Protestants, however, refused to surrender Kate — one of them being William Shakespeare, who seems to have liked the name. With the multiplication of the Puritans in

☺ ☺ ☹ ☺ ☺ ☹ ☺ ☺ ☹ ☺ ☺ ☹ ☺ ☺ ☹ ☺ ☺ ☹ ☺

America, Katherine lost much ground. In most of the birth records of New England in the 17th and 18th centuries, Katherine is missing. Then, in the 19th century, the situation began to improve, with the name's popularity increasing considerably — a trend that continued throughout the 20th century and into the 21st. Variations and nicknames include **Catherine, Catharine, Katharine, Kathy, Cathy, Katie, Katy,** and **Kat.** (See also KARA, KAREN, KATHLEEN, KATHRYN, KATRINA, and KAYLA.) The actress Katharine Hepburn's lengthy career included starring roles in *The Philadelphia Story, The African Queen,* and *On Golden Pond.* Other notable bearers of this name include the writers Katherine Anne Porter and Katherine Mansfeld, the actresses Kathy Bates and Cate Blanchett, and the comic-strip character Cathy.

Kathleen: An Irish form of KATHERINE. This name became highly popular in the mid-20th century. Although it began as a derivative, in many lists it outranks the basic Katherine. Notable carriers of this name range from actress Kathleen Turner, to Olympic skater Kathleen Blair, to opera soprano Kathleen Battle.

Kathryn: This variation of KATHERINE became popular in the 20th century, in some lists being more popular than Katherine itself. It is occasionally spelled **Cathryn.**

Katlyn: See CAITLIN (but note that this version is usually pronounced "CAT-lin" rather that "KATE-lin").

Katrina: A Russian variation of KATHERINE. It became somewhat popular in the 20th century and currently ranks among the top 300 names in use. Fans of 1980s pop music probably remember the hit song "Walking on Sunshine" by the group Katrina and the Waves.

Kayla: See KATHERINE. The name's popularity may be one reason that Mattel's mermaid Barbie doll is named Kayla. Up-and-coming author Kayla Perrin has been dubbed a writer to watch. Spelling variations include **Kaila, Kaela, Cayla,** and **Caila.** Short forms are **Cay, Cai, Kay,** and **Kai.**

Kayleigh: This name is likely a blending of several origins. The main sources appear to be (1) an English compound of the names KAY and LEIGH; (2) a variant of KYLIE; (3) a variant of KELLY; and an adaptation of the Irish word *céilidh* or *céilí,* "a musical get-together." Ranked among the 25 most popular name for baby girls in the 1990s, Kayleigh has many variations: **Caileigh, Cailey, Caylea, Caylee, Cayleigh, Cayley, Kailey, Kali** (an Indian goddess who personifies feminine power), **Kaylea, Kayleah, Kaylee, Kayley,** and **Kaylie,** to name a few.

Kaylin: English. A common variant is **Kaylyn,** which is a combination of the name KAY and the popular suffix *–lyn.* Or it may be from the Irish Caoilinn, meaning "slender and fair." Kaylin has made its way onto the top 500 names list, ranking 478th in 2002.

Cool names for the 21st century

Some names that have become quite popular just don't have the history that old names like ELIZABETH and MARY do. If you'd like to give your daughter a cutting-edge name without a lot of historical baggage, consider these options:

- Anahi
- Eliana
- Imani
- Kyla
- Leilani
- Lexi
- Makayla
- Marina
- Nayeli
- Nevaeh
- Perla
- Raven
- Shayla
- Taryn
- Tiana

Kelly: Gaelic; from a shortening of Mac Ceallaigh or O'Ceallaigh, both from the given name Ceallach, the meaning of which is debated. Possibilities include "strife," "frequenter of churches," and "bright (haired)." An all-purpose, all-gender name suitable as a first or middle name for either a boy or a girl, Kelly is used more often as a girls' name these days. Its popularity is declining, but it's still the 119th most popular name for girls. Kelly Rowland is part of the successful R&B singing group Destiny's Child. Kelly Ripa was a soap-opera star who became a cohost of television talk show *Live! with Regis and Kelly.* Kelly Clarkson parlayed her win on the contest show *American Idol* into high-profile singing and acting gigs. Other ways to spell Kelly include **Keli, Kelli,** and **Kellie.**

Kelsey: English; "Ceol's island" where Ceol is an Old English man's name. Kelsey and its variations, which include **Kelcey, Kelcie, Kellsey, Kelsea, Kelsee, Kelsi,** and **Kelsy,** was a very popular name for girls in the 1990s, breaking into the top 25 early in the decade. Its prominence has slid, and

136

Chapter 3: Gennifer, Gina, or Genevieve? Names for Girls

☺ ☻ ☹ ☺ ☺ ☹ ☺ ☺ ☹ ☺ ☺ ☹ ☺ ☺ ☹ ☺ ☺ ☹ ☺ ☺

it currently ranks just above KELLY. Probably the best-known Kelsey in the United States is a male — actor Kelsey Grammer, who has won accolades for his spinoff *Frasier,* from the hit comedy *Cheers.*

Kendall: English; "valley of the Kent River." Kendall is a name that started out as a boy's name and has gradually become almost exclusively female. Historically, it's been an unusual name, rarely seen outside the boundaries of daytime drama, but since the mid-1990s, it's broken into the top 200 a few times. A famous soap-opera bearer of the name is Sarah Michelle Gellar, now famous for her title role in the television series *Buffy the Vampire Slayer,* who was the first actress to play Erica Kane's long-lost daughter. Alternative spellings include **Kendal, Kendel,** and **Kyndall.**

Kendra: American; possibly from a blending of KENNETH and ALEXANDRA, or something similar, with no known meaning. Kendra is a fairly feminine and adaptable name for a girl. It's used modestly, ranking near such names as Nancy and Alison. Spelling variations include **Kendrah** and **Kindra.**

Kennedy: Gaelic; from a shortened Irish surname, O'Cinneide, meaning "ugly head." Kennedy was almost exclusively a surname until the second half of the 20th century, when parents started using it to honor president John F. Kennedy and his brother Robert Kennedy. Lisa Kennedy Montgomery got more than 15 minutes of fame during the 1990s when she worked as an MTV VJ, going simply by the name Kennedy. A feminized spelling of the name is **Kennedi.**

Kezia: Hebrew; "cassia." In the last chapter of Job, we're informed that the once-again-prosperous Uzzite had seven sons and three daughters. Curiously, considering the prevailing attitude toward women in those benighted times, the names of the sons were not listed, while those of the three daughters were carefully recorded. And a strange trio they were — Jemima, Kezia, and Kerenhappuch. In the early New England records, all three of these names appear. Today, it's a very rare name.

Kiley: See KYLIE.

Kimberly: English; from an English place name meaning "Cyneburg's meadow," where Cyneburg is an Old English woman's name meaning "royal fortress." For a long time, Kimberly was primarily a boy's name, but these days, it's given almost exclusively to girls. As a girl's name, Kimberly is quite popular, ranking among the top 50 in the 1990s and slightly lower today. Runner Kim Graham won a gold medal at the 1996 Olympic games in Atlanta as part of the women's 400-meter relay team. Actress Kim Basinger won an Academy Award for her work in the film *L.A. Confidential.* Alternate spellings include **Kimberlea, Kimberle, Kimberlee, Kimberley,** and **Kymberly.** In addition to the usual **Kim,** nicknames may be **Kym, Kimba,** or **Kimber.**

Kira: See KYRA.

Parent's Success Guide to Baby Names

☺ ☺ ☹ ☺ ☺ ☹ ☺ ☺ ☹ ☺ ☺ ☹ ☺ ☺ ☹ ☺ ☺ ☺ ☹ ☺

Kirsten: Latin; "a Christian." Kirsten is a perennial favorite but not an over-used girls' name. It's less popular than it was a decade ago but remains among the top 300 names given to baby girls. Kirsten Dunst won kudos for her performance opposite Tom Cruise and Brad Pitt in *Interview with the Vampire* and continues to impress in such roles as girl-next-door Mary Jane Watson in the *Spider-Man* movies. Nicknames and variations include **Kirstie, Kirsty, Kiersten,** and **Kyrsten.** Kirstie Alley won an Emmy and a Golden Globe for her work on the popular sitcom *Cheers.*

Kristin: Latin; "a Christian." This name had universal appeal during the mid-20th century, but then lost some of its luster at the dawn of the 21st, sinking from 54th in 1992 to 188th in 2002. The fetching actress Kristin Davis made a name for herself playing Charlotte on HBO's *Sex and the City,* while the equally beautiful — and prodigiously talented — Kristin Scott Thomas has starred in numerous acclaimed films, such as *Four Weddings and a Funeral, The English Patient,* and *Gosford Park.* The alternate spelling **Kristen** is now more popular than Kristin. Other variations include **Kristyn, Christa, Krista,** and **Krysta.**

Kristina: See CHRISTINA.

Krystal: See CRYSTAL.

Kylie: Australian; "boomerang." A name that gained popularity in the 1990s, cracking the top 50, Kylie is open to a number of alternate spellings, including **Kylee, Kyleigh, Kiley,** and **Kyli.** Pop singer and some-time actress Kylie Minogue, a native of Australia, has captured the hearts of American music fans with hits like "Can't Get You Out of My Head."

Kyra: Greek; "lady." The feminine form of CYRIL. That name was borne by several saints, chiefly associated with the Eastern Church. The name Kyra is used moderately in the United States today. Actress Kyra Sedgwick receives accolades for her movie career, having starred in such films as *Phenomenon* and *Singles,* and for her successful Hollywood marriage — a rare thing indeed! — to fellow actor Kevin Bacon since 1988. Alternate spellings include **Kira, Kiera,** and **Keera. Kierra** and **Kiara** are similar but have an extra syllable.

L

Lane: English; "narrow road." Lane is a flexible name in that it can be used for a boy or a girl and as a first, middle, or last name. The so far few famous Lanes are male: Lane Smith, a character actor and children's book illustrator as well as a sometime writer; and Lane Kirkland, a labor organizer and president of the AFL-CIO for 16 years.

Laura: Latin; "laurel." The actual origin in modern English may be from its literary use in Petrarch's poetry, which was largely addressed to a woman

138

☺ ☺ ☹ ☺ ☺ ☹ ☺ ☺ ☹ ☺ ☺ ☹ ☺ ☺ ☹ ☺ ☺ ☺ ☺ ☹ ☺

named Laura. Short, euphonic, and romantic in its associations, Laura has been a well-established and active name in United States in recent years. Notable Lauras include First Lady Laura Bush, Welsh fashion designer Laura Ashley, and Laura Linney. **Lora** and **Lara** are alternate spellings. See also LAUREN.

Laurel: One of many names that come from a flower or plant. See LILY.

Lauren: Latin; "crowned with laurels." Lauren, the 20th-century feminine form of LAWRENCE, is the 13th most popular girls' name today. The most famous Lauren is probably Lauren Bacall, the film actress best known for her performances opposite her husband, Humphrey Bogart. She took Hollywood by storm at the age of 19 when she starred in *To Have and Have Not*. She and Bogart made three additional films together: *The Big Sleep, Dark Passage,* and *Key Largo.* Another famous Lauren is Lauren Hutton, a former model for Revlon and an actress who starred in such films as *Paper Lion* and *American Gigolo.* Nicknames and derivatives include **Lauryn** (used by singer Lauryn Hill) and **Loren.** Hip-hop singer Lauryn Hill is the best-known holder of the former spelling variation.

Layla: Arabic; "night." Eric Clapton's band Derek and the Dominos brought fame to the fairly uncommon name with the guitar-driven hit "Layla." **Leila** and **Laila** are alternate forms. Leila Ali is doing her best to carrying on her father's legacy in the boxing ring, competing against both women and men. She's also known to have her dad's way with words.

Leah: Hebrew; "(wild) cow," "weary." In the Bible, Leah was the first wife of JACOB. We're informed that she was "tender eyed," whatever that means. There seems to be little reason for people to have used this name, but it had a continuing usage in early New England and lingered on into the 19th century until the general decline of biblical names. In modern times, the name consistently ranks among the 100 most popular names given to baby girls. Notable Leahs include actress Leah Remini of TV series *The King of Queens.* This name is generally pronounced "LEE-ah" but can be pronounced "LAY-ah," with the alternate spelling **Leia.** In the original three *Star Wars* films, Princess Leia (played by Carrie Fisher) has one of the most famous hairdos of all time.

Lee: English; from the family name, which is derived from the Anglo-Saxon *leah,* meaning "meadow, glade, clearing," and signifies a dweller at such a place. It began to appear in the early 19th century, but its chief vogue arose after Robert E. Lee had become the heroic symbol of the Confederacy. Because Southern usage allowed a family name to be bestowed on a girl, many women were called Lee. As the memory of the Civil War faded, the name spread to other parts of the country, used chiefly for men. Today, it's rarely given to girls.

Leigh: Pronounced identically with LEE, this name derives from the Anglo-Saxon form *leah,* from which Lee also descends. It has always been rare

☺ ☺ ☹ ☺ ☺ ☹ ☺ ☺ ☹ ☺ ☺ ☹ ☺ ☺ ☹ ☺ ☺ ☺ ☹ ☺

and is becoming even less common; in its place, names that end in -leigh, such as Ashleigh, Kayleigh, and Ryleigh, are on the rise. Famous first-name Leighs are hard to come by, but actresses like Janet Leigh *(Psycho)* and Vivien Leigh *(Gone with the Wind)* have employed it as a surname.

Leslie: From the family name (especially Scottish), in literal meaning probably to be distantly connected with Latin *laetitia,* "gladness." In the United States, Leslie began to be used as a given name in the late 19th century. It soon became a woman's name, perhaps because the ending suggests a feminine usage. It remained viable, but not common, in the 20th century. Its popularity has risen a bit in recent years, and it's currently among the top 100 names for girls. **Lesley** and **Lesly** are alternate spellings. The reporter Lesley Stahl has been a reporter for CBS News since the early 1970s; she has been a correspondent on TV's *60 Minutes* since 1991. Leslie Silko is a writer of Native American heritage.

Liberty: American; "freedom." In the aftermath of 9/11, names that embody American values have become increasingly popular. Liberty wasn't among the 1,000 most popular name for baby girls in the year 2000, but it ranked 783rd in 2001 and 485th in 2002.

Lila: Arabic; "night." Lila has proven to be a popular character name in literature and cinema — usually for women who are troubled in some way. Lila is the title character of Robert Pirsig's novel *Lila,* which is a continuation of Pirsig's bestselling novel *Zen and the Art of Motorcycle Maintenance.* In Alfred Hitchcock's *Psycho,* the character Lila Crane visits the Bates Motel to investigate the disappearance of her friend Marion (yes, Marion is the one in the infamous shower scene). The Lila Cheney character has made several appearances in *X-Men* comics as a troubled young woman who happens to have the ability to teleport herself anywhere. Similar names include **Delilah, Leela,** and **Leila.**

Lillian: Likely a derivative of ELIZABETH. Lillian has enjoyed some popularity, standing 23rd in one list from the early 20th century and currently ranked 97th. It was known from the actresses Lillian Russell and Lillian Gish. The former, however, had adopted it as a stage name before becoming well known. An alternate spelling is **Lilian.**

Lily: English; "flower." Except for special cases (see ROSE), the naming habits of English speakers didn't generally include the giving of flower names to women. The uncommon custom began about 1850, and by 1900 had exhausted what little vigor it had possessed. Later came Iris, Violet, Viola, and the flowering bushes, such as Heather. Individually, the flower names were negligible; as a group, they gave a touch of variety to the late 19th century. Lily and its alternate spelling, **Lilly,** remain moderately popular today; **Lili** is a lesser-used option. Actress/comedian Lily Tomlin had audiences howling with laughter in the films *All of Me* and *9 to 5*; she took on more serious roles in Robert Altman's *Nashville, The Player,* and *Short Cuts.*

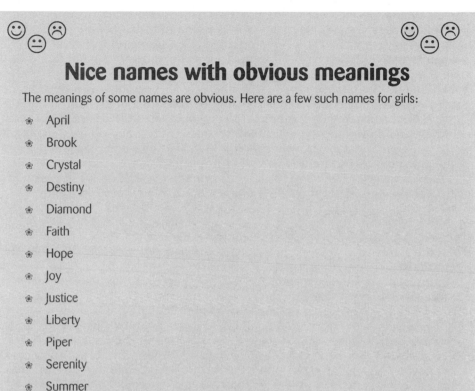

Nice names with obvious meanings

The meanings of some names are obvious. Here are a few such names for girls:

- April
- Brook
- Crystal
- Destiny
- Diamond
- Faith
- Hope
- Joy
- Justice
- Liberty
- Piper
- Serenity
- Summer
- Willow
- Wren

Linda: Old German; "serpent, dragon," probably via short forms of names like Rosalinda. Linda has had a strange history. It began to appear in America only in the final decades of the 19th century. It advanced in a remarkable thrust, and in the 1940s can be found — on one list, at least — as the most common name. The reaction, however, hit sharply, and Linda became somewhat rare. It remains so today. Famous actresses who bear this name include Linda Evans, who played a diva on both *Dallas* and *Dynasty*, and Linda Lavin, best known for her role as the tart-tongued wait-ress Alice on the show of the same name. A spelling alternative is **Lynda,** borne by *Wonder Woman* portrayer Lynda Carter.

Lindsey: English; "Lincoln's island." Lindsey and its alternate form, **Lindsay,** can be used as either a female or a male name. Today, both ver-sions are much more popular for girls than for boys; they rank 122nd and 257th, respectively. Lindsay Wagner will forever be known as heroine Jamie Sommers from television's *The Bionic Woman,* for which she won an Emmy Award.

Lisa: Origin and meaning unknown. This name is obviously from ELIZA-BETH, but its more detailed history is not clear. English handling of the situation should give us Liz, so it's likely that Lisa is taken from some other language. One source shows Lisa in Portuguese and very similar forms in German and the Slavic languages. It scarcely existed before the 19th century, and its chief usage was been in the 20th. After ranking among the most popular names between the mid-20th century and the early 1990s, Lisa has steadily declined in popularity, coming in as the 364th most popular name for baby girls in 2002. Singer/songwriter Lisa Loeb found success when she embarked on a solo career and gained widespread radio play with the musically spare and lyrically somber "Stay," while Lisa Marie Presley is more famous for her father's singing career than for her own. If you like the sound of this name but want something more modern, consider ALYSSA or **Elisa.**

Lizbeth: Hebrew; "God's oath," "God has satisfied." Lizbeth is a common variant of the English name ELIZABETH. Spelling variants include **Lisbeth** and **Lisbet.**

Lola: A pet name for **Dolores.** Another variation of the name is **Lolita.** This name has been rare, perhaps because of its associations with Vladimir Nabokov's novel *Lolita*, which features a young "nymphette" in an amorous relationship with a much older man. Another questionable association comes from the Kinks song *Lola*, about a man who finds that the woman he loves is . . . less than feminine. However, Kate Moss named her daughter Lola, and Madonna calls her daughter Lourdes Lola, so the tide may be turning.

Lorena: Italian; "crowned with laurel." Unfortunately, this name's most well-known association is probably with Lorena Bobbit, who removed her husband's member to get back at him for abusing her. But the name's association with victory makes it an appealing selection. It remains fairly obscure in the United States.

Lucy: Latin; "light." Lucy was a martyr of the fourth century whose cult became popular in England during the Middle Ages. With the Puritan antipathy to nonbiblical saints, Lucy went out of common use in the 16th and 17th centuries. It had a revival in the 19th century, but then fell off somewhat in the 20th. Today, its popularity is again on the rise, and it's among the top 300 names for girls. Both Lucy Lawless and Lucy Liu have played action heroes, Lawless on TV's *Xena: Warrior Princess* and Liu in the *Charlie's Angels* films. **Lucinda** is apparently a 17th-century poetic coinage. Another variant is **Lucille.** Lucille Ball appeared in numerous films before earning superstardom status thanks to her TV comedy *I Love Lucy.* Folk rocker Lucinda Williams won a Grammy for her critically acclaimed 1998 release, *Car Wheels on a Gravel Road.*

Lydia: Greek; "Lydian woman." In ancient Greece, a slave was often named from the country of origin, and Lydia was apparently thus derived.

Chapter 3: Gennifer, Gina, or Genevieve? Names for Girls

☺ ☺ ☹ ☺ ☺ ☹ ☺ ☺ ☹ ☺ ☺ ☹ ☺ ☺ ☹ ☺ ☺ ☺ ☺ ☹ ☺

A certain Lydia is mentioned once in the Bible (Acts 16:14). Because women's names in the New Testament are few and far between, this one was readily adopted. Lydia was a popular name among the Puritans, often rating in the top ten. Even after the decline of biblical names, it remained viable, and it still survives today. Lydia Maria Child was a writer and abolitionist in the 1800s.

Lynn: English; as an English surname, it means "pool." In its curious history, Lynn can be traced down through many centuries. Various places took the name, and the Anglo-Saxons and Normans preserved them. In turn, various people adopted the surname Lynn (or had it thrust upon them). A few of these Lynns came to America, although they were never a large family. Nevertheless, in the 19th century the name began to turn up as a given name for a man. In the 20th century, Lynn not only became much more numerous, but it also became a woman's name. Like LEIGH, Lynn is more common today as the second half of popular names like Katelynn and Ashlynn. British actress Lynn Redgrave has been appearing in feature films since the early 1960s, with an Academy-Award nomination to her credit for her lead performance in 1966's *Georgy Girl.* **Linn** and **Lynne** are alternate spellings.

Lynette: English; from a French root meaning "moon." Lynette first appeared as a character in Arthurian literature.

M

Mackenzie: Scottish Gaelic; a surname meaning "son of Coinneach," which is a given name meaning "beautiful." This definition is appropriate for film and television actress Mackenzie Phillips, the daughter of musician John Phillips of the rock-folk band the Mamas and the Papas. She made her acting debut as the troublesome teen in *American Graffiti* and then went on to become one of Hollywood's most popular and highest-paid actresses in 1970s with her role on the hit sitcom *One Day at a Time.* Another Mackenzie of note was W. L. Mackenzie King, who served as prime minister of Canada in the early 20th century and is known for his contributions to the Statute of Westminster, which gave independence to the British Commonwealth states and dominions of Canada, Australia, New Zealand, South Africa, Ireland, and Newfoundland. Variations include **Makenzie** and **McKenzie,** both of which join Mackenzie on the list of the top 200 most popular names, with Mackenzie in the lead and 48th. **Kenzie** is a possible nickname.

Macy: French, English; derived from the medieval form of the name MATTHEW, which means "gift from God." Of course, the name Macy brings to mind the ageless and classy icon of shopping, Macy's department store. Classy in a different way is soulful rock diva Macy Gray. This name has gained some prominence in recent years, reaching 226th place in the

☺ ☻ ☹ ☺ ☻ ☹ ☺ ☻ ☹ ☺ ☻ ☹ ☺ ☻ ☹ ☺ ☺ ☻ ☹ ☺

United States in 2002. The English variant, **Macie,** is also among the top 500 girls' names in use today. **Maisie** is similar.

Madeleine: Hebrew; "woman of Magdala," known in medieval usage as St. Mary Magdalene, who was closely associated with Christ in the Gospels. **Madeline** is the French (and today, the more popular) form. The name reached some popularity in the later Middle Ages and developed the short form Maudlin, which in its turn became a common adjective meaning "excessively affectionate," probably reflecting the traditional manner in which the part was rendered in the miracle plays. The Protestants saw no reason to name their daughters after one who in earlier life was a flamboyant sinner. Its revival is essentially literary and particularly to be connected with the revival of medievalism in the Romantic period of the early 19th century. **Madelyn** and **Madalyn** are French forms, and **Maddie** is a common nickname. Madeleine Albright served as Secretary of State — the first woman to hold the post — under President Bill Clinton. Comedic actress Madeline Kahn delighted audiences with her performances in *Young Frankenstein, Blazing Saddles,* and *The Muppet Movie.* Madeline is also a beloved children's book character, a Parisian schoolgirl.

Madison: English; "son of Matthew." The fourth U.S. President, James Madison, was not widely popular and scarcely attained a hero's reception, but his name came handily to the tongue. It furnished a moderately popular name, originally for boys but now more commonly for girls. It's been among the top ten girls' names for six years running. **Madisyn** and **Madyson** are alternative spellings; **Maddie** is a common nickname. Famous female Madisons are few, but, given the name's popularity, there are sure to be several of them in the future!

Makayla: Scandinavian; a variant of MICHELLE, the feminine name for MICHAEL. This popular name has numerous spellings, many of which also appear on the list of the top 500 baby names, including **Mikayla, Michaela, Mckayla,** and **Mikaela.**

Mallory: French; "unlucky." In spite of its meaning, this name has achieved moderate popularity, consistently ranking among the top 250 names for baby girls. Actress Justine Bateman played the role of the ditzy teen Mallory on the classic 1980s sitcom *Family Ties.* Alternate spellings include **Mallorie, Malorie,** and **Malory.**

Marcia: Latin; from *marcius,* having to do with the family of that name; the tribal name is probably from the name of the god Mars, which means "martial, warlike." Marcia is commonly regarded as the feminine of MARK or MARCUS. In recent times, when Mark has increased in popularity, Marcia also has shown considerable growth. In modern usage, it's sometimes spelled **Marsha,** although neither version is popular today. Actress Marcia Gay Harden won an Academy Award for her supporting role in *Pollock.* The most famous Marsha is probably 1970s TV teen Marsha Brady, from *The Brady Bunch.*

Chapter 3: Gennifer, Gina, or Genevieve? Names for Girls

☺ ☺ ☹ ☺ ☺ ☺ ☹ ☺ ☺ ☹ ☺ ☺ ☹ ☺ ☺ ☹ ☺ ☺ ☹ ☺ ☺ ☺ ☹ ☺

Marcy: Latin; "martial, warlike." This name is a feminine form of MARCUS. Marcy has almost become obsolete for today's babies, failing to rank among the 1,000 most popular names for baby girls. The name has a geographic connection: Mount Marcy is not only the highest peak in the Adirondacks, but it's also the highest peak in New York State. Derivatives include **Marci**, **Marcie**, and **Marcee**.

Margaret: Greek; from the word *margarites,* which means "pearl." The popularity of the name derives from St. Margaret of Antioch (third century), who became one of the four great virgin martyrs. In a colorful apocryphal biography, she is made a dragon slayer. She was known in England even in Anglo-Saxon times. Equally early, she seems to have become established in Scotland, where she was extremely popular. A clear evidence of her popularity is to be seen in the myriad abbreviations and diminutives, both English and Scottish — **Marge, Madge, Maisie, Maggie,** and others. As a nonbiblical saint, Margaret almost disappeared with the Reformation, and even in the 19th century, it wasn't a common name in the United States. A strong revival, however, occurred in the early 20th century. The French form **Margot** has become somewhat common, sometimes being spelled **Margo** to correspond more closely to the pronunciation. **Marguerite,** also a French form, was popular in the 19th century but declined in the 20th. A third French form, spelled **Margery** or **Marjorie,** dates from the 12th century and has been considered an independent name. Canadian writer Margaret Atwood has garnered widespread praise for works such as *The Handmaid's Tale, Cat's Eye,* and *The Robber Bride.* Margaret Mitchell created the unforgettable characters Scarlett O'Hara and Rhett Butler in her classic novel *Gone with the Wind.* Another scribe, Margaret Truman, has earned kudos for her mystery novels; she is the daughter of President Harry Truman and his wife, Bess.

Maria: The Latin form of MARY, a Hebrew name meaning "wished-for child" or "rebellion." Maria also occurs in Spanish, Italian, and several other languages. The 18th century was notable for its cultivation of the classics, and this Latin form became popular at that time. Its popularity has fluctuated, but Maria has always remained a viable name. Today, it stands at 39th. The traditional pronunciation in English has called for the *i* to be pronounced as is the sound in "high." In recent times, probably because of Spanish analogies, the *i* is often pronounced as is the double *-e* in "see." Famous Marias include nun turned governess Maria von Trapp, played beautifully by Julie Andrews in the Academy Award-winning film *The Sound of Music,* and Maria Shriver, a journalist, children's book author, and the wife of Arnold Schwarzenegger. **Mariana** and **Marina** are derivatives that have gained popularity in recent years.

Mariah: An American variant of MARIA, which in turn derives from MARY, a Hebrew name that means "wished-for child" or "rebellion." This newer name has been reasonably popular for the last decade, having peaked at No. 62 in 1998. Singer and songwriter Mariah Carey is one of the most

☺ ☺ ☹ ☺ ☺ ☹ ☺ ☺ ☹ ☺ ☺ ☹ ☺ ☺ ☹ ☺ ☺ ☹ ☺

popular recording artists in history, selling more than 80 million records worldwide. Alternate spellings include **Maryah**, **Moriah**, and **Maraya.**

Marian: From MARY, a Hebrew name meaning "wished-for child" or "rebellion." In the Middle Ages, English made much use of diminutive suffixes, one of which was -*in*, also appearing as -*on*, -*un*. Thus with MARY, it yielded **Maryon** — or, as commonly spelled, **Marion.** Both the popular characters Robin Hood and Maid Marion bore names formed with this diminutive. The family name Marion also was derived in this way. In the early 19th century, Marion (referring regularly to women) became more common. From the pronunciation, the idea developed that the name was really Mary Ann. Apparently, by this route, the form Marian developed, being restricted to women. The status of the -*on* ending thus suggested a new name for men. Today, Marion is suitable for a boy or a girl, while Marian remains primarily a girls' name. Actress Marian Ross played the sweet-natured mother Mrs. Cunningham on the TV show *Happy Days.*

Marie: The French form of MARY. Until the 19th century, it wasn't used much except in French context. However, since the opening of the 19th century, it has been a well-used name in wholly American situations. Famous bearers of this name include bubble-gum pop singer Marie Osmond and two-time Nobel Prize-winning chemist and physicist Marie Curie.

Marisa: Italian, Spanish. An elaboration of the name MARIA (the name for MARY in some Romance languages) or of the name **Maris,** which means "of the sea." Actress Marisa Tomei won an Academy Award for her comedic role in *My Cousin Vinny* and was nominated again for the drama *In the Bedroom*. An English variation is **Marissa,** which television fans might be familiar with from *Early Edition's* strong yet compassionate character Marissa Clark.

Martha: The derivation is from the local (Aramaic) speech of New Testament Palestine, meaning "woman" or "lady." The biblical Martha (Luke 10; John 11, 12) performs domestic duties, such as preparing meals. With a touch of modernism, she complains that her sister doesn't help, and Martha is therefore gently rebuked by her Lord. The Puritan father, who was largely concerned with the naming of his children, was thus in an ambivalent position with the name: He approved of Martha's devotion to family duties, but he couldn't escape the rebuke. Martha was in use from the earliest colonization, after showing up as fairly common and reaching low positions in the top ten. It was about equally used in the Puritan colonies and in the South, where Martha Washington gave it almost regal status. Less common in the 19th century, Martha was one of the few biblical names to throw off the suggestion of being out-of-date and to attain, in the 20th century, moderate popularity. Today, it has come to be seen as somewhat old-fashioned once again. Martha Stewart became a household name as an expert on decorating and cooking — a reputation she parlayed into a publishing and housewares empire.

Chapter 3: Gennifer, Gina, or Genevieve? Names for Girls

☺ ☻ ☹ ☺ ☻ ☹ ☺ ☻ ☹ ☺ ☻ ☹ ☺ ☻ ☹ ☺ ☺ ☻ ☹ ☺

Mary: Hebrew; "wished-for child," "rebellion." This name arose from an unusual development of the name **Miriam,** which the Greeks rendered as Mariam. Speakers of Latin apparently took the final *m* as a sign of the accusative case and assumed a nominative, Maria. In English, the accent shifted to the first syllable, in accordance with the usual practice of the language. The name wasn't in general use before 1200 — partly, it would seem, because it was considered too holy. But the development of the so-called "cult of the Virgin" apparently brought Mary into common use. In the first half of the 16th century, the Reformation de-emphasized the role of Mary, and the popularity of the name suffered somewhat. The Protestants didn't actually reject it, but its use fell off during the late 16th century — partly because of the unpopularity of "Bloody" Mary and of Mary Queen of Scots. By the time of the English colonization of America, Mary had again risen in popularity, and it generally shows up in any American list as the most common name. In the late 20th century, however, it fell off once again, although it usually remained in the top ten. At the dawn of the 21st century, the name's strength continues to fade, and it ranked as the 52nd most popular name for baby girls in 2002. The *l*-form of Mary was originally Mal or Mally, but it eventually became **Molly,** which is considered a name in its own right today. Actress Mary Tyler Moore received her big break when she landed the role of Laura Petrie on *The Dick Van Dyke Show*. She later became America's sweetheart as Mary Richards on *The Mary Tyler Moore Show*. Other notable Marys and Mollys include writers Mary Shelley and Mary Higgins Clark, painter Mary Cassatt, gymnast Mary Lou Retton, Titanic survivor Molly Brown, and "Brat Pack" actress Molly Ringwald.

Maureen: Gaelic; an anglicized rendering of the Irish name Mairin, a diminutive of MARY. It began to appear in the 20th century but has never attained great popularity. The actress Maureen Stapleton played Archie Bunker's ditzy wife, Edith, on the 1970s television show *All in the Family*.

Maya: Greek; "mother." It can be said that Maya Angelou is a "mother" of America, as she has become arguably the most celebrated poet and writer of the 20th century. Her work crosses all genres, from poetry and essays, to film and music, and her work has garnered numerous awards and nominations, from Pulitzer Prizes to Tony and Emmy awards. She was also the second poet in U.S. history to perform an original work at a presidential inauguration — that of President Bill Clinton in 1993. The Mayans is also the name given to the ancient Indian civilizations of Central America, Known for their pyramids, artwork, and rich culture. It's believed that the Mayan civilization spanned over 2,000 years, and the Mayans are considered to be the mother of all Native American civilizations. Another Maya of note is Maya Plisetskaya, one of Russia's most beloved ballerinas of the Bolshoi style. Alternate spellings include **Maia**. See also MIA.

McKenzie: See MACKENZIE.

Popular Irish names

If you're of Irish ancestry, you may want to choose a baby name of Irish origin or association. Here are ten popular Irish names.

- Aileen (or Eileen)
- Breanna (or Brianna)
- Bridget
- Caitlin
- Cassidy
- Ciara
- Colleen
- Kyla
- Mckayla (or Makayla or Michaela)
- Megan
- Norah

Megan: Gaelic; "gentle and soft." This perennially popular name has fallen a bit in popularity in the past few years, but it remains among the top 25 girls' names. A famous modern-day Megan is Megan Mullally, the star of the television sitcom *Will and Grace,* on which she plays the boisterous Karen Walker. Nicknames and derivatives of **Megan** include **Meagan, Meghan, Meighan** (often pronounced "MEE-gan"), and **Meg.**

Melanie: Greek; "black." It's also the name of two saints. Melanie has never been a very popular name, although it was made known from its use for a character in *Gone with the Wind.* The actress Melanie Griffith gained star power during the 1980s, with leading roles in *Something Wild* and *Working Girl.*

Melinda: This name came into general use in the 19th century and was part of a fad for coining new names ending in -*inda.* Melinda was fairly popular in the later 20th century, but it has since fallen from common usage. **Mindy** is a common nickname.

Melissa: Greek; "bee." This name traditionally has been rare but viable. In the mid-20th century, it became suddenly popular, for no easily determined reason, and it has remained fairly common since. One of Southern rock group The Allman Brothers' most famous tunes is titled "Melissa."

☺ ☺ ☹ ☺ ☺ ☹ ☺ ☺ ☹ ☺ ☺ ☹ ☺ ☺ ☹ ☺ ☺ ☺ ☹ ☺

Melody: No source of this name is known other than the ordinary English word that relates to music. It occurs sporadically in England from 1800 on. In the United States during the mid-20th century, it showed some activity. Today, Melody regularly appears in the list of the 500 most popular names for girls, although it has ranked no higher than 296th over the last decade.

Mercedes: Spanish; "mercies." The name derives from *Maria de Mercedes,* an epithet of the Virgin. The curious history is that the name originated (as the language indicates) in Spain, then passed to France, and finally to England, probably in the early 19th century. At more or less the same time, the name Mercy was common in the colonies — it may even have sprung from Catholic piety in rare instances. On the other hand, Mercedes maintains only a loose connection with Catholicism, and it more likely owes its usage to Romantic poetry. Mercedes remains a viable name today, perhaps because of its association with the German luxury car-maker of the same name. Actress Mercedes Ruehl has appeared in such films as *Married to the Mob* and *Big.*

Meredith: Welsh; a compound with an unidentified element and an element meaning "lord." Although it's never been wildly popular, this name has remained fairly in use over the last several decades. In Wales, the name is purely masculine, while it's feminine in the United States. It also appears as a surname. Among well-known Merediths, the actress Meredith Baxter-Birney will always be remembered as the progressive mother Elise Keaton on TV's *Family Ties.* Meredith Vieira is a cohost of *The View.*

Mia: Latin; "mine" (as in "not yours" — you'll probably hear this word a lot from your daughter, regardless of whether you choose this name for her). Mia Farrow, who has been married to both Frank Sinatra and Woody Allen, has played roles in such films as *Rosemary's Baby* (which made her a star), *The Purple Rose of Cairo,* and *Hannah and Her Sisters.* Another notable Mia is Mia Hamm, the soccer star who led the U.S. women's team to victory in the 1999 World Cup. **Maria** is a related name, and **Mya** is an alternate spelling. See also MAYA.

Michelle: A French feminine version of MICHAEL (see Chapter 2). This name isn't quite as popular as it once was, but it's still among the top 60 names for girls. Famous Michelles include actress Michelle Pfeiffer and singers Michelle Branch and Michelle Phillips (of the 1960s group the Mamas and the Papas).

Mikayla: See MAKAYLA.

Miranda: Latin; "to be admired." Shakespeare coined the name Miranda for the heroine of *The Tempest.* It's been very rare; today, it ranks 148th, down from a high of 57th in 1995. Miranda Richardson has twice garnered Academy Award nominations: Best Actress in *Tom and Viv* and Best Supporting Actress in *Damage.* Actress Cynthia Nixon plays a fictional, and feisty, Miranda on the HBO series *Sex and the City.*

Miriam: Hebrew; "wished-for child," "rebellion." Because Miriam was the sister of Moses, an Egyptian origin is possible. Historically, Miriam has been a fairly rare name, although it's currently among the top 300 names in use.

Molly: See MARY.

Monica: Origin and meaning uncertain. Monica was the name of the mother of St. Augustine, herself a saint. The name may be of African origin. In the 20th century, it became somewhat popular, but it has since fallen out of the top 100 names for girls. Monica Seles dominated women's professional tennis before being stabbed by a deranged fan during one of her matches. Seles survived the stabbing, but she hasn't been able to regain her previous level of tennis-playing excellence. Another notable Monica is Monica Lewinsky, a former White House intern who was found to have had an affair with the President, leading to his impeachment.

Morgan: Welsh; "edge of the sea." In the 16th century, Morgan was a given name in Wales, much used. It became a family name, and in the colonies was primarily so regarded — for example, General Daniel Morgan of the Revolutionary War. Morgan has evolved to became a popular name for boys and girls, particularly the latter. From 1994 to 2002, it has ranked among the 30 most popular baby names for girls. The actress Morgan Fairchild has appeared in countless TV shows, films, and commercials over the last 25 years.

Mya: See MIA.

N

Nadine: A French borrowing of the Russian name Nadezhda; "hopeful." This name is rare in the United States today. South African novelist Nadine Gordimer's work embodies the definition of Nadine, as she writes about the issues of racism and repression in her homeland with hope and optimism. Her body of work earned her the Nobel Prize for Literature in 1991. Similar-sounding names include **Nadia** and **Nadya.**

Nancy: The origin of Nancy seems to be ANNE. For reasons that are by no means clear, Nancy became a highly popular name in the 20th century, often attaining a place in the top ten. The name's fortunes have dipped in recent years, though; Nancy ranked as the 231st most popular name for baby girls in 2002. Notable bearers of the name include former First Lady Nancy Reagan, "These Boots Are Made for Walkin'" singer Nancy Sinatra, and Sluggo's comic-strip sweetheart Nancy.

Naomi: Hebrew; "pleasant," which stands in contrast to Marah, "bitter." The name of the mother-in-law in the biblical Book of Ruth, Naomi was used by the Puritans, but didn't attain the popularity of Ruth. It has

Chapter 3: Gennifer, Gina, or Genevieve? Names for Girls

☺ ☺ ☹ ☺ ☺ ☹ ☺ ☺ ☹ ☺ ☺ ☹ ☺ ☺ ☹ ☺ ☺ ☺ ☹ ☺

survived, and Naomi is still viable. Since 1991, it has risen more than 100 spots to No. 169. Feminist social critic Naomi Wolf took on the cosmetics industry with her book *The Beauty Myth*, while Naomi Judd has made a name for herself in the world of country music as part of the mother-daughter duo the Judds.

Natalie: French; a feminine form from *dies natalis*, "birthday" — that is, Christmas. The Latin form is **Natalia.** A diminutive form in Russian yields **Natasha,** a popular Russian name — the heroine of Tolstoy's *War and Peace*. Natalie increased in usage in the 20th century, that trend continues today. Over the last decade, the name has slowly but steadily risen up the charts, ranking as the 30th most popular name for baby girls in 2002. The beautiful Natalie Wood successfully made the transition from child actress to Hollywood starlet and is known for her roles in such films as *West Side Story* and *Splendor in the Grass*. Singer Natalie Merchant earned praise for her sonorous voice and thoughtful lyrics as lead singer for the 10,000 Maniacs; she has since embarked on a fruitful solo career.

Nicole: French; "victory of the people." Nicole is a form of NICHOLAS (see Chapter 2). The contemporary actress Nicole Kidman is probably the most famous Nicole to date. Raised in Australia, she has forged a film career that is second to none. Her early role in the film *Days of Thunder* introduced her to her future husband (and now ex), Tom Cruise. She is known for her gutsy performances in such films as *To Die For, Eyes Wide Shut,* and *Moulin Rouge,* for which she won a Golden Globe. Her performance as Virginia Woolf in *The Hours* won her an Academy Award. Nicknames include **Nicky, Nicki,** and **Nikki.**

Nina: English; a borrowing of the Irish name Niamh, meaning "brightness, radiance." It has been used occasionally since the mid-19th century. Variations include **Nia** and **Nena.** One-hit-wonder Nena received airplay for "99 Luftballons." In contrast, soulful singer Nina Simone's acclaimed career spanned many decades.

Noel: French, from the Latin *natalis;* "having to do with birth," (that is, with Christmas). Though not a common name, Noel is appropriate for a boy or girl. British playwright Noël Coward wrote more than 60 plays, including *Private Lives* and *Blithe Spirit*. **Noelle** is an alternate — and more feminine — spelling.

Nora: Of uncertain origin, Nora is most simply explained as an abbreviation of the name **Honora.** Its popularity in Ireland, since at least the time of the Norman Conquest, suggests that it was originally used because of its similarity to some Celtic name. In the United States, the name retained its Irish associations, but, like BRIDGET, suffered a loss of social status. By the late 19th century, it may be classified as relatively uncommon. A spelling variation is **Norah.** Solo artist Norah Jones shocked the music world when she dominated at the 2003 Grammy Awards, winning in all five categories for which she had received nominations. Writer Nora Ephron is known for her screenplays of the popular romantic comedies *When Harry Met Sally* and *Sleepless in Seattle.*

O

Olivia: The Latin or Italian form of the name Olive, which you don't see much today. Olivia lingered in the 16th century in England and was used by Shakespear in *Twelfth Night.* In the United States, the name Olivia probably didn't appear before the late 19th century. Since the adoption of the name of an obscure saint seems unlikely at that time and place, the name may be connected with the use of plant names which arose at that period. In the United States, it used to be rare, although it was known from the Shakespearean use. These days, however, it's the tenth most popular name in the U.S. Aussie pop star Olivia Newton John made a name for herself opposite John Travolta in the film version of the musical *Grease.* She later scored a hit with the song "Let's Get Physical." **Liv** is a possible nickname — it's the name of stars like Liv Tyler (daughter of Aerosmith lead singer Steven Tyler) and Liv Ullman.

Names that rock!

Since the birth of rock 'n' roll, female names have been fixtures in song titles. Pick a name from one of the following songs, and you'll have a ready-made lullaby for your daughter. Bear in mind, though, that some of the songs contain lyrics that aren't befitting a cherub-cheeked baby girl.

- ❀ "Allison" by Elvis Costello
- ❀ "Amanda" by Boston
- ❀ "Amy" by Pure Prairie League
- ❀ "Angie" by Rolling Stones
- ❀ "Cecilia" by Simon & Garfunkel
- ❀ "Gloria" by Van Morrison
- ❀ "Julia" by The Beatles
- ❀ "Layla" by Derek and the Dominos
- ❀ "Lola" by The Kinks
- ❀ "Maybelline" by Chuck Berry
- ❀ "Melissa" by Allman Brothers Band
- ❀ "Roxanne" by The Police

P

Paige: French; "page, assistant." The name Paige is popping up more and more often as a female name — today, it ranks 49th on the list of the most popular names for baby girls. Paige Turco is a talented actress known to television audiences for recurring or starring roles in several hit series, including *Party of Five, NYPD Blue,* and *The Agency.* Another popular Paige is Paige Davis, the perky host of the Learning Channel's home-improvement series *Trading Spaces;* this Paige also happens to be a talented Broadway singer and dancer, having toured with the national touring company for the Broadway show *Beauty and the Beast.* If five letters seems like too many, try the shorter version **Page,** which has a more literary feel.

Pamela: Greek; "all honey." This name was coined by Sir Philip Sidney for a character in his *Arcadia* (1590). The name made little impression on the world until Samuel Richardson chose it for the heroine and title of his novel *Pamela* (1740). The great popularity of that work led to the use of Pamela as a personal name, but its popularity died out, and the name may never have crossed the Atlantic in the colonial period. In the mid-20th century, however, Pamela and its diminutive **Pam** became popular in the United States. Its popularity has lagged of late, though; it currently ranks as the 488th most popular name for baby girls. One famous Pam is tennis player Pam Shriver.

Paris: Although the French city name certainly springs to mind immediately, other (unrelated) sources for this name include the Trojan prince in the *Illiad* and a French version of the name PATRICK. Paris is known as a romantic, sophisticated city, and a girl with this name might be expected to be the same. Hotel-chain heiresses Paris Hilton, with her younger sister Nicky, gets a great deal of media coverage for her social exploits, shopping sprees, and fashion sense.

Patricia: Latin; "patrician." In England, the feminine of PATRICK came into general use after the birth and naming of Princess Patricia (1886); its use in the United States developed in the 20th century (probably from this English usage). Unlike Patrick, the name hasn't had close associations with the Irish. Its short forms are **Patty, Patti, Pat,** and **Patsy** — the first being the favorite. Notable holders of the name include the Colorado politician Pat Schroeder, the kidnapped and rescued Patty Hearst, and the singers Patty Griffin and Patsy Cline.

Paulina: Latin; "small." An appropriate name for a model, as in Paulina Porizkova. The name has never been more than moderately popular in the United States. Variations include **Paula** and **Pauline**.

Penelope: Greek; "bobbin." Penelope was the name of Odysseus' wife, who devoted much of her time to weaving. With some stretching of etymological information, the meaning of this name is associated with weaving. But, like so many Homeric names, it may actually be of non-Greek origin. The American tradition has made little use of Greek mythology as a source for names. Penelope appeared as an English name in the late 16th century but didn't become common. The Homeric lady was a paragon of domestic virtues — an almost ideal role model for the Christian housewife — but the Puritans never really adopted her name, either. The nickname **Penny** sometimes appears, although it may seem a bit old-fashioned today. Spanish-born actress Penelope Cruz brings a modern edge to this name.

Peyton: Old English; "Pacca's ridge" or "Paega's village." This name is suitable for a boy or a girl, although Peyton is more closely associated with girls, while the variation **Payton** is considered more masculine. Peyton ranked as the 189th most popular name for baby girls in 2002.

Phoebe: Greek; "shining one." The name is well known in ancient Greek mythology — Phoebus being, among other things, a common term for Apollo in the Homeric poems. The actual source of the female name for the American settlers, however, was the passage in Romans 16:1, in which the writer commends "Phebe our Sister." In New England and other colonies, the name (often spelled Phebe), though never really popular, was viable down through the 19th century. The accepted pronunciation is of two syllables, although the spelling **Phebe** suggests a monosyllable. Phoebe rose in popularity over the course of the 1990s, perhaps due to the success of the TV show *Friends*, which features a character named Phoebe, played by actress Lisa Kudrow.

Piper: English; "flute player." This androgynous name seems to have come out of nowhere in recent years. It's still rare, but it's broken into the top 500 names after being outside the top 1,000 prior to 1999. One of Hollywood's celebrated actresses, Piper Laurie has starred in more than 60 films throughout her long career. She's also known for her fiery performances on many television shows, from *St. Elsewhere* and *Twin Peaks* to *ER* and *Frasier*. Piper Perabo is an up-and-coming actress, having appeared in *Coyote Ugly* and *The Adventures of Rocky & Bullwinkle*.

Priscilla: Latin; a diminutive and feminine form of *priscus*, meaning "previous, former." A Priscilla is mentioned in Acts 18:2, and a Prisca (probably the same person) appears in II Timothy 4:19. Priscus had a number of meanings, among them "old, primitive, strict." The use of the name in the United States probably wasn't directly influenced by those meanings, the name rather being taken directly from the biblical text. Priscilla appeared chiefly in the period of biblical names, with a New England background. It was rare, and Prisca was even rarer. The diminutive was Prissy, and the adjective *prissy* may have arisen from this name, some of whose meanings point in that direction. Priscilla Presley is best known as the wife to Elvis and mother to Lisa Marie, but she's had a successful career in her own right as an actress and a model.

☺ ☺ ☹ ☺ ☺ ☹ ☺ ☺ ☹ ☺ ☺ ☹ ☺ ☺ ☹ ☺ ☺ ☺ ☺ ☹ ☺

R

Rachel: Probably Hebrew; "ewe, lamb." In Genesis, Rachel bore a sweetly poetic name, was "beautiful and well-favored," and was the subject of a romantic tale of her wooing by Jacob. In short, she topped off this good press by dying young in childbirth. Yet for some reason, her name was never greatly favored — her counterpart, REBECCA, was much more common. When biblical names went out of style, the name almost died out. It experienced something of a revival in the late 19th century, became very rare in the 20th, and then experienced another resurgence in the 1970s. For more than a decade, it has remained among the top 25 names, having peaked at No. 9 in 1996. This peak is probably related to the TV show *Friends*, which features a main character named Rachel, played by Jennifer Aniston. A famous real-life Rachel is environmentalist Rachel Carson, whose influential book *Silent Spring* (1962) criticized the use of DDT and other pesticides and, some say, helped launched the environmental movement. **Rachael, Rashel** and **Rachelle** (the French form with a slightly different pronunciation) are variants of this name. See also RAQUEL.

Ramona: Old German; "might and protection." Ramona is the feminine form of RAMÓN, which came into American usage from the Spanish. The English version is Raymond. The popular 1884 novel *Ramona*, by Helen Hunt Jackson, brought some prominence to the name, and it became common in the late 19th and early 20th centuries. Gen Xers may remember the sassy young character Ramona Quimby from the Beverly Cleary's series of children's books that included *Ramona the Pest*.

Raquel: The Spanish form of RACHEL. With the growth of the Spanish-speaking population in the United States, this name is increasingly in popularity; it's among the top 400 names in use. Born Raquel Tejada, Raquel Welch was known more for being a sex symbol than for being an actress of any great talent.

Reagan: Irish; "regal." A name that has risen in popularity in recent years, Reagan is appropriate for a boy or a girl. Whether or not this upswing has anything to do with former president Ronald Reagan, or his "Just Say No" wife Nancy, is anyone's guess, but if the apparent Republican connection doesn't sit right with you, try **Regan,** the name of a character in Shakespeare's *King Lear* (albeit a not-so-nice one — one of two manipulative daughters of the king, she ends up being poisoned to death by her evil sister).

Rebecca: Hebrew; meanings range from "heifer" to "a noose." This name first appeared in Genesis. Brought to America by early immigrants, Rebecca became established immediately in the colonies, especially in New England, where it commonly appeared in the top ten. After a long decline along with the other biblical names, Rebecca recovered in the 20th century, again becoming a viable name. The reasons for this popularity aren't

☺ ☺ ☹ ☺ ☺ ☹ ☺ ☺ ☹ ☺ ☺ ☹ ☺ ☺ ☹ ☺ ☺ ☺ ☹ ☺

easy to determine, aside from the fact that she was a prominent character in the story of the patriarchs and was one of the few biblical characters to show regard for animals. She was, however, by no means wholly admirable. For example, she was underhanded in her aid to her son Jacob. Her great moment is that of her blessing: "Thou art our sister, be thou the mother of thousands of millions," to which is added the belligerent note, "Let thy seed possess the gate of those which hate them." The New Testament spelling, Rebecca, was regularly employed in America, as opposed to the Old Testament spelling, **Rebekah.** For years, **Becky** was the common diminutive, but today, **Becca** has become more popular. Daphne de Maurier's novel *Rebecca* is a classic work of fiction that the *Library Journal* called "arguably the most famous and well-loved gothic novel of the 20th century."

Reese: Welsh; "splendor," "abundance," "onslaught." That's a good descriptor for actress Reese Witherspoon, who has become one of Hollywood's most popular actresses. In 1999, she made a splash as the nice one in the movie *Cruel Intentions,* and she came into her own as a leading lady in 2001's *Legally Blonde.* Gospel singer Della Reese also starred in the once-popular TV series *Touched by an Angel.* **Reece** is another option, although it's used more often for boys than for girls (as is the name in general).

Renee: French; "reborn." Although this name has been declining in popularity in the past couple of decades, it's still in use. The fame of actress Renee Zellweger, who has starred in much-loved films such as *Chicago, Jerry Maguire,* and *Bridget Jones's Diary,* may well bring about a revival in the coming years.

Rhonda: Welsh; "noisy, babbling." This name, which is uncommon today, will forever be associated with the Beach Boys. Their song "Help Me, Rhonda," written by Brian Wilson, is about a guy looking to Rhonda to help him get over a previous love. No one knows if Rhonda ever succeeded, but this classic rock tune established the feel-good Beach Boys sound that influenced many other bands. Another Rhonda of note is Rhonda Gowler Green, the author of such children's books as *Jamboree Day* and *When a Line Bends . . . A Shape Begins.* **Rhoda** is similar.

Riley: English/Irish; the English name means "rye clearing." The Irish is an anglicized shortening of the Irish surname *O'Raghallaigh.* Traditionally, Riley is a male name, but it has quickly gained acceptance as a feminine name as well. Today, it's even more popular for girls than it is for boys, sitting at No. 77 in 2002. Given that the phrase "life of Riley" has come to mean "the good life," this name is an optimistic and hopeful choice. Variants include **Rylee** and **Ryleigh.**

Robin: English. This name, traditionally male, consists of the shortening of ROBERT with the addition of the common diminutive *-in.* It was used often in the Middle Ages, as evidenced by its use for the folk hero Robin Hood and by the commonness of the family name Robinson. In the 17th and 18th centuries, it was seldom used as a given name. In America, the name was applied to a bird (although not the same bird as the one called a robin in Britain). At some point, probably in the early 19th century, the name began to be thought of as a feminine one, and a small movement toward birds' names was thus inaugurated. It's still used as a male name, too — think of Robin Williams and Robin Gibbs of the Bee Gees. Among female Robins, actress Robin Wright Penn has appeared in numerous films, including *Forrest Gump* and *The Princess Bride.* **Robyn** is an alternate spelling.

Rose: To American namers, the association with the flower is obvious. In actual history, however, Rose apparently originated in such names as ROS-ALIND. (Note that the character Rosalind of Shakespeare's *As You Like It* is familiarly called Rose.) Rosalind is a typical two-element Germanic name, from *ros*, meaning "horse," and *linda*, meaning "serpent." Equally likely to have generated Rose is ROSAMOND, which means "horse protection." (But perhaps you'd prefer not to think of that somewhat strange meaning.) Although the name Rose has never been common, it appeared in English during the Middle Ages. Being of non-Christian origin, it existed in spite of the church. After the 13th century, however, the name was connected to St. Rose of Viterbo. The pleasant suggestion and the brevity of Rose led to its use in compounds, such as **Rosalie, Roseanne,** and **Rosemary.** The Latin form **Rosa** also exists, and Rosie is a possible nickname. Actress Rose McGowan has made a splash as one of three witches on the TV show *Charmed.* Comediennes Roseanne Barr and Rosie O'Donnell both found fame as actresses, Barr on television and O'Donnell on the silver screen. A positive association is with Rosie the Riveter, a symbol of female strength and determination during World War II.

Ruby: English; a precious stone. This rich red gem is the second hardest natural mineral on Earth and is the July birthstone. Like **Diamond,** it has maintained a fairly steady place among the top 200 girls' names. Ruby has appeared in a number of songs, from Dion's "Ruby Baby" to the Rolling Stones' "Ruby Tuesday" to Kenny Rogers' "Ruby, Don't Take Your Love to Town" to the Smashing Pumpkins' "Through the Eyes of Ruby."

Ruth: Hebrew; possibly "friend, companion." The name was already in use among the first white immigrants to America, and it seems to have increased in popularity. In Boston births from 1630 to 1690, Ruth stood in seventh place for girls. In the 18th and 19th centuries, the name suffered during much of that antibiblical period. Toward the end of the 19th century, however, it became common again, and it remained popular in the 20th century. As for the causes of this continuing popularity, Ruth is not only a book of the Bible, but also the name of its chief character, highly praised and sympathetically conceived. As a noun, the word means "compassion," and this coincidence may have been a factor in its popularity as a name. One detail of Ruth's story came especially close to that of early American women. Like her, they had migrated, and they faced the problems of being "strangers in a strange land" and the heartbreaking dilemma of "to go or to stay" when families had to be divided forever. An occasional man, as merchant or seaman, might visit England, but a woman had no such hope. Well-known Ruths have shown themselves to be symbols of

☺ ☺ ☹ ☺ ☺ ☹ ☺ ☺ ☹ ☺ ☺ ☹ ☺ ☺ ☹ ☺ ☺ ☹ ☺

strength and compassion. Diminutive Dr. Ruth Westheimer, who escaped Nazi Germany as a girl, found great success in the United States as a psychologist and sex therapist, bringing comfort to many. Ruth Bader Ginsburg sits on the bench of the U.S. Supreme Court. Before being named to the Court by President Clinton, she made a name for herself by arguing women's rights cases.

Rylee: See RILEY.

Ryleigh: See RILEY.

S

Sabrina: Brittonic; meaning unknown. The name Sabrina appears in the Celtic legend as the goddess of the Severn River; according to the legend, Sabrina drowned in the river, and the river is said to be named after her. A famous fictional Sabrina is the title character from the 1954 film *Sabrina*, played perfectly by Audrey Hepburn. Sabrina Fairchild embodies the definition of "princess" in this modern-day fairy tale. She starts out as the awkward daughter of the chauffer of a wealthy family who returns after a two-year stay in Paris to become the object of affection for both of the family's sons. The name has been fairly popular for decades, having ranked between 50 and 140 in recent years.

Ten names from Shakespeare

If great literature inspires you, a name from one of the Bard's many plays just might fit the bill for your baby. Here are some names from Shakespearean classics that still sound modern today:

- ❀ **Ariel:** *The Tempest*
- ❀ **Beatrice:** *Much Ado about Nothing*
- ❀ **Bianca:** *Othello, The Taming of the Shrew*
- ❀ **Cordelia:** *King Lear*
- ❀ **Isabella:** *Measure for Measure*
- ❀ **Miranda:** *The Tempest*
- ❀ **Paris:** *Romeo and Juliet*
- ❀ **Phebe:** *As You Like It*
- ❀ **Portia:** *The Merchant of Venice, Julius Caesar*
- ❀ **Regan:** *King Lear*

Sadie: Hebrew; "princess." A related name is SARAH, from which Sadie derives. This name has become increasingly common in recent years, jumping from 439th in 1992 to 215th in 2002. A famous Sadie is Sadie Hawkins, the character from the early 20th century's *Lil' Abner* comic strip who was anything but a princess. Instead, she was "the homeliest gal in the woods." Her father began Sadie Hawkins Day, on which the unmarried girls of the town would enter a footrace to catch the town's bachelors. Not exactly a positive image to look up to, although this comic strip event served as the basis for real-life Sadie Hawkins Days, on which it's traditional for women to take the initiative to ask the men of their choice out on dates. So you might say that Sadie Hawkins helped to encourage women's independence.

Sage: English. The word *sage* means "wise one." The androgynous name remains rare, but the positive association makes it worthy of consideration if you're looking for something different. Sylvester Stallone has a son named Sage.

Salma: Probably a variation of the name SELMA. *Frieda* star Salma Hayek has brought fame to this otherwise uncommon name.

Samantha: American; see SAMUEL in Chapter 2. Samantha has become one of the most popular names in the United States — it's been in the top ten for more than a decade. On television, you may remember the character Samantha Stevens, portrayed by actress Elizabeth Montgomery on the sitcom *Bewitched*. This Samantha was a witch — but a good one — who chose to listen to her heart and marry a mortal. Another fictional Samantha is Kim Catrall's saucy single on the racy television series *Sex and the City*. Real-life Samanthas include British actresses Samantha Morton, who received an Academy Award nomination for her role as a mute woman in Woody Allen's *Sweet and Lowdown*, and Samantha Bond, who is known for her performances in several film versions of Shakespeare's works and who took over the role of Miss Moneypenny when Pierce Brosnan became the new James Bond. **Sam** is a common nickname.

Sandra: See ALEXANDRA, its more popular cousin. Well-known Sandras include actress Sandra Bullock and Supreme Court Justice Sandra Day O'Connor. **Saundra** is another possible spelling (with a slightly different pronunciation), and **Sandy** is the usual nickname.

Sarah: Hebrew; "princess." The name Sarah has its origins in the Bible; Sarah of Sarai was the wife Abraham and the mother of Isaac. Although Sarah wasn't a particularly significant or lovable character, the name is one of the more popular biblical names you'll find. It came into use with the Reformation and was well established by the 17th century. It fell off considerably toward the end of the 19th century and came to be regarded as old-fashioned, often losing out to its own variant, **Sallie.** Of course, there's Sarah Ferguson (also known as Fergie), who became a real-life princess by marrying Prince Andrew. And in the show business world, one

of the most popular actresses today is Sarah Jessica Parker, best known for her portrayal of newspaper columnist Carrie Bradshaw in *Sex and the City.* Sarah Vaughn, the 20th-century jazz singer, ranks right up there with Ella Fitzgerald and Billie Holiday as having one of the finest voices in jazz history. Another Sarah with a voice to remember is Sarah McLachlan, who came onto the music scene in the late 1980s. **Sara** is a shorter version.

Savannah: Spanish; "treeless plain." Savannah was the first city established in the state of Georgia, and it remains a center of Southern culture with a rich history. The actress Savannah Haske is beginning to make a name for herself in both television and film, starring as Tatiana in the TV drama *Third Watch.* If you like, you can drop the *h* and name your daughter **Savanna.** The name has ranked near No. 40 on the the list of most popular names for baby girls for seven years running.

Selena: Origin and meaning uncertain. It may be from the French name **Celine**, with an unusual alteration of spelling. Celine may be from the Latin name **Coelina,** which means "heavenly." The name is commonly related to the Greek word *selene,* meaning "moon." It's still a fairly rare name in English, although it has gained popularity in the Latino community due largely in part to Tejano singer Selena, whose career was advancing by leaps and bounds until she was murdered at age 24 by the president of her fan club. **Selina** is an alternate spelling. If you like the sound of this name, you might also consider **Serena,** a Latin name that means "calm, serene." Tennis star Serena Williams has brought prominence to this name in recent years.

Selma: A short form of **Anselma,** from an Old German root meaning "god and helmet." Actress Selma Blair has appeared in such movies as *Cruel Intentions* and *Legally Blond.*

Shania: English; either a variant of **Shayna,** which means "beautiful" in Yiddish, or a variant of Shan, which is an Old English form of JEANNE. Despite its questionable roots, the name is experiencing a resurgence. Shania Twain probably has something to do with that — she remains the most popular country singer of her era, having successfully fused country with pop and rock.

Shannon: Gaelic; "old, ancient." Another possible origin is the river Shannon. This traditional Irish name (which can also be used for boys) brings to mind dark-haired beauties like Shannon Doherty (from TV's *Beverly Hills 90210* and *Charmed*) and Shannon Elizabeth (from the movie *American Pie*). It's been consistently popular in the United States, reaching as high as 21 in the 1970s. It remains in the top 200 today. For variety, try **Shanon** or **Shannan.**

Sharon: In the Old Testament, Sharon is the name of a place. As "rose of Sharon," it appears in the Song of Solomon as the symbol of the beloved. Since Rose was a well-established name in English, 18th-century usage could easily adopt the longer form, so the name appeared as Rose-of-Sharon. (See also ROSE.) It was shortened in pronunciation, with the spelling Rosasharn. The appearance of a character so named in John Steinbeck's *The Grapes of Wrath* (1939) must have disseminated the knowledge of this form. A shorter form produced Sharon, which established itself later in the 20th century, sometimes making the top ten. Today, it's much less common, although there are several Sharons of note, including actress Sharon Stone and Sharon Osbourne, wife and manager of heavy metal legend Ozzy. Alternate spellings include **Sharron, Sharin,** and **Sharyn.**

Shelby: English; probably "farm on a slope or plateau." Although it began as a male name, Shelby has been among the top 75 girls' names in the United States in recent years, peaking at No. 35 in the early 1990s. It's often associated with Southerners, from the country singer and Grammy Award winner Shelby Lynne to Julia Roberts' character in the tearjerker *Steel Magnolias.* **Selby** is a similar name.

Sidney: See SYDNEY.

Long and flowery names

A long name can sound dignified and formal. If you're looking for these qualities in a name, consider the following options. But think twice if your last name is long as well; you don't want to give your child a lifetime of hand cramps from writing out all those letters!

- Adriana
- Alexandra
- Anastasia
- Cassandra
- Dominique
- Francesca
- Genevieve
- Jacqueline
- Madeleine
- Samantha (but watch out — this one is often shortened to the very unflowery Sam)
- Savannah
- Veronica
- Yesenia

☺ ☺ ☹ ☺ ☺ ☹ ☺ ☺ ☹ ☺ ☺ ☹ ☺ ☺ ☹ ☺ ☺ ☺ ☹ ☺

Sierra: Spanish; "mountain." This popular name conjures up images of far-away places. The African region of Sierra Leone has faced a dark and troubled history since its 1961 independence from Britain, despite the fact that it's home to some of the largest and richest diamond and other mineral deposits in the world. However, reforms are beginning to take hold there, with the help of the United Nations, and it's hoped that the region will once again become hospitable to visitors. The Sierra Nevada is a mountain range in eastern California that extends into western Nevada. Another famous Sierra is an organization called the Sierra Club, which was established in 1892 and continues to fight for environmental issues. So any way you look at it, this is a name that's associated with the earth. Ciara and Cierra are alternate spellings.

Simone: French; "it is heard." Simone, a rare name today, is the French form of SIMON (see Chapter 2). French feminist and philosopher Simone de Beauvoir made herself heard when she published her study *The Second Sex,* the 1949 work in which she explored the position of women in society. Her conclusion that women hold a secondary status in society helped fuel the feminist movement. Another famous Simone was the French actress Simone Signoret, who is known for her strong performances in such films as *Les Diaboliques, Room at the Top,* and *Ship of Fools.*

Skye: Gaelic; from the Isle of Skye. In northwestern Scotland, the Isle of Skye is known for its dramatic and unspoiled scenery, so this name is likely to make others think of beauty. It's never been a wildly popular name, but its uniqueness and lack of negative associations make it worthy of consideration.

Skylar: Scandinavian; "scholar." Suitable for a girl or a boy, Skylar has risen dramatically in popularity in recent years. In 1992, it ranked as the 595th most popular name for girls; in 2002, the name had risen to 144th for girls.

Sonia: Russian; a diminutive of SOPHIA, which means "wise." Probably transmitted at the literary level by the reading of Russian works in translation, Sonia survives in American use, but it has remained a fairly rare name. Actress Sonia Braga has been in a number of acclaimed films, from *Kiss of the Spider Woman* to *The Burning Season.* **Sonya** is an alternate spelling.

Sophia, Sofia: Greek; "wise." The name Sophia makes a brief appearance in Gnostic mythology as she leads the ancient Greek gods on a mission to retake Mount Olympus. St. Sophia's Cathedral is a famous church in Russia that was named in honor of God's wisdom. Perhaps the most famous Sophia, however, is Italian actress Sophia Loren, who was primarily known as an international sex symbol until her role in the film *Two Women,* for which she won an Academy Award and was finally taken seriously as an actress. Sofia Coppola is the daughter of acclaimed film director Francis Ford Coppola and first appeared in his *Godfather* films. This talented actress has also played roles in such films as *Peggy Sue Got*

Chapter 3: Gennifer, Gina, or Genevieve? Names for Girls

☺ ☺ ☹ ☺ ☺ ☹ ☺ ☺ ☹ ☺ ☺ ☹ ☺ ☺ ☹ ☺ ☺ ☺ ☹ ☺

Married and *The Cotton Club,* in addition to having directed two of her own movies, *The Virgin Suicides* and *Lost in Translation,* starring Bill Murray. **Sophie** is a popular variation.

Stella: Latin; "star." The name apparently was first used as a fictional one by Sir Philip Sidney in his sonnet sequence *Astrophel to Stella (1591).* In the United States, it's appeared occasionally from the mid-19th century on, probably arising from its literary usage. In the film version of the play *A Streetcar Named Desire,* Marlon Brando made this name famous, desperately, drunkenly calling up to his wife, Stella, after having been tossed out into the street. Stella McCartney, daughter of Beatle Paul, is a rising star in fashion design.

Stephanie: Greek; "crown." The feminine of STEPHEN (see Chapter 2), Stephanie is a borrowing from the French that has maintained the Greek *ph* in the name. Until the mid-20th century, its use was generally negligible, but then it became popular. It remains quite popular today, although slightly less so than it was ten years ago, when it cracked the top ten. True to her name, Princess Stephanie, the daughter of King Rainier III and actress Grace Kelly (Princess Grace), wears the crown of Monaco. Alternate spellings include **Stefanie** and **Stefani,** and **Stef** and **Steffie** are possible nicknames.

Summer: English. Although modern use of this name is likely to be connected to the season, the English surname Summer is likely to derive from "sumpter, pack-horse." Olympic swimmer and Stanford University graduate Summer Sanders sets an excellent example for girls with her combination of athletic prowess and intellect.

Susan, Susanna(h): Hebrew; "lily." The name of the chief character of the famous tale Susanna and the Elders. This story, found in the biblical Apocrypha, was highly popular in the Christian tradition of the Middle Ages and has maintained itself to some degree in modern times by being anthologized as the first detective story. The name was already established in England before the colonization, and early American listings include it as a common name, spelled Susanna or Susannah. Susan, an obvious contraction, appeared rarely at first but became the predominant form in the 18th century. Generally standing in the second ten, the name occasionally reached the top ten (and would have ranked higher except that Susanna and Susan are generally listed as separate names). By the late 19th century, the name had declined sharply and was old-fashioned to most people. However, it revived in the 20th century, as such names are likely to do. In two lists of the 1950s, Susan stands in second and third place. And if the French form **Suzanne** is included, the combined count would edge the name up even further. **Sue, Susie, Suzie,** and **Susy** developed as nicknames. Susan B. Anthony was an American suffragist and, before the Sacajawea dollar was released, was the only woman to have appeared on American currency. Actress and political activist Susan Sarandon has received critical acclaim for her roles in such films as *Dead Man Walking* and *Bull Durham;* a lesser-known fact is that she starred as the naïve

Janet in *The Rocky Horror Picture Show*. Suzanne Somers starred as Chrissy Snow in the television series *Three's Company* and has since become known as a diet and exercise guru.

Sydney: French; an English surname derived from a French place name. Mark Twain used Sid Sawyer for the unpleasant younger brother of the typically American older brother named Tom. In spite of Twain, the name Sidney continued to be used. In fact, it shows a marked increase from 1870 to 1890, including the year of publication of *Huckleberry Finn*. The heroic figure of Sydney Carton in Dickens's *Tale of Two Cities* (1859) probably stimulated the use of the name as well. The variation between *i* and *y* is a matter of no importance, since early printers used the two letters interchangeably. With the passage of time, the aristocratic aura of the name faded out, but it remained viable. **Sidney** developed as a female form, but today, both forms are more commonly given to girls than to boys. Sydney, the more popular spelling for girls, has skyrocketed up to No. 23.

Sylvia: Latin; "of the woods, sylvan." Rhaea Silvia was a figure in Roman mythology, and Silvia came into renewed use as a given name in Italy at the time of the Renaissance. Its use by Shakespeare in *Two Gentlemen of Verona* is probably one cause of its preservation in English. Somewhere along the line, a *y* form developed. Today, both versions are still in use, but their popularity has waned considerably. Among well-known Sylvias, writer Sylvia Plath achieved fame for her poetry, her stormy marriage to fellow poet Ted Hughes, and her suicide at age 31. Her semi-autobiographical novel *The Bell Jar* recounts her struggles with depression.

T

Tabitha: Aramaic; "deer, antelope," probably conceived as a symbol of grace and beauty. Tabitha was the name of a woman who was restored to life by St. Peter, according to Acts 9. Although it partook of the general popularity of biblical names, Tabitha never became really popular. Its greater use may have been prevented by the string of meanings that attached themselves to the short form, **Tabby.** At various times, it has meant a house-cat, a spinster, and a gossip. In recent years, it peaked at No. 195. Tabitha Soren was a longtime MTV news reporter, scoring a Peabody award for her coverage of the 1992 presidential election.

Talia: A pet name for Natalia. (See NATALIE.) Actress Talia Shire is the sister of famed filmmaker Francis Ford Coppola, and she rose to stardom by playing Adrian, the wife of Sylvester Stallone's Rocky Balboa in each of the five films of the series. (Who can forget Rocky's triumphant cry of "Adrian!" at the end of the first film?) She's also known for her role of Connie Corleone in the *Godfather* films, which were directed by her brother.

Tamara: Russian; possibly connected with the Biblical name Tamar, which means "date palm." Tamara McKinney was the first woman to win the

Chapter 3: Gennifer, Gina, or Genevieve? Names for Girls

☺ ☺ ☹ ☺ ☺ ☹ ☺ ☹ ☹ ☺ ☺ ☹ ☺ ☺ ☹ ☺ ☺ ☺ ☹ ☺

over all Alpine World Cup championship in skiing. In another pioneering performance, Tammy Wynette sang "Stand by Your Man," which became the bestselling single ever by a female country singer. **Tammy** and **Tami** are common nicknames.

Tara: Irish; a place name. The hill of Tara was named after a mythical woman Teamhair, whose name appears to mean "eminence." Everyone recognizes Tara as the name of the home of Scarlett O'Hara in Margaret Mitchell's *Gone with the Wind.* Mitchell placed the fictional Tara in the real-life county of Clayton in Georgia, and for her novel, she drew from the experiences of her family in that area. As a place, Tara was also the name of a mysterious castle in the hills of Ireland, and it makes an appearance in Thomas Moore's famous poem "The Harp That Once Through Tara's Halls." As for notable women with the name Tara, figure skater Tara Lipinski climbed many "hills" to win gold at the 1998 Summer Olympics, beating favorite Michelle Kwan to become the youngest gold medal winner ever in women's figure skating.

Tatiana: Origin and meaning uncertain. Tatiana is probably from the name of an early Russian martyr. Grand Duchess Tatiana Nicolaievna was the daughter of Nicholas and Alexandra, the last crowned tsars of Russia. She served as a nurse during World War I before she was executed with her parents and other siblings by the Bolsheviks in 1918. Another Tatiana of note is the 20th-century archeologist Tatiana Proskouriakoff, who is known for her examinations of Mayan artifacts.

Tatum: Old Norse; "cheerful." Tatum is the feminine form of TATE. Actress Tatum O'Neal has had plenty to be cheerful about. The daughter of respected actor Ryan O'Neal and later wife of tennis great John McEnroe, she was the youngest actress to ever win an Academy Award, for her role in *Paper Moon.* She became one of the most successful child actresses in Hollywood in the 1970s, with roles in such films as in *The Bad News Bears* and *International Velvet.*

Taylor: English; "tailor." This name is used for both boys and girls — and may be considered more of a girl's name these days. You could say that Samuel Taylor Coleridge was a master tailor when it came to the craft of poetry. The 19th-century poet was a close friend of William Wordsworth, and together they published *Lyrical Ballads* in 1798. Although Coleridge had only four poems in the book, one of them was perhaps his most famous: "The Rime of the Ancient Mariner." Although there are few famous female first-name Taylors (as of yet, that is — given that this name has been among the top 20 for more than a decade, famous Taylors are sure to emerge!), there are many well-known women with the last name Taylor, from legendary actress and serial wife Elizabeth, to supermodel Niki, to blues singer Koko.

Teresa: Origin and meaning unknown. It became widely known because of St. Teresa of Avila (1515 to 1582). The name was somewhat popular in

England after 1700 because of its alliance with Austria, whose queen was Maria Theresa. In the American colonies, the name was always rare, but it survived into the 20th century, even with some increase, perhaps because of a certain popularity of Spanish names, such as LINDA. The late Mother Teresa, Christian missionary and winner of the Nobel Prize for Peace, kept this name in the public eye throughout the 20th century. **Theresa** is an alternate, equally common spelling.

Tess, Tessa: Shortened forms of TERESA.

Thelma: Apparently a coinage by the novelist Marie Corelli, Thelma appeared as the name of the chief character in the 1898 novel *Thelma*. Today, this name is known primarily for its use in the film *Thelma and Louise*, which gives it an air of female empowerment.

Theresa: See TERESA.

Tia: Spanish; "aunt." Hawaiian actress Tia Carrere seemed like more of a goddess than an aunt to Wayne and Garth in the movie *Wayne's World*. She also provided the voice for the title character Lilo in the animated film (and ensuing TV series) *Lilo & Stitch*.

Tiffany: An English adaptation of the Greek name Theophania, another name for the day of Epiphany, meaning "the manifestation of God." The religious significance of this Tiffany dates back centuries, as it became tradition to give this name to girls who were born on the Epiphany (otherwise known as January 6) in order to honor the Magi's visit to the Baby Jesus. In modern times, few people can think of the name Tiffany without thinking of the classic Audrey Hepburn romantic comedy *Breakfast at Tiffany's*, which was based on a Truman Capote novel. Singer Tiffany's appearance on the pop music scene must have seemed like an almost religious experience to her legions of teenage fans. With her first album, she became the youngest female artist to reach No. 1 on the Billboard music charts. In the 1980s and '90s, Tiffany-Amber Thiessen played both a villain and an innocent, on TV's *Beverly Hills 90210* and *Saved by the Bell*, respectively. **Tiffani** is an alternate spelling.

Tori: See VICTORIA.

Tricia, Trisha: See PATRICIA.

Trinity: Latin; "three." The Holy Trinity refers to the Christian belief that God has three states of being: Father, Son, and Holy Spirit. The name never actually appears in the Bible; rather, the Holy Trinity as a doctrine is recognized from the Bible as a way of teaching about the existence of and belief in God. Numerous Christian schools and colleges are named Trinity. As a name, Trinity *can* carry a symbolism that's unrelated to religion. In the *Matrix* films, Carrie-Ann Moss plays a character named Trinity, a tough, strong woman who helps save the world from artificially intelligent machines.

U

Ursula: Latin; a diminutive of *ursa*, "female bear." The name, however, is from St. Ursula, legendary in medieval times because of her association with the story of the 11,000 virgins slain by a horde of Huns. The name has always been rare in the United States, whose inhabitants apparently weren't enamored of such wholesale virginity. Nonetheless, there are some famous Ursulas, including feminist science-fiction writer Ursula Le Guin and 1960s film actress Ursula Andress, who made her debut in the James Bond film *Dr. No.* On the TV series *Friends*, Phoebe's twin sister (also played by actress Lisa Kudrow) is named Ursula.

V

Valerie: A feminine form of VALERIUS, a Roman family name. As the name of two saints, one of them French, Valerie is current in French, where it means "strong, powerful." French influence has kept this name in use in the United States; since 1990, it has consistently ranked between 130th and 165th on the Social Security Administration's list of the top American names. Famous Valeries include TV actresses Valerie Harper and Valerie Bertinelli (also known as the wife of rocker Eddie Van Halen). Steve Winwood brought this name to international attention with his hit song "Valerie."

Vanessa: Greek; "butterfly." Author Jonathan Swift invented this name for in his poem "Cadenus and Vanessa," in which he wrote about the woman he loved. The name later became the genus for butterfly. The widely admired actress Vanessa Redgrave is known for her powerful performances in such films as *The Taming of the Shrew*, *Smilla's Sense of Snow*, and *Mrs. Dalloway*. Her work has garnered many awards over the years, including an Oscar nomination for *The Bostonians* and an Academy Award for *Julia*. Another famous Vanessa is Vanessa Williams, the first African-American woman to win the Miss America Pageant. Williams has had successful careers in both music and film, as well as on Broadway. Vanessa remains among the top 100 names used in America, having ranked between 50th and 70th for more than a decade.

Venus: This name, from the ancient Roman goddess of love, originally occurred as a slave name. Today, however, it has a much more positive connotation, largely due to the success of tennis star Venus Williams (along with her younger sister, SERENA). It remains rare, however.

Veronica: Latin; from the phrase *vera iconica*, "having to do with the true image." The reference is to the representation of the face of Christ on the handkerchief of the woman who became St. Veronica. The name has declined in popularity since its peak at No. 89 in the early 1990s, but it remains among the top 200 girls' names. Actress Veronica Lake was known for her sculpted blond hair and her "peek-a-boo bang." In the 1990s, singer Elvis Costello had a hit song called "Veronica" about a spunky old woman.

Victoria: Latin; "victory." Queen Victoria, herself named after her German mother, brought the name into English usage. Her reign was long and successful, and she was personally popular. The era in which she ruled is even known as the Victorian age, which has come to be associated with propriety and restraint (not to mention beautiful, stately homes). Queen Victoria's name, however, was only moderately popular as a personal name among the British, even though it appeared on cities, states, and natural features all over the world. In the United States today, it's quite popular; since 1990, it has been in the top 25. Well-known Victorias include actress and beauty expert Victoria Principal, comedian Victoria Jackson, "Posh Spice" Victoria Beckham, and actress Victoria "Tori" Spelling. **Tori, Vicki,** and **Vicky** are nicknames.

Virginia: Latin; "virgin." In the United States, this name is inescapably tied to the state of Virginia, the name of which was bestowed in 1584 by Queen Elizabeth I. Because Elizabeth was frequently celebrated as the Virgin Queen, the naming was really a naming for herself. In 1587, the first English child to be born in America was christened Virginia Dare. She was, however, lost along with the rest of the Raleigh colony, and no tradition of naming baby girls Virginia resulted directly from her. The name began to appear in the 19th century and enjoyed a sudden burst of popularity around 1900. It still remains fairly common, although less so than it was a few decades ago. Writer Virginia Woolf is known for her groundbreaking book *A Room of One's Own* and other works; her novel *Mrs. Dalloway* served as the catalyst for Michael Cunningham's novel *The Hours*, which was made into a highly acclaimed film in 2002.

Vivian, Vivien: Latin; "full of life, vibrant." Theoretically, Vivian should be a man's name; Vivien is the equivalent for a woman. Vivian (the more popular version today) comes from the name of several saints. Vivien may be a misreading of the Celtic name Ninian, and it appears in Tennyson's *Idylls of the King* as a woman's name. Actress Vivien Leigh, born in India (interestingly, her given name was Vivian with an *a*), will forever be known as the Scarlett O'Hara she portrayed in the 1930s movie *Gone with the Wind*. **Viviana** is another form of this name.

W

Wendy: This name seems not to have existed before being used by J. M. Barrie for a character in the beloved 1904 children's story *Peter Pan* — he probably coined the name. Its close resemblance to WANDA may be coincidental. The remarkable feature about this name is its growth in popularity from that recent origin. In the late 20th century, it became a popular name in the United States, even acquiring a variant spelling, **Wendi. Wenda** is an older alternative. Everyone knows this name from the hamburger chain

Chapter 3: Gennifer, Gina, or Genevieve? Names for Girls

☺ ☺ ☹ ☺ ☺ ☹ ☺ ☺ ☹ ☺ ☺ ☹ ☺ ☺ ☹ ☺ ☺ ☺ ☹ ☺

Wendy's, named for late founder Dave Thomas' daughter. Wendy Wasserstein is an acclaimed playwright who won a Pulitzer Prize for *The Heidi Chronicles*, while Wendy O. Williams fronted the punk band the Plasmatics and made waves with her wild outfits.

Whitney: English; "white island." Perhaps the most famous Whitney is singer Whitney Houston, who achieved stardom in the 1980s with her No. 1 hit "Saving All My Love for You." Her songs continued to win her Grammy awards, but she will always be known for her amazing 1991 performance of the national anthem at the Super Bowl — it expressed on a wide public scale the patriotic sentiments of an entire nation during the Gulf War. Whitney also has an artistic connection: The Whitney Museum of American Art in New York City was founded by artist Gertrude Vanderbilt Whitney in 1931 and remains one of the city's most respected art museums. This name was popular in the 1990s, making the top 100 for four straight years, but its use has dropped off a bit in the years since.

Y

Yasmin, Yasmine: Persian; "jasmine flower." Actress Yasmine Bleeth is probably the best-known Yasmine; she was a favorite on television's *Baywatch*, where she played a sexy lifeguard. Pretenders lead singer Chrissy Hynde named one of her daughters Yasmin, as did actress Rita Hayworth. See also JASMINE.

Z

Zelda: German; "gray + battle." Zelda is a shortened form of the name **Griselda,** which has fallen from popular use. This name became known in the mid-20th century as the name of writer F. Scott Fitzgerald's wife. It's also the name of a popular Nintendo game starring Zelda the Wind Waker. Given that association and the fact that Z names are uncommon, Zelda has a free-spirited, outside-the-ordinary feel to it.

Zoe, Zoey: Greek; "life." Zoe, an old name, was the name of two early Catholic saints. The first was the wife of Hesperus; she and her husband were Christian slaves under the reign of Emperor Hadrian and were martyred for refusing to worship their master's pagan gods. The second St. Zoe was captured by the forces of Emperor Diocletian as she prayed by the tomb of the apostle Peter and then was tossed into the Tiber River. Zoe is also the name of an empress who ruled Byzantium from 1028 to 1050. A modern-day Zoe of note is Zoe Akins, an early 20th-century playwright who won a Pulitzer Prize for her dramatization of the Edith Wharton novel *The Old Maid.* A fictional Zoey is Zoey Bartlett, the daughter of the president on the hit television series *The West Wing.* **Zoie** and **Zooey** are variations. Actress Zooey Deschanel (of *Almost Famous, Big Trouble,* and other films) makes use of the longer version, which comes from the J. D. Salinger novel *Franny and Zooey.*

Short-and-sweet names

Do you want to make sure that no one takes your child's beautiful given name and short-ens it to something you can't stand? Or do you have a long and complex last name that you'd like to balance with something simpler? Try giving your baby one of these five-letters-or-fewer names that are virtually impossible to shorten:

* Ava
* Bella
* Chloe
* Ella
* Hope
* Ivy
* Jade
* Kira
* Lucy
* Mia
* Rose
* Ruby
* Sage
* Skye
* Zoe

The Top Ten Names from the 1950s

Based on a 5 percent sampling of Social Security card applications, the Social Security Administration came up with this top ten list of names from the 1950s. Notice how names change quite a bit even in a relatively short time: Only one boys' name on this list, Michael, appears on the latest top ten list (see Chapter 1), and none of the girls' names are duplicated.

Rank	Boys	Girls
1	Michael	Mary
2	James	Linda
3	Robert	Patricia
4	John	Susan
5	David	Deborah
6	William	Barbara
7	Richard	Debra
8	Thomas	Karen
9	Mark	Nancy
10	Charles	Donna

The Top Ten Names from the 1900s

At the turn of the 20th century, these were the top ten names for boys and girls. If you're looking for a name that sounds classic, Victorian, and perhaps quaintly old-fashioned, those on this list may be worth considering.

Rank	Boys	Girls
1	John	Mary
2	William	Helen
3	James	Margaret
4	George	Anna
5	Joseph	Ruth

continued

Rank	Boys	Girls
6	Charles	Elizabeth
7	Robert	Dorothy
8	Frank	Marie
9	Edward	Mildred
10	Henry	Alice

Ten Names That Work for Boys or Girls

If you're the type who plans to buy green or yellow rather than pink or blue so as not to unintentionally treat your baby a certain way because of its gender, these androgynous names are sure to appeal to you:

* Bailey
* Casey
* Chris
* Dakota
* Harley
* Jessie
* Jordan
* Peyton
* Riley
* Skylar/Skyler

Index

☺ ☺ ☹ ☺ ☺ ☹ ☺ ☺ ☹ ☺ ☺ ☹ ☺ ☺ ☹ ☺ ☺ ☺ ☺ ☹ ☺

Index

☺ ☻ ☹ ☺ ☻ ☹ ☺ ☻ ☹ ☺ ☻ ☹ ☺ ☻ ☹ ☺ ☺ ☻ ☹ ☺

Index

Index

Index